The Real Money Guide

The Missing Manual for Financial Recovery

DAVID KIM

COPYRIGHT

ISBN:
979-8-9925330-0-2 (Ebook)
979-8-9925330-1-9 (Paperback)
979-8-9925330-2-6 (Hardback)

Publisher: Self-Published

Contact Information: David Kim www.therealmoneyguide.com

IMPORTANT DISCLAIMERS

The content in this book is for informational and educational purposes only. It should not be considered as financial, investment, legal, or tax advice. The author is not a licensed financial advisor, investment advisor, attorney, or tax professional.

The stories, experiences, and personal accounts in this book are based on the author's recollections and memories. To protect the privacy of individuals involved and to maintain the narrative flow, certain details have been modified:

- Names of people, places, and organizations may have been changed.
- Timelines and specific dates may have been modified.
- Certain identifying details may have been altered to preserve anonymity.

These modifications do not impact the essential truth and lessons of the experiences shared. The core insights, personal growth, and financial lessons remain authentic and genuine. Readers should understand that these adaptations are made solely to protect privacy and enhance the storytelling experience. The events described are true to the author's lived experience, even if the specific details have been thoughtfully reimagined.

INVESTMENT AND FINANCIAL RISK NOTICE:

All investments carry risk, including the potential loss of principal. Past performance is not indicative of future results. Individual results may vary significantly based on personal circumstances. Investment strategies that work for one person may not be suitable for another

TAX AND LEGAL NOTICE:

The tax and legal information provided is general in nature and may not apply to your specific situation. Tax laws and regulations vary by jurisdiction and are subject to change. Always consult with qualified tax and legal professionals regarding your specific circumstances before making any decisions.

PROFESSIONAL ADVICE:

Before making any financial, investment, legal, or tax decisions, you should consult with appropriate licensed professionals who can review your personal circumstances and provide tailored advice. The author and publisher specifically disclaim any liability, loss, or risk taken by individuals who directly or indirectly act on the information contained herein.

CURRENCY OF INFORMATION:

The information contained in this book is current as of December 2025. Laws, regulations, market conditions, and other factors affecting financial decisions change frequently. Readers should verify all information independently and consider its currentness before making any decisions.

GEOGRAPHIC LIMITATIONS:

The information provided primarily relates to the United States of America and may not be applicable in other jurisdictions. Readers from other locations should consult local professionals familiar with their specific regulatory environment.

THIRD-PARTY CONTENT:

Any reference to third-party services, products, or websites is provided for informational purposes only and does not constitute an endorsement. The author and publisher are not responsible for the content or services provided by third parties.

EMPLOYMENT DISCLAIMER:

The views, opinions, advice, and financial strategies expressed in this book are solely my own and do not reflect the official position, policy, or views of Amazon.com, Inc., or any of my previous employers, including but not limited to Raytheon, Honeywell, and Genpact. This book is written in my personal capacity and is not sponsored, authorized, or endorsed by any of these companies.

Any references to my professional experiences are presented for illustrative purposes only and have been carefully written to avoid disclosure of confidential or proprietary information. No content in this book should be interpreted as financial advice specific to any company, its compensation structures, or benefits programs.

My employment status, affiliations, and professional roles are accurately stated as of the time of writing but may change after publication. Readers should not make financial decisions based on any presumed inside knowledge of these organizations or their practices.

By reading this book, you acknowledge that you understand and agree to these disclaimers. If you do not agree with or do not accept these disclaimers, do not read this book.

DEDICATION

This book is dedicated to those who have faced financial hardship, who have stumbled and fallen, yet found the strength to rise again; and to the countless individuals who struggle silently, burdened by debt or the weight of unmet financial goals. This is for the corporate employees who have dedicated years of their lives to their careers, only to encounter layoffs, downsizing, or stagnant salaries, and for those who navigate the complexities of corporate life with resilience and determination.

It is a testament to the human spirit's resilience and the power of perseverance in overcoming adversity. It is for those who believe a better financial future is possible

To those who have shown me kindness and support during my darkest hours, thank you for your unwavering belief in me. This journey has been a testament to the enduring power of human connection and the transformative impact of supportive relationships during times of immense challenge.

This book is for you, because your strength is the inspiration for its existence. May it guide you, support you, and empower you to build a solid foundation for a life of financial well-being and personal fulfillment.

CONTENTS

PREFACE

I remember the exact moment when I realized I had lost everything. Sitting across from the bankruptcy attorney's wooden desk, the fluorescent lights harsh above me, I stared down at the stack of paperwork that represented the final collapse of my financial life. Despite my MBA and Certified Financial Planner designation framed proudly on my home office wall, I managed to lose it all; my savings, my investments, my home, and nearly my family.

The journey to true financial mastery requires traveling through both valleys and peaks. My path wasn't a straight line of ascending success, but rather a cycle of building, losing, and rebuilding that taught me many lessons.

Looking back at over thirty years of military service, corporate career advancement, entrepreneurial ventures, and ultimately rebuilding from bankruptcy, I realize now that my real financial education came not from textbooks or degrees, but from hard-lived experience. The nights spent awake worrying about bills, the moment I had to tell my children we were moving to a smaller home, the humiliation of having my credit card declined for a $27 dinner; these were my most powerful teachers.

Financial success isn't just about numbers; it's about transformation. My journey taught me that sustainable wealth comes from understanding both the technical and human elements of money management.

This book isn't just my story. It's a comprehensive guide born from hard-won experience and professional expertise. Through my roles as a small business owner, consultant, technology leader, and real estate investor, I've learned that financial success requires more than just knowing what to do; it requires knowing how to implement that knowledge in real-world situations when emotions, family pressures, and life's complexities are factored in.

The lessons in these pages reflect not just my deep personal journey, but the experiences of countless others I've guided through similar challenges. From managing complex equity compensation to building sustainable passive income streams, each chapter provides actionable strategies tested in the crucible of real life.

This isn't just another personal finance book; it's the guide I wish I'd had during both my struggles and successes. My hope is that by sharing both my failures and victories, along with the practical tools and strategies I've developed along the way, I can help you avoid the pitfalls while accelerating your path to financial security.

INTRODUCTION

The phone call came on a Tuesday afternoon as I prepared for a virtual meeting with my team at my Big Tech employer. When I saw my son's name on the screen, I almost let it go to voicemail; the quarterly business review materials weren't finalized, and I was running out of time. Instead, something made me hit "accept," and I heard a mix of excitement and confusion in his voice.

"Dad, I need your help with something," my son said, his words tumbling out faster than usual. "Meta just granted me RSUs worth more than my salary, and I have no idea what to do with them."

As he spoke, I found myself staring at my home office wall where, years earlier, a different set of papers had hung; bankruptcy documentation. Now, the wall was lined with stock certificates. The irony wasn't lost on me. Less than a decade prior, I sat in a bankruptcy attorney's office, watching my own financial life crumble. Now, my twenty-three-year-old son was asking me to help him navigate a compensation package larger than anything I'd earned before age forty.

I still remember the tightness in my chest as I closed my laptop, postponing my meeting prep to focus on my son's questions. As I walked him through RSU vesting schedules and tax implications, the conversation deepened into 401(k) withholding and mega backdoor Roth elections which he was unaware he had access to. His questions brought me back to my own early career, when I'd made catastrophic mistakes despite my education; mistakes I was determined to help him avoid. This moment crystallized exactly why I needed to write this book.

Money doesn't come with an instruction manual. No one hands you a guidebook for making smart financial decisions. This reality becomes painfully clear when facing major financial choices or recovering from setbacks.

Part I traces my journey from Marine Corps service through early corporate success at Raytheon, to financial collapse from a failed restaurant venture, and ultimately to progressively rebuilding to today. This raw account demonstrates how someone with an MBA and financial certifications could still lose everything; and more importantly, how the lessons learned through failure and recovery created stronger financial principles than any formal education could provide.

My story serves as a living case study in navigating both success and setback in today's financial landscape, offering practical insights for anyone facing financial challenges or managing sudden success. I share my story because I know that somewhere, someone reading this is experiencing that same pain right now. And they need to know that it's possible to come back stronger.

My hope is that everyone can benefit from the tested lessons and principles in Part 1 regardless of where they are on their financial journey. The experiences which shaped these principles cover a wide ground, from early success to having to restart and rebuild, and a recovery which has led to stronger, more stable success.

Part II transforms these hard-learned lessons into "The Missing Manual," a comprehensive guide organized into five essential sections that progress logically from fundamental concepts to advanced strategies. While my story demonstrates these principles in action, this manual breaks them down into practical, actionable steps you can apply to your own financial life. The Missing Manual is organized into five core sections:

Core Financial Foundations lays the groundwork with battle-tested approaches to budgeting, debt management, banking, emergency funds, and student loans.

Protection & Security focuses on defending what you build, covering everything from credit management to digital financial security. In our increasingly complex financial world, protection isn't optional; it's fundamental to lasting success.

Wealth Building explores multiple paths to financial growth, from traditional investments to real estate opportunities. These chapters help you build wealth strategically while managing risk appropriately.

Career & Income addresses maximizing your earning potential while optimizing tax efficiency, recognizing that your career is often your biggest financial asset. You'll learn to navigate modern compensation structures while maintaining work-life harmony.

Family & Legacy shows you how to extend your financial success beyond yourself. These chapters address building strong financial partnerships, teaching money management across generations, and protecting your legacy through thoughtful estate planning.

Each section combines personal experiences with practical guidance, turning complex financial concepts into actionable strategies. You'll find not just theory, but specific tools and techniques tested in real-world situations; many of them learned during the darkest moments of my own financial journey.

Consider this book your missing manual for life's financial decisions. Each chapter builds upon the previous ones, creating a comprehensive approach to financial mastery. While you might be tempted to jump directly to specific topics, understanding how these elements work together will significantly improve your outcomes.

PART I: A JOURNEY THROUGH FINANCIAL SUCCESS, COLLAPSE, AND REBIRTH

Before diving into financial strategies and systems, you deserve to understand the journey that shaped them. This section shares my financial life story, not because it's uniquely special, but because within it are universal lessons that might illuminate your own path.

My journey spans multiple financial extremes: from Marine Corps service to early corporate success at Raytheon, from bankruptcy following a failed restaurant venture to rebuilding through consulting, and finally to senior leadership at Amazon Web Services. Each phase taught crucial lessons about money, success, and resilience that inform the strategies presented in later chapters.

For readers currently facing financial crisis, this narrative offers both hope and practical guidance. For those managing newfound success, particularly in technology careers, my son's experience starting at Meta with significant equity compensation mirrors challenges you may face.

For those somewhere in between, the contrast between my bankruptcy experience and later success in Big Tech provides perspective on building financial security at any stage. Through both failure and success, I've learned that sustainable financial achievement requires more than just technical knowledge. It demands understanding how money decisions affect every aspect of life.

Let's begin the journey together.

CHAPTER I
SUCCESS AND TROUBLE
(1992-2004)

MILITARY FOUNDATIONS (1992-1999)

Growing up in a Korean immigrant household in the 1980s, I witnessed firsthand the delicate balance between sacrifice and survival. My mother had arrived in America with little more than determination and dreams of providing their children with better opportunities. Our small two-bedroom apartment in Riverside, California on Olivewood Avenue housed not just our family of five (me, my mother, stepfather, brother, and grandmother) but also the weight of expectations and cultural values that would profoundly shape my relationship with money.

My parents, hardworking and resourceful, prioritized providing for their family but formal financial discussions were rare. Their focus was on providing for immediate needs, not long-term financial strategy. This lack of financial literacy was a significant oversight, a gap in my foundation that would eventually crumble beneath the weight of unforeseen circumstances. There was so much I wish my parents had taught me about money, but they never did.

THE MARINE CORPS DECISION

My decision to enlist in the Marine Corps in 1992 wasn't driven by patriotism alone. It represented an escape from tradition, financial constraints and a path to independence. At seventeen, watching my parents work endless hours for modest returns, I saw military service as a route to education and opportunity that seemed otherwise out of reach.

What I didn't realize was that I was wholly unprepared for managing even the modest income the military provided. My first paycheck, approximately $700 per month take home as a Private First Class, quickly became a lesson in poor financial decisions. Without any formal financial education or guidance, I immediately fell into patterns that would haunt me for years.

My first major financial mistake came within weeks of receiving my first paycheck. I purchased a used car at nearly 30% interest with prepayment penalties, committing myself to $300 monthly payments that consumed nearly half my take home pay. The predatory lending practices targeting young service members were common then, though I lacked the financial literacy to recognize them as such.

The remaining money disappeared quickly into a cycle of immediate gratification. While the base dining facility provided meals, I spent freely on alcohol and cigarettes, sometimes even floating checks just before payday. The Marine Corps offered minimal financial education, with only a single voluntary correspondence course titled "Personal Finance" that few Marines, including myself, took seriously.

MARRIAGE AND FAMILY LIFE

In 1994, while stationed at Camp Pendleton, I married at nineteen. Despite my wife's periodic employment, including a six-month position as a cashier before our daughter's birth, we maintained a traditional single-income household. This decision, while aligned with our values, created significant financial strain.

By 1999, my final year in service, my annual gross pay as a Sergeant (E-5) had reached only $19,368. This translated to approximately $1,200 monthly pay plus a $1,100 non-taxable monthly housing and subsistence allowance. Even with this combined $2,300 income, we struggled continuously. After paying $1,200 for rent and $500 for car payments, the remaining $600 barely covered essential living expenses. We relied on the WIC (Women, Infants, and Children) program to help with basic nutrition needs, yet still lived paycheck to paycheck.

The structured environment of military life provided comprehensive healthcare benefits and regular paychecks, creating an illusion of somewhat financial stability that masked our precarious financial reality. Each promotion brought slight increases in pay and allowances, but our financial habits remained unchanged. We simply spent more as we earned more, never developing the fundamental skills needed for long-term financial security.

EDUCATION AND TECHNICAL GROWTH

During my service from 1996 to 1999, I balanced military duties with college studies, taking advantage of the GI Bill and tuition assistance. Working with the Marine Corps' advanced communications systems sparked an interest in technology that would shape my future career. I discovered an aptitude for technical work that went beyond basic military requirements, leading me to pursue a bachelor's degree in computer science.

My combination of military experience and technical education made me an attractive candidate in the defense sector. Raytheon's offer came before my discharge. This offer seemed to validate our single-income model, that a second income wasn't needed for us to survive. The transition appeared perfect on paper, though we couldn't foresee how civilian life would test our financial assumptions.

EARLY SUCCESS AT RAYTHEON (1999-2001)

Stepping into Raytheon's Tucson facility in May 1999 felt like entering a new world. The corporate environment echoed military structure in some ways, but it also introduced entirely new challenges. My starting salary of $60,000 seemed enormous compared to military pay, especially with the added signing bonus, stock options, and benefits package. This initial success reinforced our decision to maintain a single-income household, a decision that would ultimately jeopardize our long-term financial stability.

EARLY CAREER GROWTH

The defense contracting world of the late 1990s buzzed with opportunity. Post-Cold War defense spending remained high, and the tech bubble hadn't yet burst. As the sole provider for my family, I threw myself into work with the same intensity I'd brought to military service. My role as a software engineer on missile defense systems positioned me perfectly to ride this wave of growth. At the time, I didn't realize how this single-minded focus would eventually affect our family life.

Success came quickly in those early days. Within my first year, I received a promotion and a hefty salary increase, bringing my annual compensation to $75,000. Each achievement felt effortless, validating my belief that technical expertise alone could provide an increasingly comfortable lifestyle for my family. This rapid advancement, while exciting, reinforced dangerous assumptions about the relationship between career success and financial security.

THE FIRST TRAP: LIFESTYLE INFLATION

Our lifestyle began shifting dramatically with my increasing income. The combination of my rising salary and exposure to successful colleagues changed our reference point for "normal" spending. Despite being a single-income household, we moved from our $1,200 monthly apartment to a new construction house in an upscale neighborhood in May 2000. The mortgage payment consumed a significant portion of my income, but I justified it as providing a better environment for our children.

The lifestyle upgrades extended beyond housing. We replaced our practical Honda Passport with a new Lexus ES 300. It was a purchase I rationalized as "projecting success" in the corporate world. Each upgrade seemed reasonable in isolation, considering my growing income and apparent career security. However, these choices were creating a lifestyle that consumed all my income, leaving no margin for error or emergencies.

The Lifestyle Inflation Trap

How My Spending Outpaced Even My Growing Income

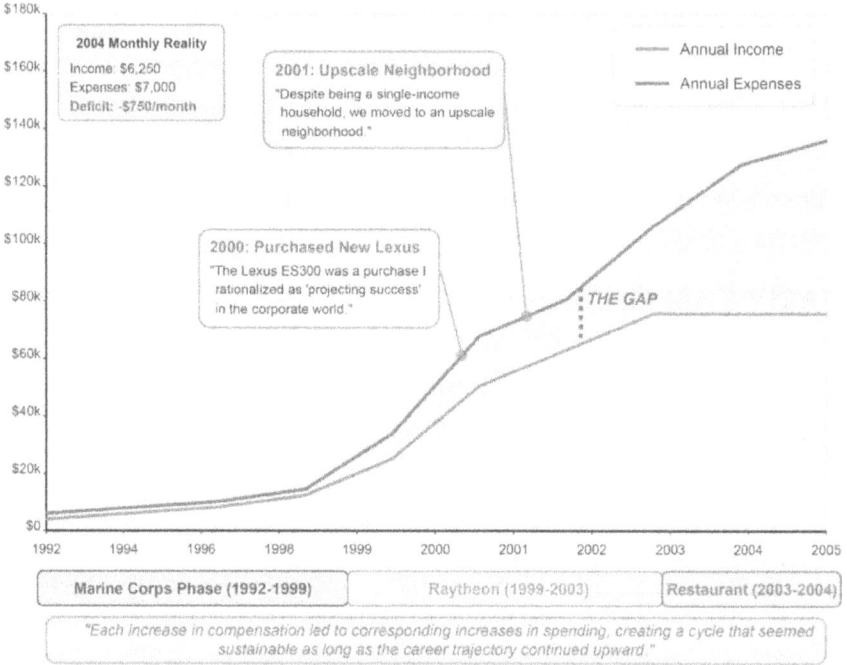

2004 Monthly Reality
Income: $6,250
Expenses: $7,000
Deficit: -$750/month

2001: Upscale Neighborhood
"Despite being a single-income household, we moved to an upscale neighborhood."

2000: Purchased New Lexus
"The Lexus ES300 was a purchase I rationalized as 'projecting success' in the corporate world."

THE GAP

- - - - Annual Income
- - - - Annual Expenses

Marine Corps Phase (1992-1999)   Raytheon (1999-2003)   Restaurant (2003-2004)

"Each increase in compensation led to corresponding increases in spending, creating a cycle that seemed sustainable as long as the career trajectory continued upward."

CORPORATE CULTURE IMPACT

The corporate culture at Raytheon subtly encouraged lifestyle inflation. Success became visible in the neighborhoods where people lived, the cars they drove, and the schools their children attended. I didn't just participate in this culture; I embraced it wholeheartedly, wanting to provide my children with advantages I never had growing up. Our kids enrolled in private activities including piano lessons, ballet, and advanced tutoring. We justified each expense as an investment in their future.

By late 2001, my base salary had grown to $90,000. With bonuses, I consistently earned six figures. Each increase in compensation led to corresponding increases in spending, creating a cycle that seemed sustainable provided my career trajectory continued upward.

THE MBA JOURNEY AND PROFESSIONAL GROWTH (2001-2003)

My decision to pursue an MBA while working full-time at Raytheon reflected both ambition and growing financial pressure. With two young children at home and increasing lifestyle commitments, the company's tuition reimbursement program made this decision financially feasible. The company would cover 80% of the costs, and my remaining Montgomery GI Bill benefits covered the other 20%, once again making my education free.

Even with everything covered, I took out subsidized student loans to help enhance my finances. My wife's support in managing our home life made it possible to balance work, studies, and family obligations, though this period began to strain our relationship.

The University of Phoenix MBA program seemed perfectly suited to my situation. Evening classes and weekend sessions allowed me to work while advancing my education. I didn't realize that this additional commitment would further distance me from family life and carry long-term consequences.

PROFESSIONAL CERTIFICATIONS AND GROWTH

During this period, as part of one of the MBA course tracks, I completed the Certified Financial Planner (CFP) curriculum. I saw this as a way to complement my technical and business education. The CFP courses demanded extensive study across areas such as insurance, investments, tax planning, retirement planning, and estate planning. This knowledge should have informed better personal financial decisions on my part.

The combination of MBA coursework and CFP studies provided both broad business acumen and specialized financial expertise. I could calculate net present values, analyze market trends, develop comprehensive business plans, and create detailed financial strategies. This dual knowledge base, while valuable, created a dangerous illusion of mastery over financial matters. It created an illusion that would influence many future family financial decisions.

CAREER ADVANCEMENT AND COMPENSATION

My professional growth at Raytheon accelerated alongside my educational pursuits. Project responsibilities expanded, and my role grew to include program management oversight of multimillion-dollar defense contracts. The increased responsibility came with higher pay and more stock options, but also with greater stress and longer hours. The demands of being the sole provider pushed me to work increasingly longer hours, which led to missed family dinners and children's activities.

To compensate for my absences, I justified more luxury purchases as "making it up to the family." A pool for the backyard, premium family vacations, the latest gaming systems, each seemed reasonable given my position and income. The correlation between missing family time and increased spending became a pattern I wouldn't recognize until much later.

IMPACT ON FAMILY LIFE

The MBA program's demands, combined with growing work responsibilities, fundamentally changed our family dynamics. My wife shouldered an increasingly disproportionate share of parenting responsibilities while I focused on career and education. Our children, though young, began adapting to a father who was physically present but mentally absorbed in work or studies most of the time.

Weekend study groups and late-night preparation for Monday presentations became routine, gradually eroding family time. The financial benefits of career advancement seemed to justify these sacrifices, but we didn't recognize how this pattern was affecting our family bonds. The pursuit of professional success was creating a deficit in family connections that no amount of material compensation could offset.

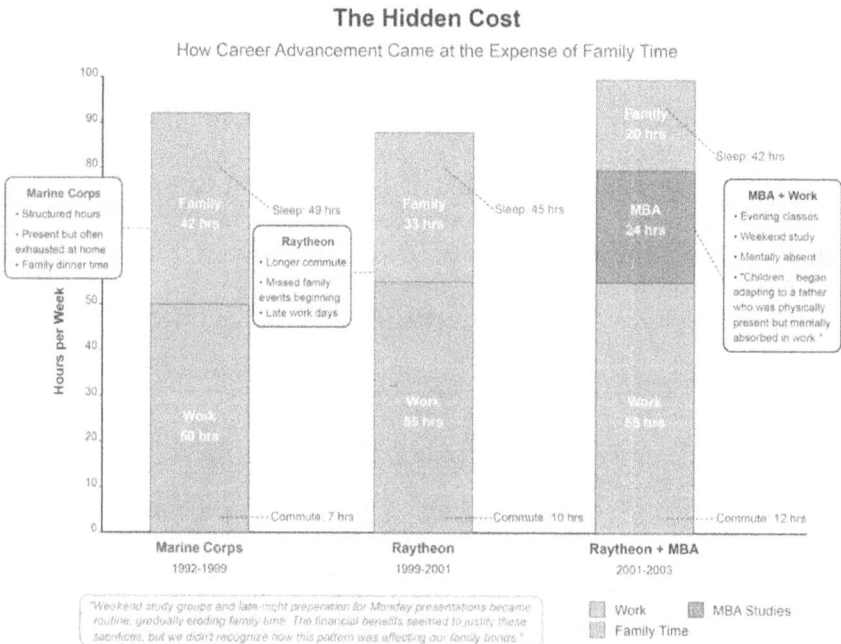

The Hidden Cost

How Career Advancement Came at the Expense of Family Time

8

EDUCATIONAL SUCCESS AND PROFESSIONAL IDENTITY

By 2002, completing my MBA program and CFP studies added prestigious credentials to my resume. These achievements, combined with my technical background and military service, created what seemed like an unassailable professional foundation. Each accomplishment reinforced my belief that I could provide an increasingly comfortable lifestyle for my family through sheer force of will and professional advancement.

This triple-threat of credentials, MBA, CFP studies, and technical expertise, should have positioned me perfectly for sound financial decision-making. Instead, it contributed to my overconfidence. The theoretical knowledge of financial planning didn't translate into practical wisdom in personal financial matters. Understanding complex financial concepts didn't automatically lead to making better financial decisions.

THE RESTAURANT VENTURE (2003-2004)

Success can be intoxicating, especially when you're responsible for providing for a family of four. By 2003, my corporate career was thriving, my MBA was completed, and I felt invulnerable.

The pressure to maintain and improve our family's lifestyle, combined with what I recognize as dangerous overconfidence, led me to venture into restaurant ownership. The idea seemed perfect: a Japanese restaurant in a growing high-end area of Tucson, leveraging what I'd learned in business school while creating an additional income stream.

The numbers looked promising on paper. My MBA coursework had taught me about business plans, market analysis, and financial projections. The $600,000 restaurant venture would require $150,000 of my own capital. It was money I cobbled together from savings, a 401(k) loan, stock option exercises, and credit cards.

I convinced myself this was a sound investment, one that would provide not just additional income but also potential future employment for our children. My wife expressed concerns about the risks, but I dismissed them with projections and promises of even greater financial security.

INITIAL CHALLENGES AND PARTNERSHIP STRAIN

The first signs of trouble appeared during the construction phase. Delays in permitting, cost overruns, and unexpected building requirements began eating into our capital reserves before we even opened the doors. I told myself these were normal startup challenges, drawing parallels to case studies from my MBA program. What those case studies hadn't prepared me for was the emotional toll of watching savings drain away while construction dragged on.

The partnership with my co-investors, initially strong, began showing cracks as we faced decisions about operational priorities. We disagreed about everything from menu pricing to staffing levels. Each disagreement required additional capital injections to resolve, and I found myself dipping deeper into personal savings and credit cards to keep the project moving forward.

FAMILY IMPACT AND FINANCIAL STRAIN

The restaurant's demands took an immediate toll on family life. My daughter, six at the time, and my son, four, saw less and less of their father. I was either at Raytheon, at the restaurant, or poring over financial statements at the dining room table, most days getting only four to five hours of sleep. My wife's initial concerns proved prophetic, but pride prevented me from acknowledging the venture's failure. Instead, I doubled down, pulling our savings and maxing out credit cards, convinced that just a little more time and money would turn things around.

Our home life became centered around the restaurant's needs. The strain showed in small ways at first. I missed school events, postponed family activities, and casual family time disappeared. I rationalized these sacrifices as temporary, necessary steps toward greater financial security, not recognizing how they were eroding our family bonds.

OPERATIONAL CHALLENGES AND FINANCIAL BLEEDING

Once fully opened, the restaurant faced the typical challenges of any new business, but our depleted capital reserves left no room for error. Labor costs ran higher than projected, food costs fluctuated unpredictably, and customer traffic built more slowly than our business plan anticipated. Each week brought new financial demands, and I found myself injecting more personal capital to keep operations running.

The complexity of restaurant management exceeded my business plan projections. Despite my MBA training, I was not ready for the intricacies of food service operations. Staff turnover, inventory management, liquor laws, and quality control consumed more time and resources than expected. My attempts to manage these challenges while maintaining my corporate career created an unsustainable schedule.

THE BEGINNING OF THE END

By early 2004, the restaurant's failure became impossible to ignore. Monthly losses mounted, and my personal financial reserves were completely depleted.

The same analytical skills that had made me successful at Raytheon now showed me the mathematical impossibility of turning the business around. Each day brought new evidence that the venture was unsustainable, yet pride and fear kept me from accepting reality.

The timing couldn't have been worse. As the restaurant was failing, Raytheon announced a major restructuring. Despite my years of service and technical expertise, I was laid off, which I know was partly due to my declining performance as I focused more on the restaurant. The double impact of a failing business and job loss shattered not just my illusion of invulnerability but threatened everything I'd worked to provide for my family.

THE AFTERMATH AND TRANSITION (2004)

The immediate aftermath of the restaurant closure and Raytheon layoff created a new reality. The financial implications extended far beyond just lost income. This loss affected every aspect of our family's life. Our savings had been depleted by the restaurant venture, credit cards were maxed out from trying to keep the business afloat, and the loss of my Raytheon position eliminated our primary source of income. The carefully constructed lifestyle we'd built unraveled with frightening speed.

Our children's private school requested immediate payment or withdrawal, forcing a mid-semester change to public education. Even basic expenses became a challenge as we faced the reality of our financial situation with no immediate prospect of replacement income.

FAMILY IMPACT

The strain on our family relationships intensified during this period. My wife, who expressed concerns about the restaurant venture from the beginning, now faced the consequences of my entrepreneurial decisions. Our dinner conversations shifted from talks about the future to tense negotiations about which bills to pay and which to delay.

My children, though young, sensed the shift in our family's circumstances. The sudden changes in their daily lives, from private to public school, cancelled activities, and the visible stress between their parents, created an uncertainty they'd never experienced before. My role as the reliable provider, a core part of my identity, had been fundamentally shaken.

Luckily, within two months, I secured a position with a management consulting firm in their Dallas office, starting at $100,000. It was an impressive recovery on paper but one that would require relocating our family from Tucson. The move itself became an expensive proposition that added to our already strained finances. Our children had to leave their friends and schools behind, adding emotional stress to our financial burden.

Yet I saw it as a fresh start, a chance to rebuild. The salary was excellent and the career potential seemed unlimited. I told myself the restaurant failure was just a temporary setback, a learning experience that would make me stronger. What I didn't realize was that I was carrying forward not just financial debt, but also dangerous habits and assumptions that would eventually lead to a more devastating collapse.

The Knowledge-Action Gap

Having Financial Education Doesn't Guarantee Financial Wisdom

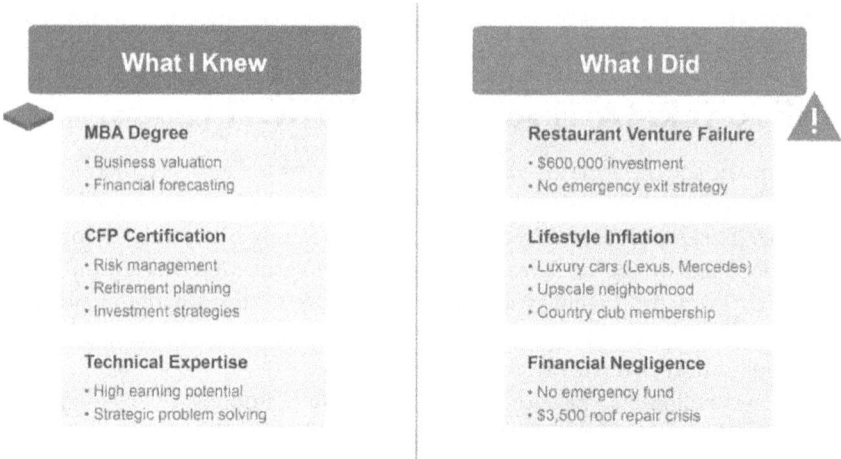

What I Knew	What I Did
MBA Degree • Business valuation • Financial forecasting	**Restaurant Venture Failure** • $600,000 investment • No emergency exit strategy
CFP Certification • Risk management • Retirement planning • Investment strategies	**Lifestyle Inflation** • Luxury cars (Lexus, Mercedes) • Upscale neighborhood • Country club membership
Technical Expertise • High earning potential • Strategic problem solving	**Financial Negligence** • No emergency fund • $3,500 roof repair crisis

KEY LESSONS FROM THIS CHAPTER:

Success without wisdom creates vulnerability: Technical skills and career advancement don't automatically translate to financial wisdom. My rapid rise at Raytheon created an illusion of financial capability that masked fundamental misunderstandings about sustainable wealth.

Appearance-based spending creates hidden fragility: The pursuit of looking successful undermines actual security. Our lifestyle upgrades, the luxury car, upscale neighborhood, and country club membership were motivated more by appearance than actual need or value.

Financial education without application leads to overconfidence: Knowledge (MBA, CFP studies) without implementation creates dangerous blind spots. My advanced education paradoxically increased my financial risk-taking by creating unwarranted confidence without corresponding wisdom or experience.

Single-income households require additional security measures: Traditional family structures need stronger financial safeguards. Our reliance on my income alone magnified every career and financial decision, creating vulnerability without adequate protection.

Entrepreneurial risks need separate financial structures: Business ventures should be insulated from personal finances. My failure to maintain separation between personal and business finances amplified the restaurant's failure into a family financial crisis.

FINANCIAL REALITY CHECK

- Annual Gross: $120,000
- Monthly Take-Home: $6,250
- Monthly Expenses: $7,000
- Monthly Deficit: -$750
- Total Assets: $20,000
- Total Debt: $120,000
- Net Worth: -$100,000

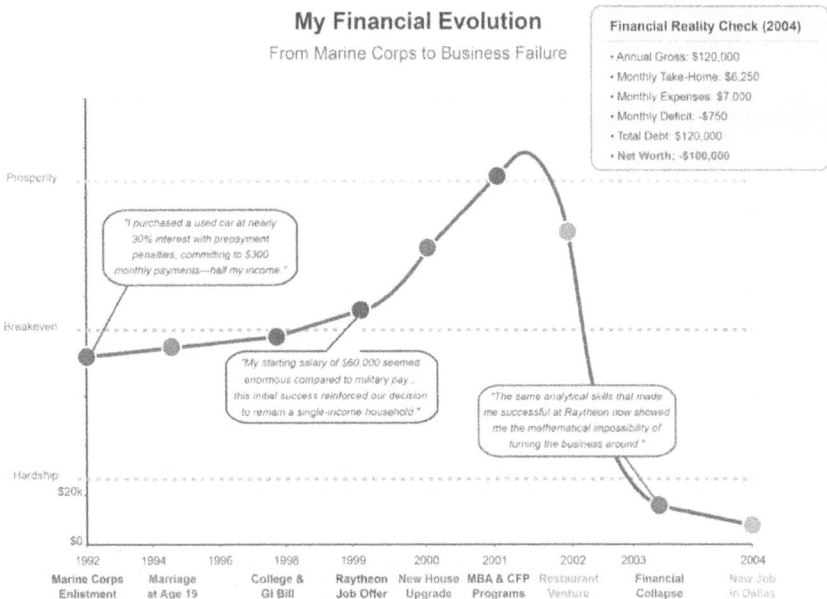

My Financial Evolution
From Marine Corps to Business Failure

Financial Reality Check (2004)
- Annual Gross: $120,000
- Monthly Take-Home: $6,250
- Monthly Expenses: $7,000
- Monthly Deficit: -$750
- Total Debt: $120,000
- Net Worth: -$100,000

"I purchased a used car at nearly 30% interest with prepayment penalties, committing to $300 monthly payments—half my income."

"My starting salary of $60,000 seemed enormous compared to military pay ... this initial success reinforced our decision to remain a single-income household."

"The same analytical skills that made me successful at Raytheon now showed me the mathematical impossibility of turning the business around."

| 1992 | 1994 | 1996 | 1998 | 1999 | 2000 | 2001 | 2002 | 2003 | 2004 |
| Marine Corps Enlistment | Marriage at Age 19 | | College & GI Bill | Raytheon Job Offer | New House Upgrade | MBA & CFP Programs | Restaurant Venture | Financial Collapse | New Job in Dallas |

My journey from military service through corporate success to first financial failure demonstrated how early career achievements without proper financial understanding can create dangerous patterns. The foundations built during this period, both strengths and weaknesses, would shape future decisions in ways I couldn't yet imagine.

CHAPTER II
THE SLOW DESCENT (2004-2014)

FAST FORWARD: A STORM OF RECKONING

June 13, 2012, began like any ordinary summer day in Dallas. By evening, tornado sirens wailed across the neighborhood. Huddled in the closet under our staircase, my wife and I wrapped blankets around our terrified children as hail pounded our roof and ferocious winds tore through our community. In the darkness of the power outage, their crying penetrated deeper than the storm's fury. It was one of the most frightening moments we'd ever experienced as a family.

When morning revealed a partially destroyed roof, the $3,500 insurance deductible presented a more personal storm. Despite earning six figures, I didn't have enough money to cover this relatively modest expense. Humbled, I had to request an advance on a future bonus from my consulting firm. This was an awakening to the precarious financial foundation beneath our seemingly successful life.

Just as the storm exposed our roof's weakness, this incident revealed the truth about our finances. The physical storm lasted hours, but it foreshadowed the financial tempest building around us that would ultimately tear apart not just our financial life but our family structure itself.

What makes a six-figure earning professional unable to handle a $3,500 emergency? The answer lies not in income but in systems, or more accurately, their absence. My journey from recovery to collapse demonstrates how even substantial income can't overcome flawed financial architecture. This chapter explores not just what happened after my initial financial setback, but why it happened.

THE RECOVERY THAT WASN'T (2004-2006)

Our move to Dallas in 2004 should have represented a fresh start. It was a chance to rebuild on a stronger foundation after the restaurant failure. With my daughter at six and my son at four, we had every opportunity to establish sound financial habits that would serve our growing family. Instead, I mistook career recovery for financial recovery as I had yet to address the underlying patterns that led to these problems.

THE PSYCHOLOGY OF FALSE RECOVERY

The transition to Dallas brought an immediate sense of relief. My consulting position offered substantial income that seemed to solve our financial challenges overnight. This created a dangerous illusion that our previous financial problems stemmed solely from insufficient income rather than flawed financial behavior.

This psychological trap, confusing income with financial health, became the foundation of our supposed recovery. Each career advancement and increase in compensation reinforced this false narrative. I believed my MBA and CFP studies provided financial sophistication while completely failing to implement basic principles like emergency savings, controlled spending, and sustainable debt management.

THE MISSING FOUNDATIONS

Our financial house lacked the most essential foundation; an emergency fund. Despite years of financial education and my CFP studies, I never established even the most basic financial safety net. Rather than building reserves with each bonus or commission, we immediately channeled these windfalls into lifestyle expansion or debt servicing. It was a pattern that would prove catastrophic when we faced with unexpected expenses like the 2012 storm damage.

More dangerously, I built no systematic approach to managing variable income. My compensation package, consisting of a base salary plus performance bonuses, created an irregular cash flow that required careful management. Instead of developing structures to smooth these fluctuations, I treated each bonus as separate from regular financial planning. I used each bonus to cover accumulated credit card debt rather than addressing the spending patterns which created that debt in the first place.

APPEARANCES VS. REALITY

Our transition to Dallas cemented a destructive pattern which prioritized the appearance of success over financial reality. The house we purchased stretched beyond reasonable limits for my income. Rather than viewing the restaurant failure as a warning to moderate our lifestyle, we treated the consulting position as permission to pursue even more luxury.

The Mercedes in the driveway, the country club membership, the extracurricular activities. Each element of our lifestyle projected an image of success while masking growing financial instability. This wasn't merely vanity; it became entwined with my professional identity. In the consulting world, projecting success often led to more client opportunities and internal advancement. This created a dangerous reinforcement cycle where career advancement both enabled and seemed to justify lifestyle inflation.

What I failed to recognize was how this appearance-focused lifestyle was creating financial fragility beneath the surface. Our ability to weather income fluctuations or economic downturns was compromised with each increase in fixed expenses such as mortgage, car payments, and school tuitions. We were building a financial structure that required perfect conditions to maintain, with no margin for error.

PSYCHOLOGICAL PATTERNS OF FINANCIAL DECLINE

As my consulting career advanced, subtle psychological patterns emerged that accelerated our financial deterioration. These patterns created a powerful system of financial self-sabotage that operated beneath my conscious awareness.

THE COMPENSATION CYCLE

By 2008, my travel schedule had intensified dramatically. I typically spent Monday through Thursday on the road, leaving only weekends for family time. This absence created significant guilt that I unconsciously addressed through financial compensation. I assuaged this guilt with expensive gifts, lavish weekend activities, and an unspoken policy of rarely denying the children's requests.

This pattern created a destructive cycle: more career success led to more family absence, which triggered compensatory spending, which required more career advancement to sustain. Each rotation of this cycle increased both our lifestyle expenses and the emotional distance within our family.

The most troubling aspect wasn't the spending itself but how it replaced genuine connection. When I missed Anabel's dance recital due to a client meeting, the expensive jewelry I brought home served as both apology and substitute for my presence. When work prevented me from attending my son's taekwondo competition, the latest gaming system became my proxy. These material compensations temporarily eased my guilt while teaching our children that emotional needs could be addressed through consumption.

IDENTITY AND FINANCIAL DECISIONS

My professional identity became increasingly entangled with financial decisions. The senior consultant role carried unwritten expectations about appropriate housing, vehicles, attire, and social activities.

Suggestions to downsize our home or reduce lifestyle expenses felt like professional failure rather than prudent financial management. My MBA and CFP studies only reinforced this distortion, creating an illusion of financial sophistication that masked fundamental missteps.

The consulting firm's culture inadvertently reinforced these patterns. Success was measured not just by client satisfaction but by visible prosperity. The unwritten rule was clear: look successful to be successful. These weren't just personal choices; they were seen as professional necessities that justified continued financial overextension.

THE FALSE PEAK (2008-2011)

The 2008 financial crisis should have served as a warning to reduce financial risk and build security. Instead, it created a false sense of invulnerability when my consulting sector initially withstood the economic downturn. While colleagues in other industries faced layoffs and financial strain, my practice area expanded as clients sought expertise in cost reduction and efficiency improvements.

This selective survival reinforced my most dangerous belief; that my technical expertise and work ethic could overcome any financial challenge. Rather than recognizing luck and timing in my continued success, I interpreted it as validation of my approach.

The crisis created another dangerous pattern; social comparison that justified continued high spending. As we witnessed other families facing financial hardship, maintaining our lifestyle became even more important as a signal of stability and success.

SYSTEMIC FINANCIAL BLIND SPOTS

Beyond the psychological patterns, specific systemic failures in our financial structure guaranteed eventual collapse. These weren't merely poor financial decisions but rather foundational flaws that no amount of income could overcome.

GEOGRAPHIC SEPARATION AND FINANCIAL FRAGMENTATION

A critical point came in May 2010 when I began working in Austin while my family remained in Dallas. What started as hotel stays and weekend commutes evolved into a fundamental separation of our lives. By May 2011, I maintained an apartment in Austin and my trips home gradually decreased from weekly to bi-weekly, then monthly. By 2014, I only visited once every few months.

This geographic separation created more than emotional distance. It established financial fragmentation that accelerated our decline. Running two households effectively doubled our fixed expenses while eliminating any natural checks on spending. Without daily financial interaction, we lost the shared visibility that might have prompted difficult but necessary conversations about our deteriorating situation.

The separate living arrangement also enabled financial compartmentalization. I could mentally separate "Austin expenses" from "family expenses," creating artificial divisions that masked our total financial picture. This fragmentation further complicated effective management of family finances.

A crucial family discussion in 2011 revealed the disconnect that would ultimately prove fatal to both our finances and marriage. When I suggested the family relocate to Austin following my major state contract award, my wife adamantly refused. She was unwilling to uproot the children from their schools and social circles.

This decision to maintain separate households doubled our living expenses while reducing our emotional connection. It turned out to be a devastating combination.

THE MISSING EMERGENCY FUND REALITY

Our lifestyle consumed every dollar of predictable income, while bonuses and commissions served to address accumulated credit card debt rather than building security. This created a perpetual cycle of high-interest debt and repayment that prevented any lasting financial progress and left us without an emergency fund.

More troubling than the missing emergency fund was my rationalization of its absence. As a Certified Financial Planner, I understood the critical importance of emergency savings. Yet I convinced myself that our high income and access to credit lines provided adequate protection. This professional knowledge without personal implementation created a dangerous blind spot. I knew better but acted as if I didn't.

THE BREAKING POINT (2013-2014)

By the end of 2013, living between Austin and Dallas led to financial strain and complete relationship breakdown. The small Austin apartment, chosen initially for its proximity to state agency clients, had become my primary residence. The distance from family reflected the growing emotional and financial divide in our marriage.

The financial impossibility of maintaining two households was apparent. Basics like rent, utilities, groceries, and daily necessities doubled across both locations. The Dallas house, once a symbol of success, now represented mounting obligations our separated lifestyle couldn't support. Credit cards bridged the growing gap between income and expenses, creating an ever-increasing spiral of debt.

THE MATHEMATICS OF FAILURE

By mid-2014, the mathematical impossibility of our situation became unavoidable. Monthly expenses far exceeded reliable income, creating a constant juggling act of minimum payments and delayed obligations. The combined weight of separated living expenses and accumulated debt was unsustainable even with my high income.

The final catalyst came in September 2014. After the loss of my major state contract renewal, I was laid off from my role as a Managing Director. This eliminated predictable income just as credit card balances reached their limits. The immediate impact rippled through our carefully balanced financial juggling act, and we missed several important payments for the first time.

The numbers told a stark story:
- Credit card balances exceeding $200,000
- Personal loans totaling $75,000
- Four Mercedes-Benz vehicles with $35,000 remaining on one loan and the rest in lease payments
- Mortgage of $360,000 plus Home Equity Line of $100,000
- Monthly obligations over $7,500 with uncertain income

My response to this setback demonstrated resilience alongside continued blind spots. The very next day after my layoff, I formed an LLC, registered to do business in Texas, and began pursuing SDVOB (Service-Disabled Veteran-Owned Business) certification. I immediately networked with state agencies and bid on relevant contracts.

Despite immediately forming my business, I secured no work until March 2015. This left me with six months without income carrying unsustainable fixed expenses. My wife's attempt to maintain appearances by borrowing money from her parents only delayed the inevitable and added family tension.

THE DIVORCE DECISION

With the decision to file for divorce, we acknowledged what our physical separation had already demonstrated. Our marriage had ended. The decision wasn't just about emotional distance; it was the first step in untangling years of accumulated financial obligations.

The house sale during our divorce proceedings brought minimal proceeds. This was due to years of equity depletion through credit lines and refinancing. The division of these limited assets proved relatively straightforward, as there was little left to divide. The agreement to assume all remaining debt reflected both my role as the primary account holder and the reality that my wife's lack of employment meant she couldn't share this burden.

The divorce finalization in February 2015 marked the end of a twenty-one-year marriage and the beginning of clarity about financial reality. The separation of our lives and finances revealed the true extent of accumulated obligations, leading to the inevitable next step.

THE BANKRUPTCY DECISION (MARCH 2015)

By March 2015, the veneer of financial sophistication had completely cracked. The divorce settlement, with its clear documentation of debts and obligations, proved what I had avoided acknowledging for years. No amount of future income could correct the fundamental flaws in my financial choices.

The decision to file for bankruptcy was an acceptance of the accumulated consequences of years of poor choices. No client project failure or market downturn had created this situation. My own decisions and denial had built this financial house of cards that now required court protection to dismantle.

The bankruptcy filing process stripped away any remaining pretense about my perceived financial sophistication. Each required form and disclosure documented years of living beyond our means, using credit to maintain appearances, and avoiding fundamental financial reality. Teaching others about financial responsibility while failing to practice basic principles myself reflected a disconnect between knowledge and wisdom.

IMMEDIATE CHANGES

The bankruptcy filing immediately altered my daily financial reality. Basic banking services disappeared as accounts closed. The remaining car loan, reaffirmed to maintain essential transportation, became one of my few ongoing obligations besides rent and child support. This stripped-down financial existence provided the first step toward honest financial rebuilding.

The most valuable lesson emerged from losing access to credit cards and traditional banking services. Each transaction required direct confrontation with available resources rather than deferred responsibility to future income or credit lines. This forced return to financial basics, while humbling, taught me lessons that my financial education had failed to instill.

KEY LESSONS FROM THIS CHAPTER:

Geographic separation compounds financial vulnerability: Physical distance creates both emotional and financial strain. Living between Austin and Dallas effectively doubled expenses while eroding family connections.

High income masks underlying financial dysfunction: Making good money can hide destructive patterns until it's too late. Despite earning six figures consistently, the inability to handle a $3,500 roof repair deductible revealed the fundamental unsustainability of our financial structure.

Small emergencies reveal systemic weaknesses: The roof repair crisis revealed that our lifestyle left no margin for even minor unexpected expenses. An otherwise manageable situation became a financial emergency.

Debt accumulation has mathematical endpoints: There's a point where even high earnings can't overcome accumulated obligations. The final months before bankruptcy demonstrated the reality of unsustainable debt.

Family financial imbalance creates relationship strain: One-sided financial responsibility creates unsustainable pressure. The combination of being the sole provider while maintaining separated households contributed to the collapse of our marriage.

FINANCIAL REALITY CHECK

- Annual Gross: $150,000
- Monthly Take-Home: $13,000
- Monthly Expenses: $14,700
- Monthly Deficit: -$1,700
- Total Assets: $320,000
- Total Debt: $770,000
- Net Worth: -$450,000

This decade-long descent from apparent recovery to complete financial collapse revealed how success without wisdom creates vulnerability. The progressive deterioration across multiple life dimensions, such as my career, family life, and financial health, highlighted the interconnected nature of financial, professional, and personal choices. These patterns, left uncorrected, led to the complete breakdown that would ultimately force fundamental changes in my approach to money, career, and relationships.

CHAPTER III
REBIRTH AND RECOVERY
(2015-2018)

STARTING OVER (2015)

The hardest part of starting over isn't the practical challenges; it's facing yourself in the mirror each morning. Living in my 400-square-foot studio apartment in Austin at the time, I learned this lesson daily. My morning routine became a ritual of rebuilding: reviewing cash balances that barely covered basic needs, scanning job boards and procurement sites for contract opportunities, and reminding myself that this was a beginning, not an end.

The contrast between my previous life as a Managing Director and my new reality proved stark. Instead of leading teams and managing million-dollar projects, I found myself piecing together IT contracts with state agencies. Each small project, often paying just enough to cover monthly child support and basic expenses, required the same dedication I once gave to corporate strategy sessions.

The financial collapse detailed in the previous chapter had left me not just bankrupt but fundamentally changed. The same poor decisions that had created my financial crisis, lifestyle inflation, insufficient emergency savings, and complex debt structures, now served as painful lessons guiding my recovery.

My first significant contract came through in April 2015, six months after the lay-off. It was a three-month database upgrade project for a state agency. The hourly rate was modest compared to my previous compensation, but what it provided was key: a chance to rebuild credibility through actual work rather than past titles. The project's success led to additional opportunities, establishing a foundation for what would become a stable consulting practice.

Rebuilding From Zero
My Post-Bankruptcy Reality

400 Square Foot Studio Apartment

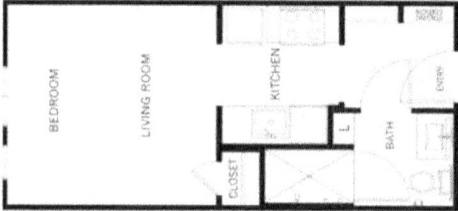

Monthly Financial Reality

Income: Variable (~$3,000)

Rent: $900

Child Support: $500

Car: $600

Other: $470

Total: $2,470/month

Banking Reality

• 3 major banks rejections

• Veteran status opened door at Chase

"The hardest part of starting over isn't the practical challenges, it's facing yourself in the mirror each morning. During those early months of 2015, living in my 400-square-foot studio apartment in Austin, I learned this lesson daily. My morning routine became a ritual of rebuilding..."

THE ESSENTIALS REALITY

Living in that studio apartment taught me valuable lessons about priorities. My twin bed, small desk, and few boxes of possessions weren't signs of failure. They were proof of resilience. When my son visited, sleeping on the IKEA sofa bed, he showed more grace and understanding than I could have imagined. These moments, though challenging, strengthened our relationship in unexpected ways. The financial reality was brutally simple. Monthly essentials included:

- Rent: $900
- Child Support: $500
- Utilities: $125
- Phone: $45
- Food: $200
- Car: $600
- Gas: $100 Total: $2,470

Each month required careful calculation and planning. Without access to credit cards or most traditional banking relationships, every expense needed cash management and precise timing. Three major banks rejected my account applications outright due to bankruptcy, but my veteran status opened an unexpected door.

A LIFELINE

Chase Bank, recognizing military service above financial history, approved me for both premium personal and business checking accounts with no fees or restrictions despite my bankruptcy filing. This acceptance provided not just practical banking services but also a small restoration of dignity during a challenging time. The relationship with Chase, beginning during my lowest financial point, would grow alongside my recovery, where I eventually reached JPMorgan Private Client status. Though at the time, simply having a checking account was a significant victory.

This period taught me that financial recovery isn't about grand strategies. It's about consistent, deliberate actions aligned with clear priorities. The veteran benefit that unlocked basic banking services served as a reminder that past service and future potential sometimes matter more than current circumstances. Each small financial decision and responsibility, managed within newly established banking relationships, built the foundation for longer-term recovery.

RECOVERY PRINCIPLES

My recovery from bankruptcy wasn't just about earning money, it required a complete reinvention of my approach to finances. The principles guiding this rebuilding process would become the foundation for the systems I teach others:

1. Cash Flow Mastery

Unlike my pre-bankruptcy life where I juggled cash flow gaps with credit, I maintained absolute clarity about money movements. Each dollar had a purpose, and my simple spreadsheet tracking system gave me daily visibility into my finances. Complete awareness of cash and obligations was a must.

"The biggest difference in my approach," I often explain to others facing similar challenges, "wasn't just spending less. It was knowing exactly where every dollar needed to go before it arrived."

2. Protection Before Growth

My previous financial approach prioritized appearance and status over security. Now, I reversed this completely. Even with minimal income, I allocated a small portion to emergency savings before considering any other optional expenses. Starting with just $25 weekly automatic transfers, I slowly built what would become my financial safety net as illustrated below.

Small Steps, Big Results

How $25 Weekly Investments Rebuilt My Financial Foundation

3. Incremental System Building

Instead of an immediately perfect financial system, I built components incrementally as resources allowed. First came basic expense tracking, then emergency savings, followed by debt management, and eventually investment. Each component built upon the previous one, creating sustainable progress without overwhelming complexity.

4. Value-Based Decisions

Perhaps most importantly, every financial decision now aligned with core values rather than external appearances. Each expense faced the same simple test: "Does this expenditure support my long-term wellbeing and goals, or merely external perceptions?" This single question eliminated countless unnecessary expenses that previously seemed essential.

These foundational principles of cash flow mastery, protection prioritization, incremental system building, and value alignment transformed my financial rebuilding from a series of reactions into a coherent strategy. While my income remained modest during these early months, these principles would eventually support much greater financial success.

A MENTOR'S IMPACT

During this challenging period, my friend Casey provided another crucial lifeline. When my divorce left me searching for both direction and shelter, he opened his home to me without hesitation. More than just offering a place to stay, Casey became a mentor whose support extended beyond the practical.

His approach to money was thoughtful, intentional, and focused on value rather than status. It stood in contrast to the financial environment that had contributed to my collapse. Where my previous professional circles often encouraged consumption and status signaling, Casey demonstrated that financial security came through restraint and purposeful spending.

"You don't need to impress anyone anymore," he told me one evening as I stressed over rebuilding my professional image. "Focus on creating value and managing what you have. The right opportunities will follow."

This perspective directly countered the status-driven approach that had led to my financial downfall. In my previous life, I had purchased luxury cars and maintained expensive appearances to project success. Casey's simple Chevy Silverado and modest lifestyle, despite his professional achievements, demonstrated a different path.

Casey's impact on my recovery went deeper than personal support. As I worked to rebuild my consulting business, he helped expand my professional network within state agencies, eventually becoming a trusted business partner on several key projects. His mentorship taught me that true friendship isn't just about emotional support. It's about believing in someone's potential even when they struggle to see it themselves. This lesson would later influence how I approached both personal relationships and professional partnerships.

BUILDING FROM ZERO (2015-2016)

Building a consulting practice from scratch taught me that success comes from consistent small actions rather than grand strategies. During the latter half of 2015, my work with state agencies evolved from individual projects into a sustainable business.

The business grew steadily through deliberate steps. By fall 2015, monthly revenue stabilized between $5,000 and $6,000. It was a far cry from my Managing Director salary, but enough to meet essential obligations while slowly building emergency savings. More importantly, this income came from actual value creation rather than borrowed money or unsustainable spending.

CLIENT DEVELOPMENT

State agencies proved ideal clients during my rebuilding phase. Their structured procurement processes meant longer payment cycles but reliable income once established. One particularly valuable relationship developed with the Department of Transportation, where a complex database migration project led to ongoing maintenance work. This stability allowed me to focus on delivery rather than constant business development.

My approach to pricing evolved through experience. Initially, I underpriced services to secure work, but this proved unsustainable. Learning from these mistakes, I developed more sustainable pricing that considered direct work hours, administrative overhead, technology requirements, professional insurance, and self-employment taxes.

The most valuable lesson came from understanding cash flow management. State agencies typically paid 45-60 days after I submitted an invoice, requiring careful planning to maintain stable income. This experience taught me to keep substantial cash reserves and stagger project timelines to ensure consistent revenue.

FINANCIAL MANAGEMENT

Managing business finances requires different skills than personal money management. The contrast between this methodical business building and my previous corporate role proved enlightening. Instead of managing large teams and budgets, I focused on delivering direct value through technical work and project management. This would later prove invaluable in corporate technology leadership.

By mid-2016, the business had grown to approximately $150,000 in gross annual revenue. While this represented significant progress from starting at zero, it also provided a stable platform for both professional and personal rebuilding.

LACEY AND NEW BEGINNINGS (2015-2016)

The hardest conversation about money isn't with a bankruptcy trustee or collections agent. It's with someone you're beginning to care about. In late 2015, as my consulting business finally provided stable income, I faced this challenge with Lacey. In her late twenties, she was over ten years younger than me, but her natural wisdom about money often exceeded her years.

The conversation about my financial past happened over dinner and a bottle of wine on one of our earlier dates. Experience had taught me that honesty about finances needed to come early in any relationship. When I shared everything about my high-flying career, layoff, divorce, bankruptcy, the lessons learned, and my new approach to money, her response surprised me. Instead of judgment, Lacey showed genuine curiosity and empathy, particularly about how these experiences had shaped my personal and financial philosophy.

"I see someone who's learned from mistakes, not someone defined by them," she said, studying me thoughtfully. "Most people never get that kind of financial education. They just keep making the same mistakes their whole lives." Her response wasn't just acceptance. It was the first moment I truly believed recovery wasn't just possible but inevitable. This conversation became a turning point in my journey, providing emotional fuel for the difficult rebuilding work ahead.

Building a Financial Partnership
How Honesty Created Trust

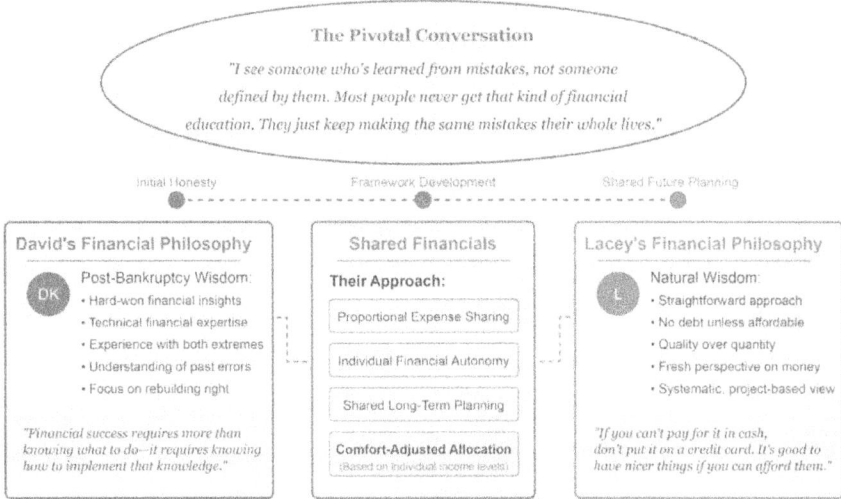

The Pivotal Conversation

"I see someone who's learned from mistakes, not someone defined by them. Most people never get that kind of financial education. They just keep making the same mistakes their whole lives."

Initial Honesty   Framework Development   Shared Future Planning

David's Financial Philosophy

DK

Post-Bankruptcy Wisdom:
• Hard-won financial insights
• Technical financial expertise
• Experience with both extremes
• Understanding of past errors
• Focus on rebuilding right

"Financial success requires more than knowing what to do—it requires knowing how to implement that knowledge."

Shared Financials

Their Approach:

Proportional Expense Sharing

Individual Financial Autonomy

Shared Long-Term Planning

Comfort-Adjusted Allocation
(Based on individual income levels)

Lacey's Financial Philosophy

L

Natural Wisdom:
• Straightforward approach
• No debt unless affordable
• Quality over quantity
• Fresh perspective on money
• Systematic, project-based view

"If you can't pay for it in cash, don't put it on a credit card. It's good to have nicer things if you can afford them."

EARLY RELATIONSHIP DYNAMICS

Our relationship dynamics contrasted sharply with my previous marriage. Where financial discussions had once triggered tension and defensiveness, Lacey and I approached money conversations with openness and curiosity. The financial patterns that had contributed to my bankruptcy had no place in our developing relationship.

Our age difference, which might have been a barrier in some discussions, proved unexpectedly valuable in our financial conversations. While I had experienced the full spectrum of financial success and failure, Lacey was still approaching many financial milestones for the first time. She hadn't yet navigated the complexities of retirement planning, investment strategies, or long-term financial goal setting.

Her financial philosophy was refreshingly straightforward: "If you can't pay for it in cash, don't put it on a credit card." Yet she wasn't afraid to spend on quality when it made sense. "It's good to have nicer things if you can afford them," she explained, "just don't buy things you can't actually afford."

As our relationship deepened through early 2016, we discovered how our different perspectives on money could complement each other. Lacey's instinctive frugality provided a natural check against my occasional impulses toward larger spending, while my hard-won financial wisdom helped her develop more structured approaches to building wealth.

MOVING IN TOGETHER

The decision to move in together in late 2016 marked a pivotal moment in both our relationship and financial journey. Despite my consulting business growing to $150,000 in annual revenue, we approached the transition methodically, reflecting both our personalities. Lacey's systematic project management background and my hard-won financial wisdom created a natural balance in planning.

Rather than rushing into the highest-end apartment we could afford, we chose a modest one-bedroom. This decision, while seemingly simple, demonstrated our shared values about building long-term security over short-term comfort. The reasonable rent left ample room for both saving and investing, supporting our individual and shared financial goals.

We developed a proportional approach to shared expenses that acknowledged our different income levels while maintaining individual financial autonomy. This early financial framework proved crucial, creating a foundation of transparency and respect that would later help us navigate much larger financial decisions. Our complementary perspectives turned what could have been challenging conversations into opportunities for deeper understanding.

DEVELOPING OUR FINANCIAL PARTNERSHIP

In contrast to my previous marriage, our financial discussions were open, productive conversations about money, goals, and values. Lacey's background in agile methodologies brought fresh perspectives to financial planning, helping me see how principles of iterative development and continuous improvement could strengthen our approach to personal finance. These conversations went beyond just numbers, exploring our hopes, fears, and aspirations around money.

The process of merging our financial lives revealed much about our compatibility. Lacey's systematic approach to money management complemented my experience-driven insights, creating a balanced framework that respected both our individual needs and shared future. Together, we built something stronger than either of us could have created alone. We built a financial partnership that would support not just our immediate plans but our long-term dreams of financial independence.

THE RETURN TO CORPORATE LIFE (2017)

My path to Honeywell emerged through an unexpected intersection of my technical work and relationship growth. What began as a casual conversation about software development methodologies evolved into an opportunity that would fundamentally shift my career trajectory.

PROFESSIONAL TURNING POINT: THE HONEYWELL INTERVIEW

The timing of this opportunity happened during a critical period. Recent changes in state contracting rules threatened the viability of my independent consulting business. At this time, a routine project presentation caught the attention of a visiting Honeywell executive. While presenting recommendations for optimizing a state agency's software development process, my blend of technical and business acumen sparked his interest.

After the meeting, a casual discussion about agile methodology uncovered an intriguing revelation: Honeywell's Software Solutions division was seeking a Director and Deputy CTO. The role would involve leading their transformation from traditional waterfall development to agile practices across multiple teams globally.

Initially, I dismissed the possibility. The position seemed beyond my reach. It was a common reaction born from lingering self-doubt after bankruptcy. That evening, I shared my hesitation with Lacey. "I've never formally led an agile team," I explained, recounting my years of traditional project management experience. "My agile knowledge is theoretical at best."

Lacey's response shifted my perspective entirely: "But you understand systems, people, and delivery. The specific methodology is just a framework you can learn. You've been adapting to new environments your entire career."

When I still hesitated, she pushed harder: "The job description is asking for what you can become, not just what you've already done. Get certified in agile this weekend, then talk to them on Monday as someone who's already closing the gap."

Her perspective, unbound by my past failures and limitations, helped me see possibilities I had overlooked. That weekend, I completed an accelerated agile certification course.

The interview process revealed how much my approach to corporate opportunity had evolved. Rather than focusing on title or status, my questions centered on team dynamics, organizational challenges, and real opportunities for impact. The technical work during my consulting years proved invaluable, giving me credibility when discussing technical and business objectives.

After three rounds of interviews, Honeywell extended an offer for the Director and Deputy CTO position with a base salary of $200,000. This represented both stability and opportunity, though it required careful consideration of the transition from consulting income.

PROFESSIONAL INTEGRATION

My return to corporate leadership demonstrated significant personal growth. No longer prioritizing title and status, I found myself genuinely concerned with building effective teams and delivering meaningful solutions. My experience doing hands-on technical work during my consulting years proved invaluable, allowing me to bridge the gap between technical and business objectives.

The timing of this career move coincided with another significant life event. Lacey and I became engaged in July 2017, just after I joined Honeywell. These parallel transitions reflected our shared approach to building a future together, making deliberate choices that aligned with our values rather than external expectations. Our engagement, like my career transition, emphasized substance over show, focusing on what truly mattered rather than superficial displays.

FINANCIAL TRANSITION

The shift from independent consulting to corporate employment required careful financial planning. While the predictable base salary provided welcome stability, managing the transition period required careful planning. We developed a three-month cash buffer to handle the gap between incoming final consulting payments and my first corporate paycheck.

The corporate environment at Honeywell revealed how much I had changed. The same structured environment that once encouraged lifestyle inflation now served as a platform for building sustainable wealth. Even with increased income, we maintained our modest living arrangements and focused on building long-term security.

CREATING A NEW FOUNDATION (2017)

Building a new foundation during my first year at Honeywell involved more than just professional transition. It required integrating lessons from both failure and recovery into a sustainable approach to success. The stability of corporate income combined with Lacey's influence helped create a framework for long-term financial security that differed dramatically from my previous corporate experience.

FINANCIAL RESTRUCTURING

Our approach to managing increased income reflected both my hard-learned lessons and Lacey's natural prudence. We maintained our modest lifestyle despite my $200,000 base salary. The one-bedroom apartment that served us well during consulting continued to meet our needs. We directed additional income toward building security rather than lifestyle inflation.

"We're making more now," Lacey observed one evening as we reviewed our growing savings, "but that doesn't mean we need to start spending like rich people. Being comfortable is enough." Her perspective helped shape our "long term, security-first" approach to allocating income:

- Essential expenses (30% of net income)
- Emergency savings (20%)
- Retirement funding (25%)
- Investment building (15%)
- Lifestyle spending (10%)

This conservative framework, maintaining lifestyle expenses at just 10% of net income, created rapid wealth accumulation while still allowing us to enjoy our increasing resources. The balance between immediate enjoyment and future security became a hallmark of our financial partnership.

PERSONAL GROWTH

Engagement and career transition created opportunities for deeper discussions about our future. Lacey and I spent evenings planning not just our wedding but our long-term life strategy. These conversations covered career development goals, family planning timeline, geographic preferences, lifestyle aspirations, and financial independence targets.

Our over ten-year age difference influenced these discussions in unexpected ways. My experience with both financial success and failure provided perspective, while Lacey's fresh viewpoint challenged assumptions about traditional career and life paths. Together, we created plans that balanced immediate needs with long-term aspirations.

INVESTMENT FOUNDATION

Building our investment foundation marked a significant departure from my previous approach to wealth building. Instead of focusing on quick gains or status symbols, we developed a methodical approach to creating lasting financial security.

The most valuable lesson from this period came from gaining an understanding how different types of investments serve different purposes. We focused on building a diversified foundation for sustainable long-term growth over seeking the highest possible returns

RELATIONSHIP GROWTH

Our engagement period provided opportunities to align our financial values more deeply. Regular financial discussions became not just about numbers but about building a shared vision for our future.

These discussions went beyond basic budgeting to include deeper questions about what we wanted from life and how financial decisions could support those aspirations. This foundation of open communication about money would prove invaluable as our financial situation grew more complex.

KEY LESSONS FROM THIS CHAPTER:

Honesty creates unexpected opportunities: Financial transparency (with Lacey) builds rather than destroys relationships. The third-date financial confession that I feared would end our relationship instead became the foundation for its strength.

Starting small builds sustainable habits: Beginning with $25 weekly investments creates patterns that scale with income. The disciplined approach to rebuilding from zero establishes habits that support wealth later.

Recovery requires both emotional and financial support: Mentors like Casey and partners like Lacey provide crucial encouragement during rebuilding.. Support systems make sustainable rebuilding possible.

Clear targets accelerate progress: Specific financial milestones ($50k, $100k, etc.) create momentum. Setting concrete net worth targets and tracking progress against them created measurable forward movement.

Past failures can become future strengths: Bankruptcy experience creates wisdom that benefits future decisions. The painful lessons from financial collapse provided invaluable perspective for building more sustainable success.

FINANCIAL REALITY CHECK (PROGRESSION 2015-2019)

Early Recovery (Early 2015)
- Annual Gross: $100,000 (projected from consulting)
- Monthly Take-Home: $5,000 (average, highly variable)
- Monthly Expenses: $3,270
    - Rent: $900
    - Child Support: $500
    - Utilities: $125
    - Phone: $45
    - Food: $200
    - Car: $600

- o   Gas: $100
- o   Other essentials: $800
- Monthly Savings: $1,730 (directed primarily to emergency fund)
- Total Assets: $2,500 (primarily emergency savings)
- Total Debt: $0 (post-bankruptcy)
- Net Worth: $2,500

Mid-Recovery (Early 2017)

- Annual Gross: $150,000 (consulting revenue)
- Monthly Take-Home: $8,500
- Monthly Expenses: $3,960 (modest lifestyle inflation)
- Monthly Savings: $4,540 (now including retirement contributions)
- Total Assets: $42,000 (emergency + beginning investments)
- Total Debt: $0
- Net Worth: $42,000

Honeywell (2018)

- Annual Gross: $295,000 (salary + bonus)
- Monthly Take-Home: $12,500
- Monthly Expenses: $5,440
  - o   Rent: $1,300
  - o   Child Support: $500
  - o   Utilities: $250
  - o   Phone: $90
  - o   Food: $600
  - o   Car: $700
  - o   Insurance: $300
  - o   Other essentials: $1,700
- Monthly Savings: $7,060 (aggressive wealth building)
- Total Assets: $180,000 (emergency + investments + retirement)
- Total Debt: $0
- Net Worth: $180,000

This financial progression demonstrates the power of maintaining lifestyle stability while income grows. My income nearly tripled from early 2015 to 2018. However, my monthly expenses increased by only 66%. I directed the majority of income increases toward building assets rather than expanding lifestyle.

The transformation from bankruptcy to new beginnings involved more than just financial recovery. Each phase, from early consulting through relationship development to corporate return, was built upon previous lessons and created a foundation for future growth. The period proved that true rebuilding requires attention to both professional and personal aspects of life.

CHAPTER IV
THE NEW FOUNDATION
(2018-2022+)

Our August 2018 wedding in Las Vegas represented more than just the union of our lives. It marked a personal and financial transformation that began in the darkest moments of bankruptcy. As I stood beside Lacey, exchanging vows in an intimate ceremony with just 25 of our closest family and friends, I couldn't help reflecting on the contrast between this moment and my financial collapse just three years earlier.

The decision to have a modest, meaningful wedding rather than an extravagant display wasn't driven by financial constraints. Both our careers were thriving, and we could have afforded something more elaborate. Instead, it demonstrated our mutual belief that true value comes from experiences shared with those who matter most, not from external validation or appearances. This shift in perspective represented the most profound lesson from my bankruptcy journey. The wedding, funded entirely in cash and planned within our means while still feeling special, embodied the balanced approach to finances we'd built together.

Having Casey as my best man and Kristen as Lacey's maid of honor, with no additional wedding party, kept the focus on what truly mattered. Casey had stood by me during the rebuilding of my life after bankruptcy, while Kristen had supported Lacey through her own life transitions, even having a small hand in our relationship. Their presence represented the importance of having people who believe in you through both struggles and successes.

PROGRESSION AT HONEYWELL (2018-2019)

From the time I started in 2017 and on to 2018, my role at Honeywell allowed me to establish both professional credibility and financial stability. As Director and Deputy CTO, I led the transformation of multiple development teams from traditional waterfall to agile methodologies. More importantly, I applied the financial lessons learned during recovery to build lasting security.

Then, a transformative opportunity emerged that would deepen both my technical expertise and leadership capabilities. I was tasked with leading the migration of Honeywell's alarm signaling data center infrastructure to the cloud. This was a mission-critical system processing millions of security and fire alarm signals daily from IoT devices across North America. It wasn't just a lift-and-shift operation; it required reimagining how alarm signals could be processed more efficiently in a cloud environment while maintaining the stringent reliability requirements of life-safety systems.

The project pushed me to expand my technical knowledge significantly. I dove deep into cloud-native architectures, IoT device management at scale, and the complexities of maintaining real-time communication with millions of edge devices. Working closely with both the security systems team and cloud architects, we developed innovative solutions for handling legacy protocols in a modern cloud environment while ensuring the sub-second response times.

FINANCIAL PROGRESSION

With our emergency fund fully established at six months of expenses, we began implementing a more aggressive investment strategy. Our approach remained conservative by typical standards, but methodical:

- Maxing out my 401(k) to IRS limits, also with Honeywell's 6% match
- Establishing Roth IRAs for both Lacey and me through backdoor
- Maintaining our modest lifestyle despite increasing income

By the end of 2018, our net worth had grown significantly while our monthly expenses remained nearly unchanged from my consulting days. The chart below highlights the difference between our income and expenses.

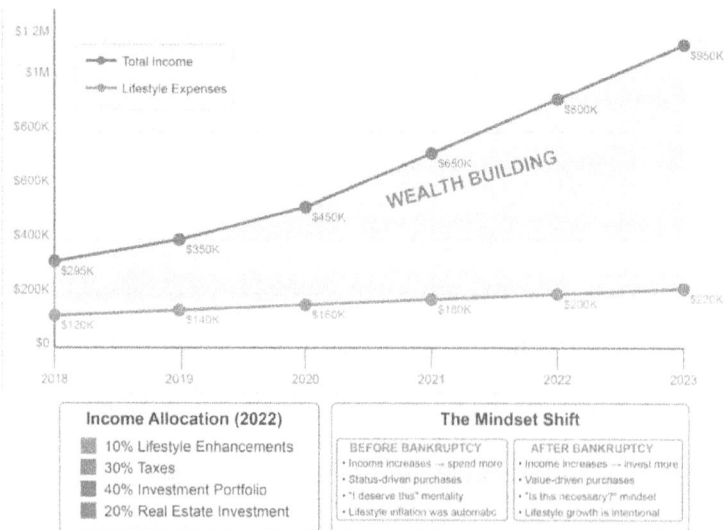

Income Allocation (2022)	The Mindset Shift	
10% Lifestyle Enhancements	BEFORE BANKRUPTCY	AFTER BANKRUPTCY
30% Taxes	• Income increases → spend more	• Income increases → invest more
40% Investment Portfolio	• Status-driven purchases	• Value-driven purchases
20% Real Estate Investment	• "I deserve this" mentality	• "Is this necessary?" mindset
	• Lifestyle inflation was automatic	• Lifestyle growth is intentional

BALANCING GROWTH WITH PROTECTION

The lessons from my financial collapse shaped our approach to this period of career growth. Despite increasing financial success, the memory of bankruptcy remained a powerful teacher guiding our decisions. I once viewed financial safety nets as optional, now I recognized them as essential components of sustainable success.

Accordingly, we implemented several concrete practices:

First, we maintained higher emergency reserves than conventional wisdom suggested. Financial advisors typically recommend saving for 3-6 months of expenses. We opted to build and maintain a full year of essential expenses in high-yield savings accounts. This wasn't fear-based hoarding but strategic risk management based on lived experience.

Second, we created intentional separation between different financial assets and accounts. After experiencing how quickly financial problems can cascade across connected accounts, we established clear firebreaks between different elements of our financial life. Career assets, investment accounts, property holdings, and emergency funds were structured to prevent contagion from any single financial setback.

Third, we developed a quarterly review of potential financial weaknesses and appropriate mitigation strategies. This practice forced us to regularly ask uncomfortable but crucial questions: What would happen if I lost my job? What if the market dropped 40%? What if we faced a major health emergency? By confronting these scenarios proactively, we built resilience into our financial system.

Perhaps most importantly, we recognized that true security comes not from eliminating all risk, but from building sufficient margins to weather inevitable setbacks. This meant making intentional trade-offs, such as accepting slightly lower investment returns in exchange for greater stability or maintaining high cash positions.

"The most sophisticated financial strategy becomes worthless if a single emergency forces you to abandon it," Lacey observed during one planning session. This insight captured our balanced approach perfectly. We pursued growth aggressively, but never at the expense of security.

THE GENPACT OPPORTUNITY (2019)

In early 2019, my former manager at Honeywell, the CTO that I had been hired by and reported to and had become both my mentor and friend, reached out with an intriguing proposition. He had joined Genpact as a senior executive and was building a new cloud transformation practice. His vision: create a consulting organization helping Fortune 100 companies establish cloud centers of excellence to accelerate their migration to AWS, Azure, and Google Cloud.

"I need someone who understands both the technical and human sides of transformation," he explained. "Someone who can talk cloud architecture with engineers while helping executives understand the business case for change, someone who has done it before at scale."

The role of Vice President of Cloud Transformation came with a substantial compensation increase to over $300,000. It also offered the chance to build something meaningful. The opportunity to help large organizations navigate their cloud journeys while building a consulting practice from the ground up aligned perfectly with my technical background and consulting experience.

THOUGHTFUL TRANSITION

The decision to join Genpact required more careful consideration than any previous career move. Unlike my earlier transitions driven primarily by compensation, Lacey and I approached this opportunity with a broader perspective. We spent many late evenings discussing how this role would shape our finances and entire life together.

"This isn't just about the money," Lacey observed one evening as we discussed the opportunity. "It's about what kind of life we want to build together." While the compensation increase was substantial, we found ourselves focusing more on how the role's travel requirements would affect our time together, how its remote work flexibility could support our future plans, and how leading a new practice aligned with our developing FIRE goals.

The geographic flexibility of the position particularly intrigued us. As we developed our long-term plans, the ability to work from anywhere opened possibilities we hadn't previously considered. We discussed how this flexibility could eventually support our dream of moving closer to family while maintaining career growth. The role's potential impact on work-life balance became a central topic, especially considering the demands of building a new practice from the ground up.

BUILDING THE PRACTICE

My role at Genpact evolved into something far more significant than initially envisioned. Taking on the challenge of creating a cloud transformation practice meant building everything from scratch. I built organizations of multiple teams, technical frameworks, consulting methodologies, and client relationships. By late 2019, our efforts had transformed an initial concept into a thriving practice serving Fortune 100 clients.

The development of our cloud architecture frameworks marked a crucial milestone, combining cutting-edge technical expertise with practical business applications. Through partnerships with Microsoft Azure and Amazon Web Services, we established ourselves as a serious player in the cloud transformation space. Our reputation grew as we developed repeatable, effective solutions for common client challenges.

Our success with several Fortune 50 clients validated our approach. Each engagement helped refine our methodologies, contributing to a growing body of proven practices and solutions. This foundation would later prove instrumental in my transition to Big Tech, though at the time I focused solely on building something lasting at Genpact.

HOME PURCHASE DECISION (2020)

By early 2020, our disciplined saving had created a substantial down payment fund, which we ended up not needing because of my VA loan eligibility. Despite our combined income at the time providing significant buying power, we maintained our conservative approach as we shopped:

- Set a firm budget keeping monthly housing costs below 20% of net income
- Chose a new construction home in a developing area
- Used my VA loan benefit for zero down payment
- Maintained significant cash reserves even after purchase
- Selected a home well below our maximum qualification

The Austin housing market was booming, but we resisted the temptation to overextend. Instead of purchasing at the top of our budget, we found a new construction home in a newly developing area that met our needs while leaving plenty of room for saving and investing.

This balanced perspective helped us avoid the trap of status-driven home purchase that had contributed to my previous financial problems. Instead, we approached homeownership as one component of our overall financial strategy rather than as a status symbol.

FINANCIAL FRAMEWORK

Our home purchase approach differed dramatically from my pre-bankruptcy real estate decisions. We prioritized sustainable affordability.

The timing of our purchase proved fortunate, though we couldn't have known it then. We closed on our home just before the market experienced its dramatic pandemic-driven surge. The pandemic lockdowns hit the week after our move-in date. However, the real victory wasn't in the timing. It was in maintaining our disciplined approach to housing costs even when we could have spent considerably more.

Our monthly housing costs, including mortgage, taxes, insurance, and maintenance reserve, consumed less than 20% of our net income. This provided flexibility which helped further other financial goals.

THE BIG TECH OPPORTUNITY (2021)

While leading cloud transformation initiatives at Genpact, our work with Fortune 50 companies caught the attention of recruiters from a major tech firm. We started with an exploratory conversation, which evolved into serious discussions about two different senior leadership roles. Both positions would leverage my technical expertise and delivery execution with strategic vision.

The choice came down to two distinct opportunities: one in their Professional Services division and another in their Public Sector division. Both aligned with my background; I had consulting experience relevant to Professional Services and had worked extensively with government agencies at both federal and state levels. While the positions offered similar levels of responsibility and comparable compensation, the Public Sector role presented more promising growth potential. The company's expanding government contracts and increasing investment in this division suggested greater opportunities for advancement and impact.

What truly resonated with me was the company's commitment to work-life harmony and their position as a technology leader; values that had become increasingly important during my career rebuilding journey.

The compensation package was nearly double my Genpact compensation, but it was structured quite differently. The base salary of $160,000 represented a significant reduction from what I was earning at Genpact. This decrease was balanced by substantial sign-on bonuses for the first two years and generous RSU grants that increase in value with time. Evaluating this offer required looking beyond immediate numbers to the long-term, especially in the faster-growing Public Sector division where my expertise could create greater impact.

Facing this complex career decision, Lacey and I applied a decision framework we'd developed through my financial recovery. I examined opportunities through multiple lenses rather than focusing solely on compensation. This multi-faceted approach had emerged directly from the lessons of my bankruptcy. I'd learned that career decisions based primarily on money often led to imbalanced outcomes. Our framework evaluated opportunities across four key dimensions:

1. **Financial Impact:** Beyond just headline compensation figures, we analyzed the complete picture including base salary, equity potential, benefits value, geographic considerations, and tax implications. We

simulated different scenarios, conservative, moderate, and optimistic, to understand the full range of possible outcomes.

2. **Life Integration:** We assessed how the role would affect our overall life quality, including work schedule flexibility, stress levels, travel requirements, and compatibility with our long-term geographic preferences. This dimension had been absent from my pre-bankruptcy career decisions.

3. **Growth Potential:** We evaluated how the position would expand my skills, network, and future opportunities rather than just immediate benefits.

4. **Alignment with Values:** We considered how the role aligned with our core values of balance, continued learning, and building meaningful impact. This values-based assessment would have seemed foreign to my pre-bankruptcy self.

We spent several evenings analyzing the opportunity from multiple angles. The compensation package, heavily dependent on stock price, required careful evaluation. I calculated a realistic range by considering both upside potential and a significant downside scenario. Even if the company's stock dropped by 50%; which seemed like a reasonable floor given the company's size and market position; the total compensation would still be only about 10% less than my Genpact package. However, with normal market performance, the same package could deliver up to 80% more.

With this wide range of potential outcomes, we looked beyond just the numbers. We evaluated the role's potential for career growth, its alignment with industry direction, and particularly the flexibility of remote work. The decision wasn't just about immediate compensation; it was about positioning ourselves strategically for our future plans.

After applying our framework, the decision became clear despite the base salary reduction. The role offered an optimal balance across all four dimensions in our framework.

Where I once would have chased the highest immediate compensation regardless of other factors, I understood that sustainable success required a more comprehensive evaluation that factored more than just compensation.

TECHNICAL LEADERSHIP AND INTEGRATION

The Big Tech role marked a full-circle moment in my career. The hands-on technical work I'd done during my consulting recovery might have seemed like a step backward at the time. It proved invaluable in understanding Big Tech's technology landscape. My experience bridging technical and business perspectives, refined through various roles, aligned perfectly with their leadership principles.

In this role, I would be responsible for developing technical strategy, building teams across multiple regions and guiding customer cloud transformation initiatives. The position demanded both deep technical knowledge and the ability to drive organizational change. This was a combination that my diverse career path had uniquely prepared me for.

MANAGING COMPLEX COMPENSATION

The equity compensation component required more sophisticated planning than any previous role. Working with Lacey, we developed a systematic approach to managing the RSUs. Her project management background was invaluable as we created structured approaches for handling vesting schedules, tax implications, and diversification strategies.

Rather than viewing the RSUs as a lottery ticket, we treated them as a component of our long-term financial strategy. We analyzed vesting schedules, planned for tax impacts, and developed clear holding period decisions that aligned with our risk management approach.

LIFESTYLE AND FINANCIAL STRATEGY

Although this role provided me with a higher total compensation potential, we maintained our conservative lifestyle approach. The lower base salary helped reinforced this discipline. Our strategy for managing the additional income reflected this cautious approach.

We allocated earnings thoughtfully: maintaining our existing living expenses at previous levels, setting aside 30% of additional income for taxes, directing 40% toward our investment portfolio, dedicating 20% to a real estate investment fund, and allowing just 10% for lifestyle enhancements. This structured approach helped us avoid lifestyle inflation.

PROFESSIONAL INTEGRATION AND REMOTE WORK

The transition to Big Tech required adapting my leadership approach while maintaining core principles. My role focused on developing cloud transformation strategies, architecting enterprise solutions, and leading global teams. The combination of my technical expertise and business acumen was instrumental as I helped clients navigate their own transformation journeys.

Big Tech's embrace of remote work created both opportunities and challenges. Leading teams across multiple time zones required new approaches to collaboration and team building. We established clear communication protocols and virtual team-building practices while maintaining strict work-life boundaries. This structure allowed us to maintain our home base while engaging with teams globally.

THE NASHVILLE DECISION (2022)

Our decision to relocate from Austin to Nashville emerged from deep discussions about quality of life and family connections. While our Austin home had doubled in value over just two years, our move wasn't primarily financially motivated. Instead, we sought to create a more sustainable lifestyle that would support both our current needs and future aspirations.

Nashville offered compelling advantages beyond just financial benefits. The comparable cost of living, lower property tax, and absence of state income tax were attractive, but the real draw was family accessibility. The dramatic reduction in travel time to Indianapolis, from a 16-hour drive to just over four hours, meant more frequent family connections. The strong healthcare infrastructure and cultural opportunities aligned with our long-term lifestyle goals.

The timing of our move proved fortunate given the housing market. The sale demonstrated the wisdom of our conservative approach. By keeping our housing costs below traditional guidelines, we built significant equity without becoming house-poor. The two-year ownership period qualified us for the primary residence capital gains exclusion, protecting our substantial profit from taxes.

Beyond the Numbers

How We Evaluated the Nashville Relocation

Factor	Austin, TX		Nashville, TN	
Financial Factors				
Housing Cost	Median home: $640,000+	●	Median home: $450,000	●
Tax Burden	No state income tax, high property tax	●	No state income tax, lower property tax	●
Quality of Life Factors				
Family Access	16-hour drive to Indianapolis	●	4-hour drive to Indianapolis	●
Healthcare	Good options, higher traffic	●	Vanderbilt Medical Center, less traffic	●
Future Growth Factors				
Investment Growth	Market possibly overheated	●	Strong growth, still affordable	●

● Better   ● Neutral   ● Worse

Austin Home Value Appreciation	"Our Nashville decision wasn't about fleeing Austin, but consciously choosing a lifestyle that supported our long-term goals."
Purchased: $600,000 (2020)	
Sold: $1,200,000 (2022)	

FINDING OUR NASHVILLE HOME

We relied on the same disciplined approach we'd used in Austin to conduct our Nashville home search. We committed to keeping housing costs below 20% of our net income regardless of increased income alongside proceeds from the Austin sale. As Lacey often reminded me, "Just because we can afford more doesn't mean we should spend more."

This self-imposed constraint wasn't about affordability; it was about maintaining financial flexibility. We focused on finding a home that would support effective remote work, with dedicated office spaces, robust internet infrastructure, and proper sound isolation. The inclusion of backup power options and separate work entrances was ideal for a sustainable work-from-home environment.

BUILDING MULTIPLE INCOME STREAMS (2022)

The sale of our Austin home created an opportunity to develop multiple income streams. Rather than simply banking the profits or investing everything in traditional markets, we approached wealth-building more systematically.

Our first major diversification came through real estate investment. Drawing on both the painful lessons from bankruptcy and new financial wisdom, we developed a carefully structured approach to property investment. Our first direct property investment was a single-family home, purchased using a DSCR (Debt Service Coverage Ratio) loan that qualified based on the property's potential rental income rather than our personal income. This structure created scalability for future acquisitions while maintaining separation between personal and investment finances.

As Lacey noted after closing on our first rental property, "Your bankruptcy actually taught us both to be more thoughtful real estate investors. We're approaching this as a business with proper structure and risk management, not as an extension of personal finances." Her observation captured how lessons from financial failure had transformed into wisdom that informed more successful investment approaches.

Beyond direct property ownership, we diversified into commercial real estate through crowdfunding platforms and REITs, creating exposure to different property types without the management intensity of direct ownership. Each investment vehicle served specific purposes in our portfolio, from current income generation to long-term appreciation potential.

HOUSEHOLD INCOME

Risk Exposure: Diversified

Big Tech Compensation	Real Estate Investments	Investment Portfolio
Primary Income Source	Passive Income	Market Investments
(60% of Income)	(20% of Income)	(15% of Income)
MODERATE RISK	LOW RISK	MODERATE RISK

Base Salary	RSU Grants	Rental Property	REITs	Stock Portfolio
$160,000	$700,000+	Single-Family Home	Commercial Real Estate	Dividend Investments
LOW RISK	HIGH RISK	MODERATE RISK	LOW RISK	MODERATE RISK

VA Disability Compensation (5% of Income) - Guaranteed for Life
ZERO RISK

Pre-Bankruptcy vs. Current Risk Exposure
PRE-BANKRUPTCY: 100% SINGLE INCOME SOURCE   CURRENT: MULTIPLE DIVERSIFIED STREAMS

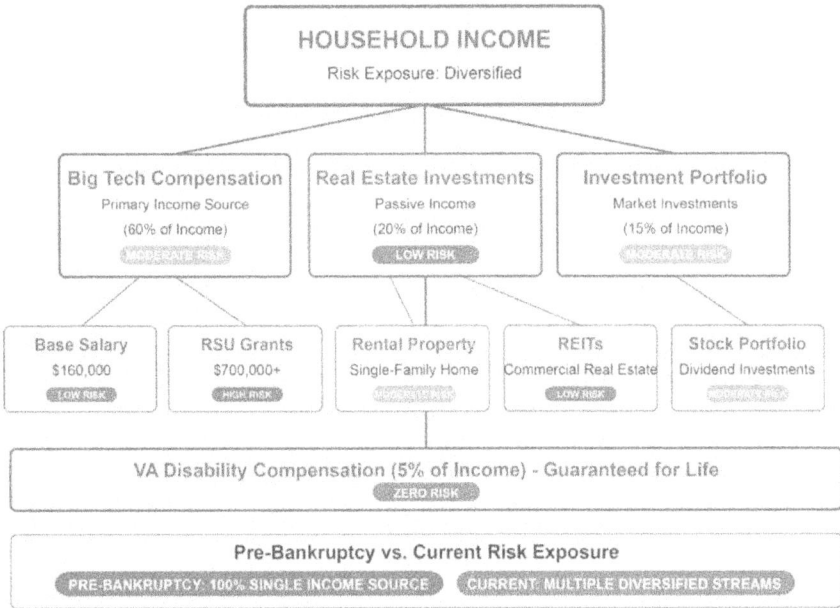

DIVERSIFYING INCOME SOURCES

Our income diversification extended beyond real estate. Our combined salaries and bonuses provided our primary income, but we strategically built additional streams: rental property income, commercial real estate returns, dividend-focused investments, municipal bond interest, and my VA disability compensation. Each stream served a specific purpose. Some provided immediate cash flow, others focused on long-term appreciation or tax advantages.

This diverse approach reflected one of the most crucial lessons from bankruptcy: **never again would we be overly dependent on a single income source.** The strategy provided immediate security and long-term resilience against potential career or market disruptions.

THE FIRE JOURNEY (2022 AND BEYOND)

As our income streams diversified and assets grew, our pursuit of Financial Independence, Retire Early (FIRE) evolved beyond savings targets. While my Big Tech compensation provided substantial current income, we focused increasingly on building sustainable wealth that could support early retirement. Our target became achieving financial independence by age 55, using a conservative 3% withdrawal rate that would maintain our lifestyle while accounting for healthcare costs before Medicare eligibility.

This FIRE journey represented a transformation of my relationship with money. Where bankruptcy had once forced a reckoning with financial reality, FIRE represented a chosen discipline. It is voluntary simplicity and intentional financial planning in service of future freedom.

The irony wasn't lost on us that my journey from financial collapse to potential early retirement spanned just over a decade. This transformation wasn't through some secret investment strategy or experiencing a sudden windfall. We applied fundamental principles consistently: living below our means, investing systematically, and aligning our financial decisions with deeper values.

PORTFOLIO CONSTRUCTION FOR INDEPENDENCE

Our approach to FIRE differed significantly from traditional models. Rather than relying solely on stocks and bonds, we built a diversified portfolio across multiple asset classes. Traditional retirement accounts formed our foundation, complemented by taxable investment accounts holding a mix of stocks, REITs, and ETFs, and my VA disability income. Our real estate holdings provided both appreciation potential and inflation protection, while a small cryptocurrency position offered exposure to emerging digital assets.

This diversified approach directly addressed the risks I'd previously experienced. My pre-bankruptcy finances had concentrated risk through excessive leverage and inadequate diversification. Our FIRE strategy distributed risk across multiple uncorrelated assets. We established guardrails like limiting crypto exposure to 5% regardless of performance.

Lacey's perspective helped maintain our focus during market volatility. "We're not trying to get rich quick," she would remind me during investment discussions. "We're building a portfolio that can weather any storm and support us for decades."

HEALTHCARE PLANNING FOR EARLY RETIREMENT

Healthcare costs emerged as one of our biggest challenges in FIRE planning. The potential impact of extended care requirements on personal and family finances makes this an increasingly important aspect of comprehensive protection. Understanding available options and appropriate timing for long-term care coverage helps create sustainable protection.

Our planning involved developing multiple scenarios for coverage between early retirement and Medicare eligibility, including maximizing HSA contributions, evaluating long-term care options, and integrating VA healthcare benefits. We even researched potential geographic arbitrage through international healthcare options, understanding that medical costs could significantly impact our withdrawal strategy.

CREATING A SUSTAINABLE WITHDRAWAL STRATEGY

We chose to target a 3% withdrawal rate, substantially more conservative than the traditional 4% rule, to further promote long-term security. This conservative approach, combined with multiple income streams and government benefits such as VA Disability and potential SSDI, created redundancy in our retirement funding. We structured our withdrawal strategy to be tax-efficient while maintaining buffers for healthcare costs and inflation protection.

The journey toward financial independence has reinforced the most valuable lesson from my financial recovery: sustainable success comes from patient, methodical progress rather than aggressive shortcuts. Each decision, from asset allocation to withdrawal planning, reflects both the wisdom gained from past failures and our commitment to building lasting financial security.

This FIRE journey represents more than just a financial strategy. It embodies a complete transformation in my relationship with money. From the unstable financial foundation that led to bankruptcy to the deliberate, values-aligned approach we follow, the contrast couldn't be more profound. While the bankruptcy taught me what doesn't work, our FIRE journey represents what does; it represents sustainable practices aligned with deeper purpose and consistent principles applied over time.

KEY LESSONS FROM THIS CHAPTER:

True success balances earning with preserving: Focus on maintaining rather than just acquiring wealth. Our decision to maintain modest lifestyle costs despite substantial income growth created accelerated wealth building and financial freedom.

Long-term planning requires proportional thinking: The 30/20/50 framework scales across income levels. Maintaining percentage-based allocation rather than fixed dollar budgets prevented lifestyle inflation as income increased.

Compensation structure matters more than headline numbers: Understanding total compensation beyond base salary is crucial. The Big Tech decision demonstrated how evaluating full compensation packages, including equity components, leads to better long-term outcomes.

Geographic flexibility creates financial advantages: Willingness to relocate can significantly impact wealth building. The Nashville move illustrated how location decisions affect both financial outcomes and life quality.

Multiple income streams create true security: Diversifying beyond employment income provides lasting stability. Our systematic development of passive income sources created resilience against potential career disruptions.

FINANCIAL REALITY CHECK

Genpact (2019-2021)
- Total Gross: $426,000
- Monthly Take-Home: $24,500
- Monthly Expenses: $13,200
- Monthly Savings: $11,300
- Total Assets: $1,357,000
- Total Debt: $652,000
- Net Worth: $705,000

Big Tech + Investing (2021-2025)
- Total Gross: $900,000
- Monthly Take-Home: $45,000
- Monthly Expenses: $20,000
- Monthly Savings: $25,000
- Total Assets: $4,480,000
- Total Debt: $1,980,000
- Net Worth: $2,500,000

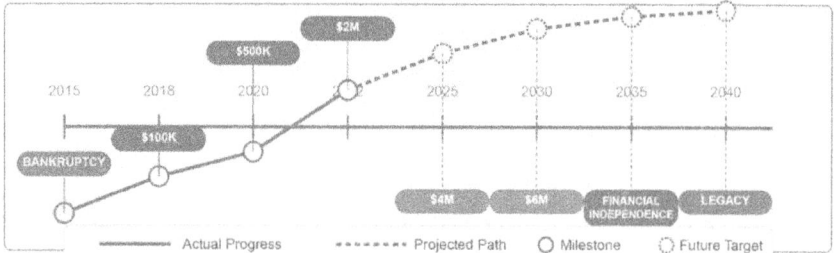

FIRE Strategy Components
- 3% Safe Withdrawal Rate
- Multiple Income Streams
- Real Estate Portfolio
- Tax-Efficient Withdrawal Planning
- Healthcare Coverage Bridge to Medicare
- Geographic Flexibility
- Continued Part-Time Work Options

Redefining Success

"The FIRE journey represents more than just a financial strategy. It embodies a complete transformation in my relationship with money. While the bankruptcy taught me what doesn't work, our FIRE journey represents what does: sustainable practices aligned with deeper purpose."

The transformation from recovery to lasting success demonstrated how fundamental principles create sustainable prosperity. Each phase of this period from corporate progression through Big Tech to FIRE planning built upon lessons learned while adapting to new opportunities and challenges.

Most importantly, this chapter showed how financial success supports life goals rather than defining them. Each decision, from career moves to investment choices, reflected careful consideration of both immediate impact and long-term implications.

The contrast between this thoughtful approach and my pre-bankruptcy financial management is stark. Where I once made decisions based primarily on status and appearance, often ignoring fundamental financial principles, I approached each choice through a comprehensive framework considering sustainability, alignment with values, and long-term impact.

FROM EXPERIENCE TO UNIVERSAL PRACTICAL APPLICATON

The journey from bankruptcy through recovery to sustainable success proved that lasting prosperity comes not from pursuing wealth alone, but from building systems that support both financial security and personal fulfillment. These lessons continue guiding decisions as we move forward, maintaining focus on fundamental principles while adapting to new opportunities and challenges.

FROM MY JOURNEY TO YOURS: HOW TO USE THIS MANUAL

If you've read this far, you've walked with me through the highest highs and lowest lows of my financial life. You've seen how an MBA and CFP training couldn't prevent catastrophic decisions. You've witnessed what happens when lifestyle inflation meets insufficient emergency reserves. And you've watched the slow, deliberate process of rebuilding; not just finances, but identity, relationships, and purpose.

Now it's time to turn these hard-won lessons into your advantage.

THE LESSONS BEHIND THE MANUAL

Every chapter in Part II emerges from a specific moment in my journey. Understanding these connections will help you see that the strategies aren't theoretical; they're battle-tested:

The $400 car repair that nearly derailed my recovery became the foundation for Chapter 4: Emergency Funds. When you read about building financial buffers, know that I'm writing from the experience of staring at an ATM screen, card declined, wondering how I'd get to work.

The bankruptcy that erased $200,000 in debt but left my student loans intact shapes Chapter 2: Debt Management and Chapter 5: Student Loans. Not all debt is created equal, and understanding these distinctions could save you years of financial pain.

The third-date conversation with Lacey; where I disclosed my bankruptcy over coffee; informs Chapter 13: Money in Relationships. Financial partnerships require honesty from the start, even when that honesty feels terrifying.

My son's call about his Meta RSUs, asking questions I wished someone had answered for me decades earlier, drove Chapter 11: Career Financial Planning and Chapter 14: Financial Literacy for Families. The gap between earning money and understanding it persists across generations unless we actively bridge it.

The 67/33 proportional split system that Lacey and I developed; respecting both our income difference and our individual autonomy; appears throughout, but especially in Chapter 13. This isn't a system I read about; it's one we built through trial, conversation, and mutual respect.

FINDING YOUR PATH

Not everyone needs to read this manual the same way. Your starting point determines your optimal path:

If you're in financial crisis right now; facing bankruptcy, foreclosure, or overwhelming debt; start with Chapters 1, 2, and 4. These foundations will stabilize your situation before you worry about wealth building. I remember those days vividly. The path forward exists, even if you can't see it.

If you're building systematically; stable income, manageable debt, ready to grow; work through the sections in order. The progression from Foundation through Protection to Wealth Building mirrors the natural journey of financial development.

If you're optimizing from strength; solid foundation, looking to maximize; focus on Sections III, IV, and V. Chapters 9-15 address the complexities of investing, career optimization, and legacy planning that become relevant once basics are secure. You might also find value in revisiting foundation chapters; I've discovered gaps in my own knowledge even now.

A NOTE ON TONE

You'll notice Part II reads differently than Part I. The narrative gives way to frameworks. The personal stories become illustrative examples rather than the main thread. This shift is intentional.

Part I was about understanding *why* these principles matter; through the visceral experience of watching them fail and then watching them succeed. Part II is about *how* to implement them in your own life, with specific strategies, action steps, and decision frameworks. But don't mistake the more instructional tone for distance. Behind every "Key Principle" box is a lesson I learned the hard way.

BEFORE YOU BEGIN

Take a moment to assess where you stand. Be honest with yourself; not about where you want to be, but where you actually are right now:

- Do you know exactly how much you spend each month?
- Could you cover a $1,000 emergency without borrowing?
- Do you understand every component of your compensation?
- Have you had an honest money conversation with your partner?
- Do you know your credit score and what's on your credit report?

If you answered "no" to any of these, you've identified your starting chapters. There's no shame in beginning with basics; I had to relearn them myself, with an MBA hanging on my wall.

The manual awaits. Let's transform experience into action.

PART II
THE MISSING MANUAL
FOR FINANCIAL RECOVERY

Theory means nothing without practical application. While **Part I** showed you the reality of financial success, failure, and rebirth through my personal journey, **Part II** transforms those lessons into actionable strategies you can implement in your own life. This is the manual I wish I'd had; both during my early success and while rebuilding from bankruptcy.

Organized into five comprehensive sections, this manual builds systematically from core financial concepts to advanced wealth-building strategies. Each chapter combines technical expertise with real-world application, making complex financial concepts accessible and actionable.

Unlike traditional financial advice books that fall into two categories; personal finance basics that oversimplify complex issues, or advanced investing guides that assume a strong financial foundation; this manual bridges the gap between crisis and wealth building. It acknowledges both the practical and emotional aspects of financial recovery and growth.

The sections progress logically from foundational concepts through advanced strategies, but each chapter also stands alone as a complete guide to its topic. You can work through the manual sequentially to build a comprehensive financial framework or focus on specific chapters that address your immediate needs.

This manual's unique structure; combining practical guidance with real-world examples; reflects what I've found most effective in helping others transform their financial lives. Each topic, from bankruptcy and debt management through investment strategies, reflects lessons learned through both success and failure.

Whether you're recovering from financial hardship, building wealth for the first time, or pursuing financial independence, the following chapters provide a practical roadmap for your journey. Every concept, strategy, and recommendation has been tested not just through professional experience but through personal application and teaching others.

Let's begin building your path to lasting financial success, one principle at a time.

FINDING YOUR PATH

This manual contains fifteen chapters across five sections. You don't have to read them in order; though you can. Your current financial situation should guide your journey through these pages.

WHERE ARE YOU RIGHT NOW?

Before diving in, take an honest inventory. Check the statements that apply to you:

Signs you're in Crisis Mode:

- You're unsure how you'll pay next month's bills
- You're receiving collection calls or past-due notices
- A $500 emergency would require borrowing
- You're considering bankruptcy or have recently filed
- You've lost income and don't know when it will return

Signs you're in Building Mode:

- You have stable income but little savings
- You're making minimum payments on debt
- You want to start investing but aren't sure how
- You're ready to get serious about your financial future
- You've stabilized after a setback and want to grow

Signs you're in Optimization Mode:

- You have emergency savings and manageable debt
- You're earning well but want to maximize your money
- You're navigating equity compensation or complex benefits
- You're planning for early retirement or financial independence

THREE READING PATHWAYS

Based on where you are, here's how to approach this manual:

Path 1: Crisis Recovery

For readers who checked multiple items in Crisis Mode

Start here: Chapter 1 (Budgeting) → Chapter 2 (Debt Management) → Chapter 4 (Emergency Funds)

Why this order: When you're in crisis, you need to stop the bleeding before you can heal. These three chapters give you immediate tools: understanding where money goes, managing what you owe, and building even a small buffer against the next emergency.

Then add: Chapter 6 (Credit) ; because your credit situation affects your options for recovery

Path 2: Systematic Building

For readers who checked multiple items in Building Mode

Start here: Begin with Section I and read through Section III

Why this order: You have the stability to build properly. The sections are designed to stack: foundation supports protection, protection enables growth. Reading in order gives you the complete framework.

Pay special attention to: Chapter 5 (Student Loans) if you carry education debt, Chapter 6 (Credit) if you're rebuilding your credit profile, and Chapter 9 (Investing) when you're ready to grow wealth

Don't skip: The temptation is to jump to investing. Resist it. I made this mistake in my pre-bankruptcy life; focusing on growth while ignoring foundational cracks. The collapse taught me that Chapters 1-4 aren't just for beginners; they're the bedrock everything else rests on.

Path 3: Strategic Optimization

For readers who checked multiple items in Optimization Mode

Start here: Section III (Wealth Building) → Section IV (Career & Income) → Section V (Family & Legacy)

Why this order: Your foundations are solid. You need strategies for maximizing what you've built and protecting it for the long term.

Circle back to: Chapters 1-5 for a foundation check. Even with my current income and assets, I regularly revisit budgeting principles and debt management frameworks. You may discover gaps you didn't know existed.

Pay special attention to: Chapter 11 (Career Financial Planning) for equity compensation strategies, Chapter 12 (Taxes) for optimization opportunities, and Chapter 15 (Estate Planning) if you haven't formalized your legacy plans

From my experience: Helping my son navigate his Meta compensation showed me that even high earners need guidance. The gap between earning money and understanding it doesn't disappear with a bigger paycheck; it just has bigger consequences.

A NOTE ON SKIPPING AHEAD

This manual is designed so each chapter stands alone. If you need information on real estate investing right now, you can turn to Chapter 10 without reading everything before it.

I encourage you to eventually read the sections you skipped. The crisis reader who stabilizes should return to wealth-building chapters. The optimizer who skimmed foundations might discover a crack that needs attention.

SECTION I
CORE FINANCIAL
FOUNDATIONS

Building a secure financial future requires starting with strong fundamentals. This section covers the building blocks everyone needs at every stage of their financial journey. Like constructing a house, your financial life needs a solid foundation before adding more complex elements.

During my recovery from bankruptcy, I learned these fundamentals through necessity. Now, watching my son manage his six-figure Meta salary, I see how these same principles apply regardless of income level.

Chapter 1: Budgeting and Cash Flow lays the groundwork with battle-tested approaches to managing your money. Whether you're struggling to make ends meet like I once did or handling substantial Big Tech compensation like I do now, understanding and controlling your cash flow creates the foundation for financial success.

Chapter 2: Debt Management addresses how to handle financial obligations effectively. Through my journey from bankruptcy to financial security, I've learned that managing debt requires more than just making payments; it needs strategic approach and clear understanding.

Chapter 3: Personal Banking explores how to build and maintain essential financial relationships. My experience losing all banking access during bankruptcy taught me that proper banking relationships provide more than just services; they create crucial financial infrastructure.

Chapter 4: Emergency Funds covers building and maintaining financial safety nets. When a $400 car repair once threatened my recovery, I learned that emergency funds provide more than just security; they enable better financial decisions by removing pressure of immediate needs.

Chapter 5: Student Loans explores managing education debt as part of your financial foundation. I discovered that student loans carried unique characteristics that affected my entire financial picture.

These chapters provide the groundwork for everything that follows. Even if you're eager to explore investing or real estate, take time to master these fundamentals first. They'll serve as your financial safety net and decision-making framework throughout your journey.

CHAPTER 1
BUDGET AND CASH FLOW

LEARNING OBJECTIVES

- Understand fundamental money flow principles
- Master practical budgeting approaches
- Learn to manage variable income effectively
- Develop sustainable financial awareness
- Create lasting money management habits

OPENING STORY

The reality of budgeting hit me hardest not during my high-income years, but during my recovery period. I discovered that effective budgeting isn't about complex spreadsheets or perfect math as I sat in my small studio apartment, calculating how to make $127 last until my next paycheck. Budgeting is about understanding how money moves through your life and making intentional decisions about where it goes. This lesson now helps others understand that successful money management starts with awareness rather than rigid rules.

INTRODUCTION

Money flows through our lives like water through a landscape; sometimes in a steady stream, sometimes in unpredictable waves. Understanding and directing these flows determines whether we build reservoirs of wealth or face constant financial drought. Yet many people approach budgeting as a restrictive exercise rather than a tool for achieving their goals.

Creating effective money management systems resembles designing irrigation for a garden; different areas need different amounts of resources at different times. Like a skilled gardener, successful money managers learn to direct their financial resources where they'll produce the best results while maintaining enough reserves for dry periods.

The most successful approach to budgeting combines clear understanding with flexible execution. Similar to weather patterns, income and expenses follow both predictable and unpredictable cycles.

Understanding these patterns helps create systems that work in real life, not just on paper.

Most importantly, you'll discover that budgeting isn't about restriction; it's about awareness and intention. The methods we'll discuss work whether you're managing a tight budget or substantial income, because they focus on fundamental principles that adapt to any financial situation.

UNDERSTANDING MONEY FLOW

KEY PRINCIPLE
Effective money management starts with understanding your unique income and expense patterns rather than forcing yourself into someone else's system.

During my first months of consulting after bankruptcy, I found myself sitting at my kitchen table with a scattered pile of bills and a nearly empty checking account. My income fluctuated wildly; some weeks I could expect substantial payments from state contracts, while others were completely dry as I waited for new projects to begin. "None of the standard budgeting advice works for me," I remember telling my friend Casey, who had been my financial sounding board. "How do I create a system when I never know when the next check is coming?"

This frustrating reality taught me a crucial truth: before you can manage your money effectively, you need to understand how it actually moves through your life.

UNDERSTANDING INCOME PATTERNS

Income flows rarely follow the traditional biweekly paycheck model anymore. Modern households often combine multiple income sources, variable payment schedules, and irregular payment amounts. Understanding these patterns requires observing both short-term fluctuations and longer seasonal trends. Some income sources provide stability while others offer growth potential. Recognizing these differences helps you create more effective management strategies.

Even people with regular paychecks often face irregular expenses. Understanding how income and expense cycles align; or conflict; helps you prevent cash flow problems and enables you to identify opportunities for better financial coordination.

The Ideal Cash Flow System

How money should flow through your accounts for maximum efficiency

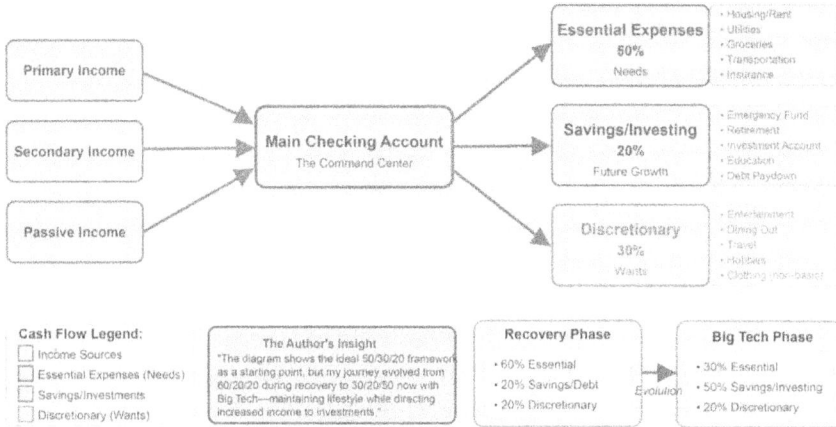

Primary Income		Essential Expenses 50% Needs · Housing/Rent · Utilities · Groceries · Transportation · Insurance
Secondary Income	Main Checking Account The Command Center	Savings/Investing 20% Future Growth · Emergency Fund · Retirement · Investment Account · Education · Debt Paydown
Passive Income		Discretionary 30% Wants · Entertainment · Dining Out · Travel · Hobbies · Clothing (non-basic)

Cash Flow Legend:
- ☐ Income Sources
- ☐ Essential Expenses (Needs)
- ☐ Savings/Investments
- ☐ Discretionary (Wants)

The Author's Insight
"The diagram shows the ideal 50/30/20 framework as a starting point, but my journey evolved from 60/20/20 during recovery to 30/20/50 now with Big Tech—maintaining lifestyle while directing increased income to investments."

Recovery Phase
- 60% Essential
- 20% Savings/Debt
- 20% Discretionary

Evolution

Big Tech Phase
- 30% Essential
- 50% Savings/Investing
- 20% Discretionary

RECOGNIZING SPENDING PATTERNS

Spending patterns reveal important truths about money habits and lifestyle needs. Most people discover their expenses fall into predictable patterns, even when they feel random. Regular expenses like rent and utilities create the foundation of these patterns, while discretionary spending adds complexity. Once you understand these patterns in your life, you can identify both problems and opportunities for better money management.

Personal spending triggers often drive financial decisions more than conscious choice. Stress, celebration, social pressure, and even the time of day can influence your spending habits. Recognizing these triggers helps you develop better responses to emotional or situational spending cues. This awareness proves particularly valuable when developing new money management habits.

BUILDING PATTERN AWARENESS

Effective money management grows from understanding personal financial patterns rather than forcing arbitrary rules. Daily expenses, weekly bills, monthly obligations, and annual costs each create their own rhythms. Learning to recognize and work with these natural patterns helps you develop sustainable financial habits.

Remember: Understanding money flow creates the foundation for effective management. Focus on observing your natural financial rhythms before trying to change them. The most successful money management systems grow from understanding rather than forcing change.

CREATING SUSTAINABLE BUDGETING SYSTEMS

KEY PRINCIPLE
Effective budgeting requires building systems that work with your natural habits rather than fighting against them.

Think of creating financial systems like establishing a morning routine; it needs to work with your natural tendencies to be effective. Many people try to force themselves into complicated budgeting systems that fight against their natural habits, which leads to frustration and abandonment.

I discovered this truth during my post-bankruptcy rebuilding phase. While consulting for state agencies, my income fluctuated with project cycles. Trying to force this irregular income into traditional budgeting methods left me constantly stressed. Some months I'd feel flush with cash, others I'd barely cover expenses. "I'm a financial professional," I remember thinking one particularly tight month, "how am I still struggling with this?"

It wasn't until I created a system that matched my actual income pattern; separating essential expenses from my income floor while banking surpluses; that I finally regained control of my financial life.

UNDERSTANDING CORE BUDGETING METHODS

Traditional Percentage Budgeting (50/30/20) provides a flexible framework that adapts to different income levels. This approach allocates 50% to needs, 30% to wants, and 20% to savings and debt repayment. Its simplicity makes it particularly effective for those with regular income who need basic guidance without complex tracking.

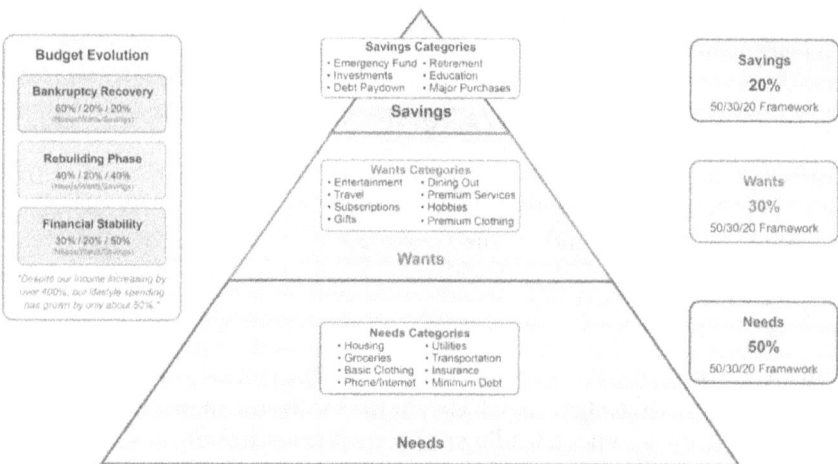

Additional allocations can be used depending on your needs and circumstances:

1. **40/20/40**: 40% needs, 20% wants, 40% saving/investing (for growing careers)
2. **30/20/50**: 30% needs, 20% wants, 50% saving/investing (for established careers)
3. **60/20/20**: 60% needs, 20% wants, 20% saving/investing (for high-cost areas or early careers)

The percentages matter less than maintaining proportionality as income grows.

Zero-Based Budgeting is a method where you assign every dollar a specific purpose, giving you complete control over spending. This method proves especially powerful for those working to eliminate debt or build savings quickly. However, it requires more intensive tracking and regular adjustments, particularly with variable income.

Value-Based Budgeting aligns spending with personal priorities rather than rigid categories. This approach focuses first on funding what matters most; whether that's debt repayment, family activities, or future goals; before allocating remaining money to other needs. Value-based budgeting creates stronger motivation by connecting spending to personal values.

IMPLEMENTING YOUR CHOSEN METHOD

To succeed with any budgeting method, you need to implement it correctly. This starts with understanding your natural money patterns and choosing a method that aligns with your personality and circumstances. Many people find success by starting with a simpler method and gradually adding complexity as their skills improve.

Once your basic plan is in place, review it regularly and adjust as necessary. Monthly reviews help you catch problems early, while quarterly assessments provide opportunities for you to adjust broader patterns. These reviews should focus more on alignment with goals than perfect adherence to categories.

Compatibility Rating:

Finding Your Budget Match

Low to ***** High Comparing different budgeting methods based on your financial personality

Budgeting Method	Detail-Oriented Analytical, Precise	Big-Picture Holistic, Strategic	Emotional Feelings-Driven	Busy/Minimal Limited Time	Good For Variable Income
50/30/20 Budget 50% Needs, 30% Wants, 20% Savings/Debt Simple percentage allocation	★★★	★★★★★	★★★★	★★★★★	★★★
Zero-Based Budget Every dollar assigned a purpose Income - Allocation = Zero Complete planning & tracking	★★★★★	★★	★★	★★	★★★★
Value-Based Budget Priorities funded first Aligned with personal values Purpose-driven allocations	★★★	★★★★	★★★★★	★★★★	★★★★★
Envelope System Cash-based physical or digital Separate "envelopes" for categories Tangible spending control	★★★★	★★	★★★★★	★★	★★★
Income-First System Income smoothing for variable earnings Holding account + personal "salary" Creates stability from inconsistency	★★★★	★★★★	★★★	★★★	★★★★★

Author: "Effective budgeting isn't about complex spreadsheets... it's about understanding how money moves through your life."

CREATING AUTOMATED SYSTEMS

To manage your budget effectively, rely on automation to reduce decision fatigue and ensure consistency. Automatic transfers for savings, bill payments, and debt reduction remove the need for constant decision-making while letting you maintain progress toward financial goals.

Technology should support your budget system rather than complicate it. While apps and software can provide valuable tracking and insights, they work best when supporting already-established good habits rather than when you're trying to create them.

MAINTAINING FLEXIBILITY

Sustainable budgeting systems must accommodate both regular expenses and irregular spending patterns. This means building in flexibility for seasonal variations, unexpected opportunities, and changing circumstances while maintaining progress toward long-term goals.

Remember: Sustainable financial systems grow from understanding and working with your natural habits. Focus on creating simple, automatic processes that support your goals while matching your actual income and spending patterns. The most successful money management often comes from systems that feel natural rather than forced.

MANAGING VARIABLE INCOME

KEY PRINCIPLE
Variable income requires creating stability through systems rather than hoping for consistent earnings.

Managing irregular income resembles sailing a ship; you need to navigate both calm seas and storms while maintaining a steady course toward your destination. Many people with variable income struggle because they try to force irregular earnings into traditional budgeting approaches designed for steady paychecks.

Consider my own transformation from financial stress to stability when rebuilding my consulting business. During those early recovery years, I'd panic during slow months and splurge during good ones. I remember one December when a major contract payment arrived; I immediately upgraded my laptop instead of setting aside funds for the predictably slow period starting in January. By March, I was taking smaller projects out of desperation.

Learning to think of my income as an annual stream rather than monthly chunks changed my approach to money management and gave me the stability I needed to rebuild.

ESTABLISHING YOUR INCOME FLOOR

The first step to stability is understanding your minimum reliable income. This "income floor" represents the lowest amount you can reasonably expect in any given month, based on historical patterns and guaranteed minimums. Using this floor for essential expenses while treating additional income differently provides stability.

Most variable income earners discover their true income floor lies lower than they initially estimate. Careful tracking over several months reveals patterns previously hidden by focusing on average earnings. This understanding helps you create realistic baseline budgets that remain sustainable even during lowest-earning periods.

Operating with this income floor might mean maintaining a more modest baseline lifestyle than income averages might suggest, but this conservative approach creates sustainability through income fluctuations. Key elements for handling variable income effectively:

- Percentage-based saving from all earnings
- Separate accounts for different purposes
- Tax reserve calculations and management
- Buffer fund for income smoothing
- Clear priorities for extra earnings

CREATING INCOME STABILITY

To build stability with variable income, you must develop multiple protective layers. The first layer, a basic emergency fund, provides protection against unexpected expenses. The second layer, an income smoothing fund, helps you maintain consistent monthly income despite earning fluctuations.

Income smoothing is key for managing variable earnings. This process involves channeling all income into a holding account, then paying yourself a consistent "salary" based on your income floor. Additional earnings build reserves for leaner periods while allowing you to maintain lifestyle stability.

TAX MANAGEMENT STRATEGY

Variable income creates unique tax challenges that require careful planning. Self-employed individuals and commission-based workers often need to manage their own tax withholding and quarterly payments. Understanding tax obligations and maintaining appropriate reserves prevents common problems with irregular income.

Creating separate savings for taxes helps prevent common pitfalls with variable income. Many successful variable income earners automatically set aside tax percentages from every payment received, treating these reserves as untouchable for other expenses.

LONG-TERM FINANCIAL PLANNING

Variable income requires different approaches to long-term financial planning. Traditional retirement planning methods often assume steady income growth, requiring adaptation for irregular earnings. Understanding how to balance current stability with long-term wealth building is important.

Remember: Variable income management requires creating your own stability rather than waiting for steady earnings. Focus on understanding your income patterns and building systems that smooth natural variations. The most successful approaches combine clear baseline planning with flexible handling of additional earnings.

BUILDING FINANCIAL AWARENESS

KEY PRINCIPLE
Financial awareness grows through consistent attention rather than occasional intense monitoring.

Developing financial awareness resembles cultivating a garden; daily attention reveals patterns and potential issues before they become problems.

Many people alternate between obsessing over every financial detail and completely avoiding their money situation, missing the balanced awareness that creates lasting success.

During my early recovery from bankruptcy, I oscillated between financial extremes; obsessively checking my bank balance ten times daily during tight periods, then avoiding it entirely when things improved. This pattern created a rollercoaster of stress and denial.

"This isn't sustainable," I finally admitted to myself one evening after a particularly anxiety-filled week. By establishing a simple daily check-in routine; just two minutes each morning; I developed balanced awareness without the emotional turbulence. This regular rhythm transformed my relationship with money. Essential elements of financial awareness include:

- Daily balance checks
- Weekly spending reviews
- Monthly bill planning
- Quarterly goal assessments
- Annual financial evaluations

UNDERSTANDING SPENDING TRIGGERS

Emotional spending patterns reveal important truths about financial behavior. Most people discover specific situations, feelings, or times of day that trigger unnecessary spending. Understanding these patterns helps you develop preventive strategies that keep you from repeatedly dealing with consequences.

Environmental factors often influence spending decisions more than conscious choice. Time of day, stress levels, social situations, and even weather can affect financial decisions. Recognize these influences in your daily habits to help you create systems that protect you against impulsive choices.

DEVELOPING PATTERN RECOGNITION

Financial patterns extend beyond basic income and expenses. Market cycles, seasonal variations and life events create predictable financial impacts that become visible through consistent awareness. Understanding these larger patterns helps you with both short-term management and long-term planning.

Conduct regular review sessions to build pattern recognition skills naturally. Weekly money dates; short, scheduled times to review recent transactions and upcoming needs; will allow you to develop awareness without creating anxiety. These reviews should focus on understanding patterns rather than judging decisions.

BUILDING SUSTAINABLE AWARENESS

True financial awareness combines attention to detail with a broader perspective. Like learning to read music, initial practice requires conscious attention to every note. Eventually patterns become naturally recognizable. This progression from deliberate monitoring to intuitive understanding marks mature financial awareness.

Digital tools support awareness without replacing personal attention. Banking apps, spending trackers, and automated alerts should serve as helpful aids rather than primary monitoring methods. Effective awareness combines technology support with personal engagement in financial decisions.

CREATING FORWARD-LOOKING AWARENESS

Focus on identifying opportunities and potential challenges before they arrive. A forward-looking perspective helps prevent problems while positioning for positive possibilities. Understanding upcoming expenses, income changes, and market trends supports better current decisions.

Remember: Financial awareness develops through regular attention rather than sporadic monitoring. Focus on building consistent habits that create natural understanding of your money patterns. Effective awareness often comes from noticing trends and patterns rather than tracking every penny.

CREATING LONG-TERM FINANCIAL SUCCESS

> **KEY PRINCIPLE**
> Sustainable financial success requires building habits that evolve with your life rather than maintaining rigid systems.

Long-term financial success requires adapting to different approaches while maintaining consistent care. Many people create financial systems that work for their current situation but fail to adapt as their lives change, eventually leading to system breakdown.

PERSONAL JOURNEY: THE EVOLUTION OF OUR BUDGETING FRAMEWORK

During my recovery from bankruptcy, necessity dictated a structure focused primarily on immediate needs with minimal allocation toward future growth.

"When I first began rebuilding," I often explain to those starting their own recovery, "my budget followed what I call a 60/20/20 framework; 60%

toward essential expenses, 20% toward debt repayment, and just 20% toward savings and future growth."

This initial allocation wasn't ideal, but it reflected my financial reality at the time. With limited income and substantial obligations, directing the majority toward essentials was necessary for stability. The modest 20% toward savings primarily built my emergency fund, while the 20% toward debt focused on strategic repayment of remaining obligations.

When Lacey and I began building our financial life together, we maintained a similar allocation initially, though the debt component had largely been eliminated post-bankruptcy. "We recognized this wasn't our forever approach," Lacey noted during one of our early financial discussions. "But it gave us stability while we established our foundation."

As our incomes grew and our essential expenses remained relatively stable, we systematically shifted our allocation model. Each raise, bonus, or income increase presented an opportunity for intentional adjustment rather than lifestyle inflation.

"What if we maintain our current lifestyle and direct all new income toward building wealth?" Lacey suggested when I received a substantial promotion. This simple but powerful question became our guiding philosophy.

By the time I transitioned to Genpact, our allocation had evolved to 40/20/40; with 40% toward essential expenses, 20% toward short-term savings, and 40% toward investments and long-term growth. Though our absolute spending had increased modestly, our expense percentage had decreased significantly as our income grew.

Today, after several years of disciplined allocation adjustments and substantial income growth with my move to Big Tech, we've reached what we consider our optimal framework: 30/20/50.

This current model allocates:
- 30% toward lifestyle and essential expenses
- 20% toward short-term savings and security
- 50% toward investments and long-term wealth building

Despite our household income increasing by over 400% since we began our journey together, our absolute lifestyle spending has grown by only about 50%. Meanwhile, our wealth-building capacity has expanded dramatically.

This evolution from 60/20/20 to 30/20/50 didn't happen overnight. It represented a series of deliberate choices over several years; saying yes to automation that directed income increases toward investments, and being selective about which lifestyle improvements truly mattered to us.

For those beginning their financial journey, I emphasize that **your starting allocation matters less than your direction**. The initial 60/20/20 framework wasn't ideal, but it started the evolutionary process that eventually enabled our current 50% investment rate. Each phase built upon the previous one, creating momentum that transformed our financial trajectory.

Most importantly, this budgeting evolution aligned with our values and goals throughout each phase. The percentages themselves matter less than creating an intentional framework that supports both current needs and future aspirations; a framework that can evolve as your financial situation improves.

BUILDING PROGRESSIVE SYSTEMS

Financial systems need built-in flexibility to accommodate life changes. Starting with basic expense tracking and emergency savings provides a foundation, but successful systems grow to include investment strategies, tax planning, and wealth-building components as circumstances evolve.

Many people increase expenses automatically with income increases, missing opportunities for accelerated wealth building. Creating deliberate decision processes for handling income changes helps you maintain financial progress. Core financial habits that support long-term success:

- Regular financial review sessions
- Automatic saving and investing
- Conscious spending decisions
- Continuous financial education
- Strategic goal adjustment

CREATING MULTIPLE INCOME STREAMS

Financial stability increases with income diversification. Beyond traditional employment, developing additional income sources; whether through investments, side businesses, or passive income; creates resilience against economic changes while accelerating wealth building.

Each income stream requires its own management approach while contributing to overall financial health. Understanding how different income sources interact with each other, particularly regarding tax implications and time requirements, helps you optimize their collective benefit.

MAINTAINING LIFE BALANCE

Sustainable financial success requires balancing present enjoyment with future security. Extremely restrictive systems often fail long-term, while too-loose approaches prevent progress. Find the appropriate balance between your current lifestyle and future goals to promote sustainability.

You can maintain this balance via regular life assessments. Conduct quarterly reviews of your financial progress alongside your life satisfaction and identify areas that could use adjustment. During these reviews, focus on aligning financial systems with broader life goals.

PLANNING FOR LIFE TRANSITIONS

Major life changes; career shifts, family changes, or retirement planning; require system adaptation. Successful transitions combine maintaining core financial principles while adjusting specific practices to match new circumstances.

Remember: Long-term financial success grows from developing adaptable habits rather than rigid rules. Focus on creating systems that can evolve with your life changes while maintaining consistent core principles. The most successful financial journeys combine steady practice with flexibility to seize opportunities.

CHAPTER SUMMARY AND KEY TAKEAWAYS

Through my journey from bankruptcy to financial stability, I've learned that successful money management combines understanding fundamentals with developing sustainable habits. The lessons from both personal experience and helping others show that effective budgeting requires active awareness rather than rigid rules.

CORE MONEY MANAGEMENT PRINCIPLES:

Patterns Over Rules: During my recovery period, I discovered that understanding personal money patterns matters more than following standard budgeting formulas. One restaurant manager's experience reinforced this; by recognizing her natural income and spending cycles, she created more effective systems than when trying to force herself into traditional budgeting approaches.

Awareness Over Avoidance: Working with others showed how regular financial attention prevents larger problems. A freelance designer's experience demonstrated this when her consistent awareness of income patterns helped her maintain stability through irregular earnings. The most successful money managers work to maintain steady awareness rather than alternating between obsession and avoidance.

Evolution Over Rigidity: Through both success and failure, I've learned that financial systems must grow with our lives. Recent experiences helping others navigate life transitions showed how flexible approaches create better long-term outcomes than rigid systems that eventually break under pressure.

ACTION PLAN

First 30 Days: Foundation Building
- Track all income and spending patterns
- Identify natural financial rhythms
- Create basic awareness habits
- Establish regular review times
- Begin emergency fund building

60-Day Implementation
- Develop sustainable systems
- Build automatic transfers
- Create conscious spending plans
- Strengthen awareness habits
- Start pattern recognition

90-Day Establishment
- Review and adjust systems
- Deepen financial awareness
- Plan for future changes
- Build long-term habits
- Maintain flexible adaptation

FINAL THOUGHTS

Money management success isn't about perfect budgeting; it's about creating sustainable systems that support your goals while matching your natural patterns. Through bankruptcy and recovery, I learned that effective financial management requires understanding yourself as much as understanding numbers. Your money management journey will be unique, whether you're:
- Managing variable income
- Building stable finances
- Growing wealth
- Planning life changes

The principles remain consistent: understand your patterns, build sustainable habits, and maintain systems that can evolve with your life. With proper development, money management becomes a natural part of life rather than a source of stress or restriction.

Remember that financial needs change with different life stages. Stay flexible, maintain awareness, and don't hesitate to adjust your approach as circumstances change. Your goal isn't perfect budgeting but sustainable financial success that supports your goals while maintaining peace of mind.

CHAPTER 2
DEBT MANAGEMENT

LEARNING OBJECTIVES

- Understand how different types of debt affect your financial future
- Master effective debt repayment strategies
- Learn to navigate complex debt situations
- Develop sustainable debt management habits
- Create lasting financial freedom

OPENING STORY

During my bankruptcy, I discovered that not all debts are created equal. While most obligations could be discharged, my student loans remained firmly in place. This taught me that debt management requires understanding not just how to make payments, but how different types of debt affect your entire financial life. This lesson now helps others understand that effective debt management starts with knowledge rather than just throwing money at the problem.

INTRODUCTION

Debt shapes our financial lives in many ways. Whether you're carrying a mortgage, student loans, or credit card balances, understanding how to manage debt can mean the difference between financial freedom and persistent struggle.

Different debts require different strategies, and the path to financial freedom rarely follows a straight line. Many people focus solely on making payments without understanding how various debts affect their broader financial picture.

The most successful approach to debt management combines clear understanding with strategic action. Like a skilled navigator, you need to understand both your current position and the best route to your destination. Different types of debt require different management strategies.

Most importantly, you'll discover that debt management isn't about perfection; it's about progress. The methods we'll discuss focus on fundamental principles that scale to any situation.

UNDERSTANDING MODERN DEBT

KEY PRINCIPLE
Different types of debt carry distinct terms, protections, and management options that significantly affect your financial future.

Understanding modern debt resembles learning a new language; each type has its own vocabulary and rules. Many people treat all debt the same, missing differences that could affect their path to financial freedom.

My own awakening about debt came during bankruptcy proceedings when the judge explained which debts could be discharged and which couldn't. Despite my financial education, I'd been making minimum payments on credit cards for years. My focus was on aggressively paying down my mortgage; contrary to traditional financial wisdom. I realized I'd paid over $12,000 in credit card interest the previous year without reducing the principal. "I've been working harder just to stay in the same place," I thought bitterly. This transformed my understanding of how different debts affect long-term financial health.

TYPES OF CONSUMER DEBT

Credit card debt operates differently from other obligations. Compound interest often exceeds 20% annually and credit cards offer minimal consumer protections. A credit card balance can quickly spiral beyond control. Unlike other debts, credit card interest compounds daily, making them particularly dangerous when carrying balances.

Personal loans and lines of credit occupy a middle ground in the debt hierarchy. While they typically offer lower interest rates than credit cards, they lack the specific protections of federal student loans or the tax benefits of mortgage debt. Understanding these distinctions helps create more effective repayment strategies.

Not All Debts Are Created Equal

Understanding the impact of different debt types

Debt Type	Typical APR	Tax Benefits	Security Type	Payoff Priority
Credit Cards	15-24%	None	Unsecured	HIGHEST
Personal Loans	7-36%	None	Unsecured	HIGH
Auto Loans	3-10%	None	Secured (Vehicle)	MEDIUM
Federal Student Loans	4-7%	Interest Deduction (Income Limited)	Unsecured	MEDIUM
Private Student Loans	5-13%	Interest Deduction (Income Limited)	Unsecured	HIGH
Home Mortgage	3-7%	Mortgage Interest Deduction	Secured (Home)	LOW
HELOC/Home Equity	4-8%	Interest Deductible (Home Improvements)	Secured (Home)	MEDIUM

Highest Priority (Pay off ASAP)　Medium Priority
High Priority　Low Priority (Pay Minimum)

SECURED VS. UNSECURED DEBT

Mortgage and auto loans use physical assets as security, creating both opportunities and risks. These secured debts typically offer lower interest rates and longer repayment terms but carry the risk of asset loss through foreclosure or repossession. This security gives lenders more confidence but requires borrowers to carefully consider their ability to maintain payments.

FEDERAL STUDENT LOAN CONSIDERATIONS

Federal student loans stand apart from other debt types through their unique protections and payment options. Income-driven repayment plans, forgiveness opportunities, and hardship provisions create flexibility unavailable with other debts. However, these loans typically can't be discharged in bankruptcy, making their management particularly important.

MODERN DEBT CHALLENGES

Buy-now-pay-later services and financial technology have created new forms of debt that blur traditional categories. These modern obligations often lack the consumer protections of traditional loans while carrying additional complexity. Understanding these new debt forms is important for effective financial planning.

Remember: Different debts require different management approaches. Focus on understanding the specific characteristics of each obligation rather than treating all debt the same. The most successful debt management strategies will prioritize addressing the most dangerous debts first while maintaining sustainable payments on all obligations.

CREATING YOUR REPAYMENT STRATEGY

KEY PRINCIPLE
Effective debt repayment requires a strategy that matches your life circumstances rather than one designed to follow generic advice.

Developing a debt repayment strategy resembles planning a long journey; you need both a clear destination and a realistic route to reach it. Many people jump into aggressive repayment plans without considering their broader financial picture, often leading to frustration and failure.

My own transformation from overwhelmed to in control came through strategic planning rather than sheer effort. During my early recovery, I desperately attacked my remaining car loan debt, putting every spare dollar toward principal reduction. "I was so focused on eliminating that one debt that I neglected building an emergency fund," I later explained to Lacey.

The consequences became painfully clear when my aging Mercedes needed a $400 transmission repair. With no savings, I reluctantly used my newly-obtained secured credit card, undoing months of progress. I learned that balance matters more than aggressive payoffs alone.

BUILDING YOUR FOUNDATION

Before accelerating debt repayment, establishing basic financial stability is crucial. This means maintaining essential bill payments while building a modest emergency fund. Even $500-$1,000 in savings can prevent minor emergencies from creating new debt as you work toward larger financial goals.

The relationship between income and debt payments requires careful balance. While conventional wisdom suggests maximizing debt payments, maintaining sustainable payment levels matters more than making occasional large payments. This often means starting with smaller, consistent extra payments rather than dramatic lifestyle changes.

CHOOSING YOUR METHOD

Two primary repayment approaches have proven successful over time, each with distinct psychological and financial benefits. Once you understand these methods, you can then craft a strategy that is aligned with both your personality and financial situation.

The Avalanche Method

The avalanche method prioritizes mathematical efficiency by targeting highest-interest debts first. After meeting all minimum payments, every extra dollar goes toward the highest-interest obligation. Once that debt is eliminated, the freed-up money "avalanches" to the next highest-interest debt. Consider Maria's situation with three debts:

- Credit card: $5,000 at 22% APR
- Personal loan: $10,000 at 12% APR
- Car loan: $15,000 at 6% APR

By focusing her extra $300 monthly on the credit card while maintaining minimum payments on other debts, Maria will save over $3,000 in interest compared to other approaches. This method is for those looking to maximize efficiency and minimize interest costs.

The Snowball Method

The snowball method creates momentum through quick wins by targeting smallest balances first, regardless of interest rate. This psychological boost often proves more valuable than mathematical efficiency for many people. James found success using the snowball method with his debts:

- Store credit card: $800 at 24% APR
- Major credit card: $4,500 at 19% APR
- Personal loan: $12,000 at 15% APR

Eliminating the store card in just three months created such motivation that he maintained his aggressive payment plan through complete debt elimination. While he paid more in total interest, the consistent progress kept him engaged with his repayment plan.

AVALANCHE METHOD (Pay highest interest rate first)			
Debt	Balance	Interest	Payment Order
Credit Card A	$3,500	22%	1
Car Loan	$12,000	5%	4
Credit Card B	$1,800	18%	2
Personal Loan	$2,500	12%	3

SNOWBALL METHOD (Pay smallest balance first)			
Debt	Balance	Interest	Payment Order
Credit Card A	$3,500	22%	3
Car Loan	$12,000	5%	4
Credit Card B	$1,800	18%	1
Personal Loan	$2,500	12%	2

RESULTS

Total Interest Paid: $1,820

Time to Debt-Free: 28 months

Card A	B	loan	Car Loan
0   14 months   28 months

Avalanche Advantage:
Saves $285 in interest (mathematically optimal)

RESULTS

Total Interest Paid: $2,105

Time to Debt-Free: 28 months

B	Loan	Card A	Car Loan
0   14 months   28 months

Snowball Advantage:
Two early wins provide psychological momentum

Creating Your Hybrid Approach

Some people find success combining these methods. Lisa prioritized her highest-interest debt but allowed herself to eliminate a small balance first to create momentum. This hybrid approach matched both her logical understanding of interest costs and her need for early encouragement.

Success requires matching your strategy to your personality and circumstances. Some people need the motivation of quick wins, making the snowball method more effective despite higher total interest costs. Others find satisfaction in maximizing efficiency, making the avalanche method more sustainable.

PAYMENT OPTIMIZATION

Understanding how payments affect different debts creates opportunities for faster progress. Making payments before statement closing dates can reduce interest charges on credit cards. Similarly, biweekly payments on mortgages or car loans can significantly reduce total interest paid while accelerating debt elimination.

Remember: Your repayment strategy needs to work with your life rather than against it. Focus on creating sustainable progress rather than seeking the fastest possible debt elimination. The most successful debt repayment often comes from consistent, strategic action rather than aggressive but unsustainable efforts.

MANAGING MULTIPLE OBLIGATIONS

> **KEY PRINCIPLE**
> Successfully managing multiple debts requires coordination and strategy
> rather than treating each debt in isolation.

Managing multiple debts resembles conducting an orchestra; each debt requires individual attention, but success comes from making them work together harmoniously. Many people handle each debt separately, missing opportunities to improve overall outcomes.

During my financial collapse, I was drowning in obligations; mortgages, credit cards, personal loans, and student debt. Each month, I'd scatter payments wherever I could in an attempt to stay afloat. "I was making payments everywhere but seeing progress nowhere," I remember telling my bankruptcy attorney.

It wasn't until I began rebuilding that I learned the power of coordination. By mapping out all my remaining obligations and creating a strategic repayment hierarchy while maintaining minimum payments, I experienced that motivating sensation of watching debts systematically disappear.

CREATING YOUR DEBT INVENTORY

Understanding your complete debt picture provides the foundation for effective management. This means more than just listing balances; it requires understanding terms, interest rates, payment requirements, and special features of each debt.

Regular review of this inventory helps identify both problems and opportunities. Monthly review sessions help track progress while quarterly deep dives can reveal patterns that need attention.

MANAGING MINIMUM PAYMENTS

Establishing reliable minimum payment systems will empower you to build the foundation for successful debt management. This often means setting up automatic minimum payments, ensuring these obligations never fall behind. Build a small buffer in your checking account to prevent payment problems.

Beyond just meeting minimums, understanding how these payments affect your debt becomes crucial. Some loans apply extra payments differently than others; some automatically apply overpayments to the next month's payment rather than principal reduction. You need a full understanding of these details to ensure your extra payments work as intended.

The Hidden Cost of Minimum Payments

How much that purchase really costs

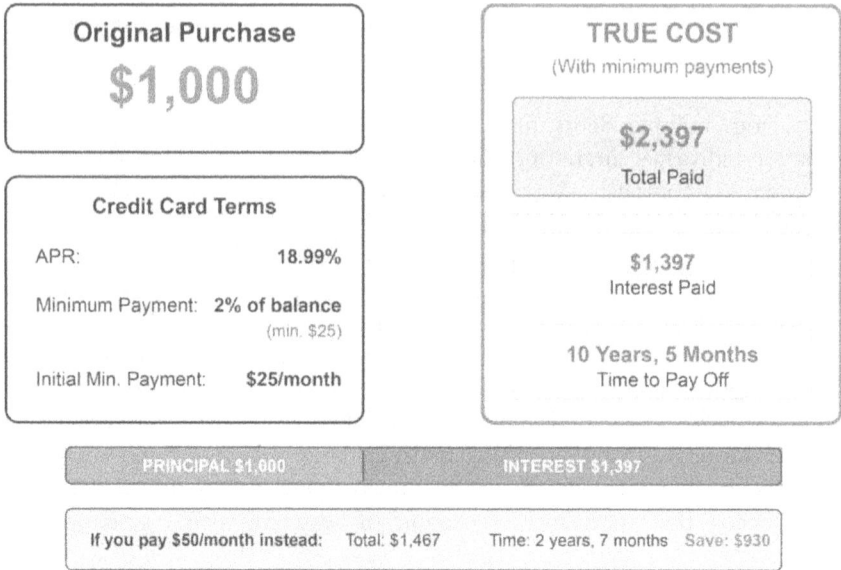

Original Purchase	TRUE COST
$1,000	(With minimum payments)

TRUE COST
(With minimum payments)

$2,397
Total Paid

Credit Card Terms

APR: 18.99%

Minimum Payment: 2% of balance
(min. $25)

Initial Min. Payment: $25/month

$1,397
Interest Paid

10 Years, 5 Months
Time to Pay Off

PRINCIPAL $1,000   INTEREST $1,397

If you pay $50/month instead: Total: $1,467   Time: 2 years, 7 months   Save: $930

STRATEGIC EXTRA PAYMENT ALLOCATION

Once minimum payments are stable, the extra money left over can be allocated strategically. This requires balancing mathematical optimization with practical reality. While putting all extra money toward your highest-interest debt typically saves the most money, maintaining momentum through occasional smaller debt elimination can provide important psychological benefits.

Creating specific "debt-free dates" for each obligation helps maintain motivation. By calculating how different payment allocations affect payoff timing, you can create meaningful milestones. These milestones maintain momentum through what often feels like a long process.

PROTECTION AGAINST SETBACKS

Building financial buffers while paying down debt helps prevent setbacks. This means maintaining a modest emergency fund even while carrying high-interest debt. While this might seem counterintuitive, protection against new debt often proves more valuable than the interest saved through aggressive payment.

Remember: Multiple debt management requires comprehensive strategy development. Focus on creating coordinated approaches that address all your obligations while maintaining clear progress toward debt freedom. The most successful multiple debt management involves strategic prioritization rather than treating all debts equally.

BUILDING DEBT-FREE HABITS

KEY PRINCIPLE
Long-term financial freedom requires developing habits that prevent future debt rather than just eliminating current obligations.

Building debt-free habits resembles developing a healthy lifestyle; it requires changing both behaviors and mindsets to create lasting transformation. Many people focus solely on debt elimination without addressing the patterns that created their debt, often leading to repeated cycles of debt accumulation and payoff.

I faced this harsh reality after my first financial recovery. Having paid off significant business debt following my restaurant failure, I celebrated becoming "debt-free" without addressing my underlying habits. Within eighteen months, I'd accumulated nearly $30,000 in new credit card debt while building my consulting business.

The late-night realization hit me hard: becoming debt-free wasn't enough; I needed to become the kind of person who stays debt-free. This painful lesson led me to focus on developing sustainable financial habits alongside debt elimination.

UNDERSTANDING MONEY PATTERNS

Financial habits often have deep roots in our personal history and emotional relationships with money. Recognizing spending triggers becomes crucial for developing better habits. Some people spend more when stressed, others when celebrating, and many struggle with social pressure to maintain certain lifestyle appearances.

Creating awareness of these patterns requires honest self-reflection. Daily spending logs help identify not just what we buy, but why we buy it. This understanding helps you uncover how emotional needs are being met through financial means. With this awareness, you can develop healthier coping mechanisms that don't involve spending.

BUILDING NEW FINANCIAL SYSTEMS

Successful habit development requires creating systems that make good decisions easier than poor ones. This starts with practical changes to how we handle daily finances. Strategies to help you curb impulse spending include:

- Setting up automatic savings transfers
- Removing stored credit card information from shopping sites
- Maintaining spending buffers in checking accounts

The power of these systems comes from reducing decision fatigue. When good financial choices happen automatically, we preserve mental energy for handling genuine emergencies or opportunities. This automation proves particularly valuable during stressful periods when decision-making abilities might be compromised.

DEVELOPING EMERGENCY RESPONSE PLANS

Even with strong habits, life occasionally presents genuine emergencies that require quick financial decisions. Having predetermined plans for different scenarios helps prevent panic-driven choices that could restart debt cycles. This might include maintaining specific emergency savings, having clear criteria for what constitutes a genuine emergency, and establishing specific steps for handling unexpected expenses. Creating these plans involves more than just saving money; it requires developing clear decision-making frameworks.

MAINTAINING LONG-TERM PERSPECTIVE

Sustainable financial freedom requires balancing immediate needs with long-term stability. This often means making peace with delayed gratification while developing appreciation for financial security. Learning to find satisfaction in growing savings rather than immediate purchases creates powerful motivation for maintaining debt-free status.

ACHIEVING LONG-TERM FINANCIAL FREEDOM

> **KEY PRINCIPLE**
> Lasting financial freedom requires building wealth beyond debt elimination rather than just reaching zero.

My perspective on financial freedom transformed after finally eliminating my bankruptcy-era debts. I still remember the day I made my final payment; the momentary euphoria was quickly replaced by an unexpected emptiness. While staring at my zero balance, a sobering realization hit me: "Being debt-free isn't the finish line; it's just the starting point."

Without wealth-building strategies, I'd remain vulnerable to future financial shocks. This prompted me to redirect my former debt payments into investments. The discipline that freed me from debt became the same discipline that would build my wealth and true financial security.

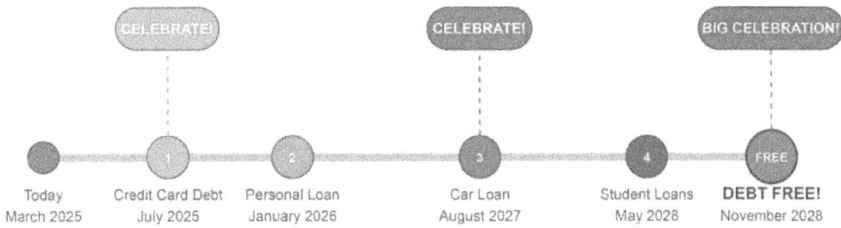

| Today | Credit Card Debt | Personal Loan | Car Loan | Student Loans | DEBT FREE! |
| March 2025 | July 2025 | January 2026 | August 2027 | May 2028 | November 2028 |

Monthly Payment Timeline

$850/mo $850/mo $850/mo $850/mo $850/mo   SAVE

Credit Card   Personal Loan   Car Loan   Student Loans   Savings

Total Debt Freedom Journey: 3 years, 8 months
Monthly Amount Freed Up for Investing: $850

MOVING BEYOND ZERO

The transition from debt repayment to wealth building requires careful planning. The same intensity that enables successful debt elimination can be redirected toward building assets. Many people find success by maintaining their "debt payment" amount but directing it toward investments and emergency savings instead.

This transition can be psychologically challenging. After years of focusing on debt elimination, shifting to wealth building requires developing new financial muscles. Understanding basic investment principles, risk management, and long-term planning are crucial for this next phase of the journey.

BUILDING FINANCIAL SECURITY

True financial security requires creating multiple layers of protection. Emergency savings provide the first line of defense against unexpected expenses, while investment accounts build long-term wealth. Understanding how different financial tools work together lets you create comprehensive protection against future debt.

It's important to balance the relationship between income, savings, and investments. While maintaining a debt-free lifestyle, successful individuals typically focus on increasing their income through career development or side businesses. This additional income, when properly managed, accelerates wealth building while strengthening financial security.

CREATING PASSIVE INCOME STREAMS

Developing income sources beyond traditional employment provides additional security against future debt. This might include dividend-paying investments, rental properties, or small business ventures. These multiple income streams help maintain financial stability even during challenging times.

Investment selection requires balancing growth potential with risk management. While aggressive investing might seem appealing after becoming debt-free, maintaining sustainable growth often proves more valuable than seeking quick returns. Understanding risk tolerance and investment time horizons helps create appropriate investment strategies.

MAINTAINING LIFE BALANCE

Financial freedom should support life goals rather than restrict them. This means finding balance between saving for the future and enjoying the present. Many people discover that mindful spending on experiences or carefully chosen purchases supports their financial freedom by preventing feelings of deprivation that lead to overspending.

Remember: Long-term financial freedom grows from building wealth beyond debt elimination. Focus on creating multiple layers of financial security while maintaining the positive habits developed during debt repayment. Successful transitions to lasting financial freedom often combine continued financial discipline with strategic wealth building.

CHAPTER SUMMARY AND KEY TAKEAWAYS

Through my journey from bankruptcy to financial stability, I've learned that successful debt management combines understanding different types of debt with developing sustainable habits. The lessons from both personal experience and helping others show that lasting debt freedom requires more than just making payments; it demands transforming our relationship with money.

CORE DEBT MANAGEMENT PRINCIPLES:

Understanding Over Action: During my recovery, I discovered that understanding how different debts affect your financial life matters more than making rushed payoff attempts. A nurse practitioner's experience reinforced this; by understanding the nature of her different debts, she created more effective strategies than those who simply threw money at the highest balance. Success comes from knowing how different obligations affect your complete financial picture.

Strategy Over Speed: Thoughtful planning creates better outcomes than aggressive but unsustainable payoff attempts. A teacher's experience demonstrated this when his balanced approach, including emergency savings, proved more successful than maximizing payments without protection against setbacks. Effective debt elimination often comes from consistent progress rather than dramatic sacrifices.

Habits Over Hurry: Through both success and failure, I've learned that developing debt-free habits matters more than quick payoff. Recent experiences helping families navigate debt challenges showed how changing financial behaviors creates more lasting success than focusing solely on debt elimination.

ACTION PLAN

First 30 Days: Foundation Building
- Create complete debt inventory
- Establish minimum payment systems
- Begin emergency fund building
- Track spending patterns
- Start habit development

60-Day Implementation
- Choose repayment strategy
- Build automatic payment systems
- Develop emergency plans
- Strengthen positive habits
- Create progress metrics

90-Day Establishment
- Review and adjust strategy
- Deepen financial awareness
- Plan wealth building steps
- Build support systems
- Maintain consistent progress

FINAL THOUGHTS

Remember: Debt freedom isn't about reaching zero; it's about transforming your financial life. Through bankruptcy and recovery, I learned that effective debt management requires changing both behaviors and mindsets while building toward lasting financial security.

YOUR NEXT STEP

Look at your debt inventory. Which obligation causes you the most stress? That's your starting point; not necessarily because it's the mathematically optimal choice, but because eliminating it will give you the psychological momentum to tackle everything else.

Debt freedom isn't a destination you reach once. It's a skill you develop, a muscle you strengthen. The strategies in this chapter will serve you not just now, but every time life presents a financial challenge. And it will.

CHAPTER 3
PERSONAL BANKING

LEARNING OBJECTIVES

- Understand modern banking fundamentals and systems
- Master effective account management strategies
- Learn to navigate digital banking securely
- Develop strong banking relationships
- Create sustainable financial infrastructure

OPENING STORY

The hardest part of bankruptcy wasn't the legal process; it was standing at an ATM, watching my card decline for a $40 withdrawal. This moment taught me that banking isn't just about storing money; it's about having the basic tools to participate in modern financial life. Now, managing multiple accounts effectively, I understand that banking is the foundation for all other success.

INTRODUCTION

Banking in today's world extends far beyond the simple checking accounts our parents knew. Modern banking resembles operating a personal financial command center; requiring understanding of digital tools, security measures, and various account types to create an effective financial infrastructure.

Creating an effective banking system resembles building a house; you need a solid foundation, rooms for different purposes, and proper security measures.

The most successful approach to banking combines understanding modern tools with traditional financial wisdom. Many people maintain basic accounts without understanding how to use banking tools effectively, missing opportunities to create stronger financial foundations.

For effective management, you need to design banking systems that support both current needs and future growth while maintaining security. Most importantly, you'll discover that effective banking isn't about having the most sophisticated accounts; it's about creating systems that work for your specific situation. The methods we'll discuss work whether you're rebuilding your finances or managing substantial assets.

UNDERSTANDING MODERN BANKING FUNDAMENTALS

KEY PRINCIPLE
Modern banking requires active management rather than passive participation in basic accounts.

My banking awakening came during my first months of consulting after bankruptcy. I quickly discovered my simple checking account couldn't handle the complexity of my rebuilding business. Client deposits would arrive, but without proper separation from personal funds, I'd lose track of what was available versus what needed to be reserved for taxes or business expenses.

One painful quarterly tax deadline taught me that proper banking isn't just about having accounts; it's about creating systems that track every dollar's purpose. The right banking structure became the foundation for my financial recovery.

UNDERSTANDING ACCOUNT TYPES

Modern checking accounts serve different purposes than their traditional counterparts. Beyond basic bill paying and debit card access, these accounts now offer features like mobile deposit, instant transfers, and automated bill payment. Understanding these capabilities helps create more efficient money management systems.

Traditional savings accounts from major banks typically offer minimal interest rates, often below 0.1% annually. However, online banks and credit unions frequently provide high-yield savings options exceeding 4% APY. This difference can significantly impact long-term savings growth, particularly for emergency funds and short-term savings goals.

The Ideal Banking Architecture

Building your financial command center

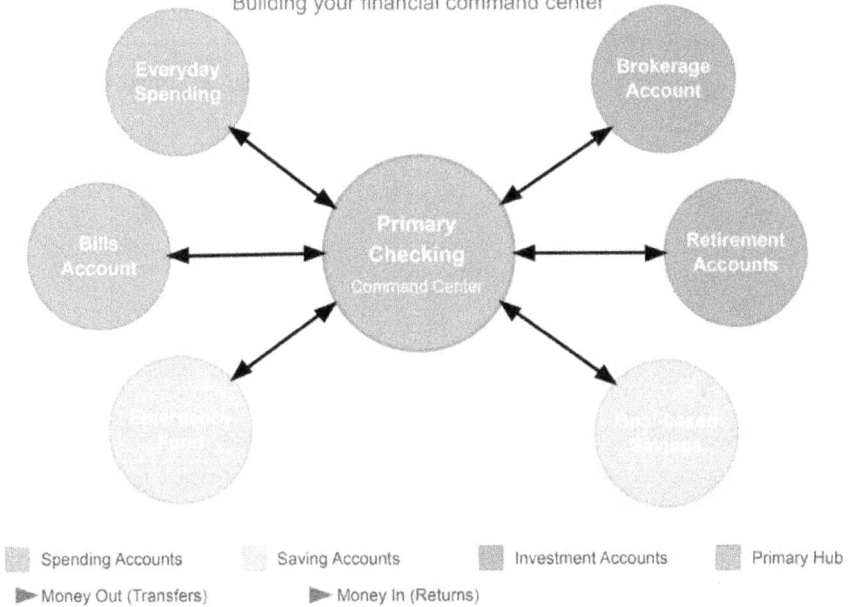

Everyday Spending

Brokerage Account

Bills Account

Primary Checking
Command Center

Retirement Accounts

Spending Accounts   Saving Accounts   Investment Accounts   Primary Hub

Money Out (Transfers)   Money In (Returns)

DIGITAL BANKING INTEGRATION

Modern banking infrastructure relies heavily on digital tools and connectivity. Mobile apps, online portals, and electronic payment systems create opportunities for better financial management while requiring understanding of proper security measures and usage patterns.

The relationship between different financial tools; payment apps, investment platforms, and traditional banking; requires careful coordination. Many people maintain unnecessary complexity by failing to integrate these tools effectively, relying on multiple accounts that could be simplified. Essential elements of modern banking management include:

- Minimum balance requirements
- Monthly maintenance fees
- Transaction limitations
- Overdraft protection options
- ATM network access

The True Cost of Banking

Identifying and eliminating unnecessary fees

Fee Type	Typical Amount	Frequency	Annual Impact	Avoidable?
Monthly Maintenance	$12.00	Monthly	$144.00	Yes
Out-of-Network ATM	$3.50	2× per month	$84.00	Yes
Overdraft	$35.00	4× per year	$140.00	Yes
Wire Transfer	$25.00	6× per year	$150.00	Partially
Paper Statements	$2.50	Monthly	$30.00	Yes
Minimum Balance	$10.00	Quarterly	$40.00	Yes

TOTAL ANNUAL COST	$588.00

Potential Savings with Fee-Free Banking: $500+ per year

BUILDING BANKING RELATIONSHIPS

Despite increasing digitization, banking relationships remain valuable. Strong banking relationships can provide fee waivers, better loan terms, and expedited problem resolution. Understanding how to build and maintain these relationships while utilizing digital tools creates an optimal banking experience.

Traditional branch banking serves different purposes in the modern era. While routine transactions move increasingly online, branches provide important services for complex transactions, document notarization, and relationship building. You'll be able to bank more effectively when you understand when to use branch services and when to leverage digital tools.

Remember: Modern banking success requires understanding both traditional principles and current tools. Focus on creating banking systems that support your specific needs while maintaining flexibility for growth. The most effective banking approaches often combine digital efficiency with strong institutional relationships.

MANAGING MULTIPLE ACCOUNTS

KEY PRINCIPLE
Effective account management requires purposeful organization rather than maintaining accounts by default.

Managing multiple bank accounts resembles conducting an orchestra; each account plays a specific role, but success comes from making them work together harmoniously. Many people accumulate accounts randomly over time, creating unnecessary complexity and missed opportunities for financial efficiency.

During my post-bankruptcy recovery period, I juggled five different accounts across three institutions: a checking account for consulting income, another for personal expenses, a savings account at a different bank, and business accounts elsewhere. "I had accounts everywhere but no real system," I confessed to my financial mentor.

My breakthrough came when I created a purposeful account structure with clear roles for each account. This simple organization transformed my recordkeeping along with my entire relationship with money, providing me with control I desperately needed.

CREATING PURPOSEFUL ACCOUNT STRUCTURE

The "Hub and Spoke" banking system provides an effective framework for most people. This approach uses a primary checking account as the hub, with specialized accounts (spokes) serving specific purposes. Understanding the function and role of each account roles informs the account types and features that you need.

Primary checking accounts require careful selection based on several factors. Beyond basic features like free ATM access and online bill pay, consider minimum balance requirements, mobile deposit limits, and transfer capabilities. This account serves as the command center for your financial life, making feature selection particularly important.

Reference the chart below to familiarize yourself with different types of bank accounts. Consider each account type's features and your financial needs to determine what goes in your banking portfolio.

Purpose-Driven Banking

Matching the right accounts to financial goals

Account Type	Key Features	Best For
C Primary Checking	• Direct deposit access • Debit card transactions • Bill payments	Daily transactions and monthly bill payments
H High-Yield Savings	• Higher interest rates • Limited transactions • Online accessibility	Emergency funds and short-term savings goals
M Money Market	• Check writing • Higher balances • Tiered interest rates	Larger savings with occasional access needs
C Certificates of Deposit	• Higher fixed rates • Term commitments • Early withdrawal penalties	Known future expenses with specific timeframes
S Specialized Account	• HSA, 529 Plans • Tax advantages • Specific usage rules	Healthcare expenses and education funding

Short-term   Medium-term   Long-term

SPECIALIZED ACCOUNT PURPOSES

Emergency savings accounts need different features from regular savings. High-yield accounts without debit card access often work best, creating both better returns and a psychological barrier to casual withdrawal. Some people maintain these accounts at separate institutions to further reduce impulsive access.

All business banking should be fully separated from your personal finances. Even small side businesses benefit from dedicated accounts. This simplifies tax preparation and financial tracking. Understanding business banking features like merchant services, ACH transfers, and cash management tools will help you select appropriate accounts.

ACCOUNT INTEGRATION STRATEGIES

Modern financial management requires an understanding of how different accounts connect. Payment apps, investment platforms, and traditional banking create an interconnected financial ecosystem. Effective management means optimizing these connections while maintaining appropriate security measures.

Key account management considerations include:
- Transfer timing and limits
- Account linking security
- Payment processing delays
- Mobile app integration
- Backup access methods

BALANCE MANAGEMENT

Maintaining appropriate balances across accounts requires a systematic approach as well. Too much money in checking earns no interest, while too little places you at risk of overdraft fees. Understanding your typical spending patterns and bill payment schedules helps you optimize balance distribution.

It's important to conduct regular balance reviews to catch and prevent common banking problems. A weekly review of all your account gives you the chance to identify potential issues before they become problems, while monthly deep dives ensure optimal account usage and fee avoidance. These reviews focus on both immediate needs and longer-term optimization.

SECURITY CONSIDERATIONS

Multiple account management requires enhanced security measures. Different accounts may need different security levels based on their purpose and access requirements. Understanding and implementing appropriate security measures for each account type helps you prevent unauthorized access while maintaining convenient usage.

Digital account access requires particular attention to security. It's imperative to protect all your digital accounts with strong, unique passwords, two-factor authentication, and regular security reviews. You need to understand how different security measures work together to ensure comprehensive protection.

Remember: Multiple account management requires purposeful organization and regular attention. Focus on creating clear purposes for each account while maintaining efficient connections between them. Successful account management combines simplicity of structure with clarity of purpose.

DIGITAL BANKING SECURITY

KEY PRINCIPLE
Digital financial security requires proactive protection rather than reactive response to threats.

My wake-up call about digital security came through a seemingly innocent coffee shop transaction during my consulting days. I used public Wi-Fi to check account balances between client meetings, which led to unauthorized access attempts on three different accounts within 48 hours. I still remember the sinking feeling in my stomach as those security alerts popped up. "I thought my complex passwords were enough protection," I wrote in my journal that night. This close call transformed my approach completely; I immediately implemented comprehensive security protocols that I maintain to this day, even as I manage significantly larger assets.

BUILDING YOUR SECURITY FOUNDATION

Digital financial security starts with fundamental protection measures. Strong, unique passwords for each financial account provide basic security, but modern protection requires additional layers. Password managers help maintain complex, unique passwords while reducing the temptation to reuse passwords across accounts.

Two-factor authentication creates crucial additional security beyond passwords. While some view this extra step as inconvenient, it significantly reduces unauthorized access risk. Understanding different authentication methods; SMS codes, authenticator apps, or physical security keys; helps choose appropriate protection levels for different accounts.

CREATING SECURE ACCESS PATTERNS

Account access habits affect security. Public Wi-Fi usage, shared computers, and mobile device security all impact financial information protection. Developing secure access patterns helps you prevent common security breaches while providing convenient account access.

Device security requires particular attention in modern banking. Mobile phones often provide primary banking access, making phone security crucial for financial protection. Regular device updates, secure app installation practices, and proper security settings help maintain financial security. Key components of comprehensive digital security:

- Unique passwords for each account
- Multi-factor authentication setup
- Regular security reviews

- Device protection measures
- Monitoring alert systems

MANAGING ACCOUNT NOTIFICATIONS

Alert systems provide critical security monitoring. Understanding different alert types and setting appropriate notification thresholds helps you identify potential security issues quickly. Leverage balance alerts, transaction notifications, and login warnings to create real-time security monitoring.

Regularly review your security processes to upkeep your protection. Monthly security checks ensure all protective measures remain active and appropriate. As you conduct these reviews:

- Check recent account activity
- Verify security settings
- Update protection measures as needed

RECOVERY PLANNING

Understanding how to quickly secure accounts, contact financial institutions, and prevent further unauthorized access helps you minimize damage from security incidents. Create clear response protocols before problems occur to ensure quick, effective reaction to security issues.

Document storage security requires particular attention. Financial documents, account information, and security recovery codes need to sit in secure but accessible storage. Understanding different storage options; digital vaults, secure cloud storage, or physical security boxes; helps create appropriate document protection.

Remember: Digital financial security requires active management and regular attention. Focus on creating comprehensive protection while maintaining practical usability. The most effective security combines strong technical measures with consistent security habits.

BUILDING BANKING RELATIONSHIPS

KEY PRINCIPLE
Strong banking relationships provide opportunities and protection beyond basic account services.

Building banking relationships resembles developing professional networks; it requires intentional effort, consistent interaction, and mutual benefit. Many people view banks as simple service providers, missing opportunities to create valuable financial partnerships that can support both immediate needs and long-term goals.

My understanding of banking relationships transformed during my business recovery phase. After bankruptcy had severed most of my banking ties, I spent a year building a relationship with a regional credit union, making sure the branch manager knew my story and witnessed my rebuilding efforts.

When I needed funding for a critical consulting contract requiring upfront equipment, that relationship proved invaluable. "We see your history, but we also see your progress," the loan officer told me. "I'm personally advocating for your application." That relationship made the difference between contract success and another missed opportunity.

DEVELOPING INSTITUTIONAL CONNECTIONS

Modern banking relationships require balancing digital convenience with personal connection. While most transactions happen electronically, maintaining contact with key banking personnel creates valuable resources for complex financial needs. Regular communication helps you maintain these connections.

Branch relationships are still important despite digital banking prevalence. Personal bankers, branch managers, and loan officers can provide services and solutions beyond standard online offerings. Understanding when to leverage these relationships helps you maximize banking benefits while maintaining digital convenience. Banking relationships provide benefits beyond basic services:

- Fee waiver opportunities
- Rate improvement possibilities
- Expedited problem resolution
- Custom solution access
- Financial advice resources

NAVIGATING FINANCIAL INSTITUTIONS

Different financial institutions serve different purposes in a comprehensive banking strategy. Traditional banks, credit unions, and online institutions each offer unique advantages.

Credit unions often provide particularly valuable relationships. Member-owned structure and community focus frequently result in more personalized service and better rates. Understanding credit union membership requirements and benefits allows you to access these advantages.

MANAGING MULTIPLE INSTITUTION RELATIONSHIPS

Maintaining relationships with several financial institutions creates both opportunities and challenges. While multiple relationships provide access to various services and benefits, they require careful management to maintain effectiveness. Establish a clear purpose for each relationship to optimize these connections.

Documentation organization becomes crucial with multiple banking relationships. Keeping clear records of accounts, contacts, and communications helps maintain effective relationships while preventing confusion or oversight. Regular review of these relationships ensures continued value and appropriate service levels.

PROBLEM RESOLUTION THROUGH RELATIONSHIPS

Strong banking relationships prove particularly valuable during problems. Account issues, fraud concerns, or service questions are often resolved more quickly through established relationships. Understanding proper escalation processes while maintaining professional relationships helps address problems effectively.

Fostering banking relationships will benefit all your future planning. Major financial decisions; home purchases, business expansion, or investment opportunities; often work better with established banking connections. Building these relationships before specific needs arise creates valuable resources for future opportunities.

Remember: Banking relationships require active development and maintenance. Focus on creating mutually beneficial connections while maintaining appropriate professional boundaries. Successful banking relationships often combine regular interaction with clear purpose and value.

LONG-TERM BANKING SUCCESS

> **KEY PRINCIPLE**
> Sustainable banking success requires adapting financial systems as your life evolves rather than maintaining static arrangements.

Long-term banking success resembles maintaining a growing business; systems must evolve to support increasing complexity while maintaining fundamental stability. Many people establish basic banking arrangements early in their financial lives but fail to adapt these systems as their needs change.

My own banking evolution from military service to Big Tech leadership demonstrates this principle perfectly. "I kept the same basic checking account

I'd had since my Marine Corps days," I realized during my financial rebuilding. After my bankruptcy, I continued using a simple account structure that had worked when my finances were straightforward.

It wasn't until Lacey encouraged me to analyze how this approach was limiting our financial growth that I understood banking needs to grow alongside your career. Creating a more sophisticated banking architecture; with dedicated accounts for different purposes; became a crucial step in rebuilding my financial foundation.

CREATING ADAPTIVE SYSTEMS

Your banking needs will change significantly through different life stages. Early on in your career, you might require simple checking and savings arrangements. On the other hand, someone in the stages of family planning will require more sophisticated money management tools. Understanding how different life stages affect banking needs helps you create appropriate system evolution.

Future planning significantly impacts banking structure. Major life goals; home purchase, business formation, or early retirement; often require specific banking arrangements. Develop a banking system that supports both your current needs and future goals to form a stronger financial foundation. Modern banking offers numerous opportunities to manage your assets more efficiently:

- Automated payment systems
- Cash management tools
- Investment integration
- Tax planning features
- Wealth building resources

MANAGING FINANCIAL GROWTH

Simple checking and savings accounts are inadequate for managing substantial assets as your wealth grows. Take the time to understand different account types, options for investment integration, and wealth management services available to you as you work to create appropriate financial structures.

Your needs for risk management become increasingly important with financial growth. FDIC insurance limits, account security measures, and institutional stability all require careful consideration. Work to create appropriate protection for growing assets while maintaining convenient access.

INSTITUTION SELECTION STRATEGY

Banking relationships require regular evaluation as your needs change. Institutions that may have served you well early on in your financial life might not provide optimal services for evolving needs. Understanding when to maintain existing relationships and when to seek new banking partners helps you optimize financial services.

Geographic considerations affect long-term banking success. Factors such as relocation, travel requirements, or business expansion might necessitate banking relationship adjustments. Maintaining effective financial access while adapting to changing geographic needs requires careful planning.

TECHNOLOGY INTEGRATION

Mobile banking features, integration with financial management tools, and emerging payment technologies all affect banking effectiveness. Staying informed about technological developments while maintaining appropriate security helps you optimize banking arrangements.

CHAPTER SUMMARY AND KEY TAKEAWAYS

Through my journey from bankruptcy to financial stability, I've learned that effective banking combines understanding modern tools with building strong institutional relationships. The lessons from both personal experience and helping others show that banking success requires active management rather than passive account holding.

CORE BANKING PRINCIPLES:

Systems Over Simplicity: During my recovery, I discovered that creating purposeful banking systems matters more than maintaining basic accounts. One business owner's experience reinforced this; by developing comprehensive banking arrangements rather than relying on simple checking accounts, she created stronger financials supporting both personal and business growth.

Relationships Over Transactions: Working with others showed how banking relationships create opportunities beyond basic services. A small business owner's experience demonstrated this when her long-term credit union relationship provided crucial support for business expansion. Successful banking approaches combine efficient digital services with valuable connections.

Evolution Over Stability: Through both success and failure, I've learned that banking needs change with life circumstances. Recent experiences helping families navigate financial transitions showed how adaptive banking systems create better outcomes than static arrangements. Success comes from growing banking relationships alongside personal financial evolution.

ACTION PLAN

First 30 Days: Foundation Building
- Review current banking arrangements
- Assess account purposes and efficiency
- Establish security protocols
- Begin relationship development
- Create monitoring systems

60-Day Implementation
- Optimize account structure
- Build institutional connections
- Strengthen security measures
- Develop digital efficiency
- Establish review processes

90-Day Establishment
- Evaluate system effectiveness
- Deepen banking relationships
- Plan future adaptations
- Build long-term strategy
- Maintain regular assessment

FINAL THOUGHTS

Remember: Banking success isn't about having the most accounts; it's about creating effective financial systems that support your goals.

YOUR NEXT STEP

Pull up your bank statements from the last three months. How many fees did you pay? How many accounts do you actually use? Sometimes the best banking optimization starts with simplification.

Banking should work for you, not the other way around. If your current setup requires constant attention just to avoid problems, it's time to redesign the system.

CHAPTER 4
EMERGENCY FUNDS

LEARNING OBJECTIVES

- Understand what truly constitutes a financial emergency
- Master practical methods for building emergency savings
- Learn to balance emergency funds with other financial needs
- Develop sustainable saving habits
- Create protection that grows with your changing life

OPENING STORY

The value of an emergency fund hit home for me late one Tuesday night when my son needed emergency dental surgery. The $2,200 bill didn't send me into panic or debt because I had gradually built my emergency savings during my recovery years. This moment crystallized that emergency funds aren't just about money; they're about sleeping peacefully knowing you can handle life's unexpected challenges.

INTRODUCTION

Emergency funds function like a financial immune system; protecting you from unexpected financial threats while maintaining your overall financial health. Many people view emergency savings as a luxury rather than a necessity, missing the crucial role these funds play in preventing minor setbacks from becoming major crises.

Building emergency savings resembles training for a marathon; success comes from consistent effort. Like physical training, developing emergency funds requires both discipline and appropriate pacing to create lasting financial protection.

The most successful approach to emergency savings combines clear understanding of protection needs with practical saving strategies. Similar to designing a safety system, different life circumstances require distinct levels of financial protection.

Most importantly, you'll discover that emergency fund building isn't about reaching a perfect number; it's about creating appropriate protection for your specific situation. The methods we'll discuss work whether you're saving your first $500 or building substantial reserves.

UNDERSTANDING EMERGENCY FUND FUNDAMENTALS

KEY PRINCIPLE

Emergency funds provide multiple layers of protection rather than just covering unexpected expenses.

My approach to emergency funds underwent a complete transformation after bankruptcy. What once seemed like an optional financial buffer became the foundation of our financial security and decision-making confidence.

During the darkest days of my financial collapse, a minor $400 car repair created a cascade of financial problems. Without adequate reserves, I had to choose between missing client meetings due to transportation issues or creating new credit card debt I couldn't afford. This experience shaped my financial philosophy.

When Lacey and I began building our financial life together, establishing proper emergency savings became our first priority; even before investing or retirement planning.

What made our approach different wasn't just the priority we placed on emergency funds, but how we structured them. Rather than creating a single emergency account, we developed a tiered system:

- Tier 1: $2,000 in high-liquidity cash for immediate needs
- Tier 2: Three months of expenses in a high-yield savings account
- Tier 3: Three additional months in a slightly less liquid money market fund
- Tier 4: A low-interest line of credit as backup protection, never used but available

"The different tiers serve different purposes," Lacey observed as we built this system. "The immediate cash prevents small emergencies from becoming larger problems, while the extended reserves protect against income disruption."

Building Your Safety Net

The four stages of emergency protection

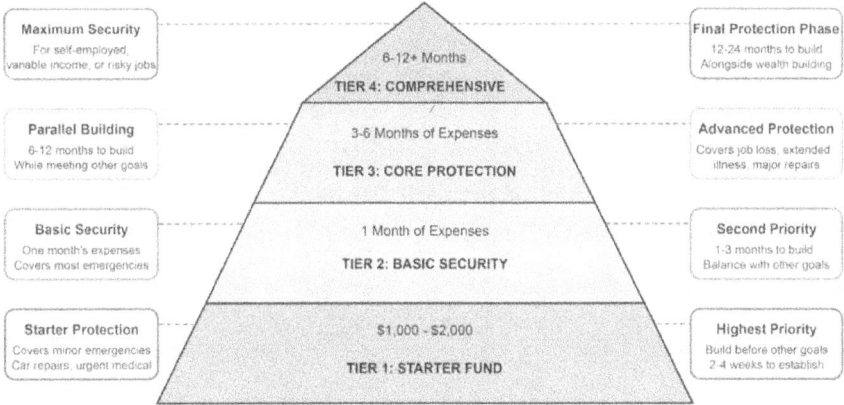

Maximum Security For self-employed, variable income, or risky jobs	**6-12+ Months** TIER 4: COMPREHENSIVE	**Final Protection Phase** 12-24 months to build Alongside wealth building
Parallel Building 6-12 months to build While meeting other goals	**3-6 Months of Expenses** TIER 3: CORE PROTECTION	**Advanced Protection** Covers job loss, extended illness, major repairs
Basic Security One month's expenses Covers most emergencies	**1 Month of Expenses** TIER 2: BASIC SECURITY	**Second Priority** 1-3 months to build Balance with other goals
Starter Protection Covers minor emergencies Car repairs, urgent medical	**$1,000 - $2,000** TIER 1: STARTER FUND	**Highest Priority** Build before other goals 2-4 weeks to establish

Build your emergency fund in stages, focusing on tier 1 first
before advancing to higher levels of financial protection

We automated the building of these reserves through direct deposits, starting with $100 weekly transfers that increased as our income grew. The discipline of treating these contributions as non-negotiable, even when other financial opportunities arose, reflected the lessons I'd learned through financial hardship.

One incident validated this approach. When Lacey needed an unexpected dental procedure costing $3,200, the decision process took less than five minutes. Rather than stressing about financing or postponing necessary care, we tapped into our Tier 2 emergency fund for immediate treatment without disrupting other financial goals.

"This is what financial security actually feels like," Lacey noted afterward. "Not just having the money but making decisions based on what's best rather than what's affordable in the moment."

As our income grew, we proportionally increased our emergency reserves. Although holding larger cash positions may be seen as inefficient, the psychological security these reserves provided was priceless. This peace of mind enabled us to make bolder decisions in other areas of our financial life.

DEFINING TRUE EMERGENCIES

Understanding what constitutes a genuine emergency is necessary for effective fund planning. True emergencies typically involve unexpected, urgent, and necessary expenses. Regular car maintenance, annual insurance premiums, or predictable seasonal expenses don't qualify as emergencies; these require separate planning and saving strategies.

It's important to define the distinction between emergencies and irregular expenses for effective financial planning. Many people deplete emergency funds for predictable but irregular expenses, leaving themselves vulnerable when genuine emergencies arise. Creating separate savings for known irregular expenses helps maintain emergency fund integrity.

Use the flowchart below to assess whether a given situation is a true emergency, or simply part of irregular expenses.

Is It Really an Emergency?

Decision framework for accessing emergency funds

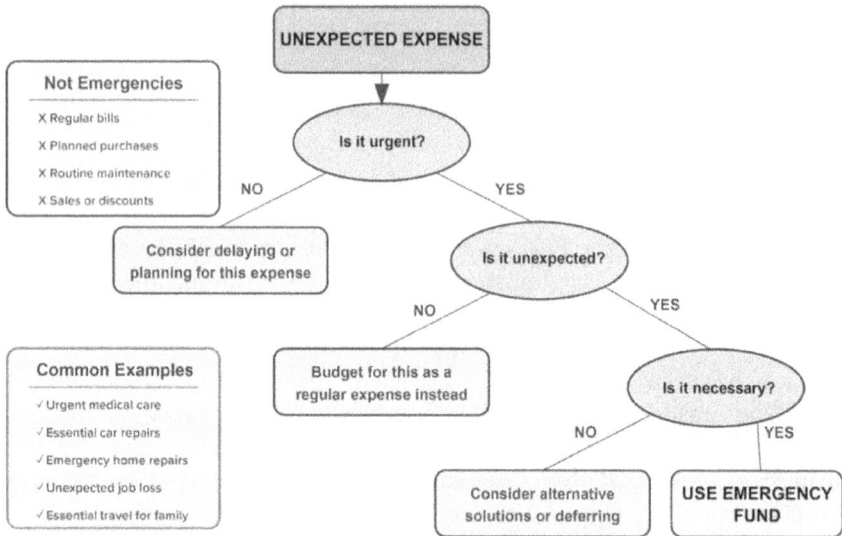

Not Emergencies
X Regular bills
X Planned purchases
X Routine maintenance
X Sales or discounts

UNEXPECTED EXPENSE

Is it urgent?

NO → Consider delaying or planning for this expense

YES → Is it unexpected?

NO → Budget for this as a regular expense instead

YES → Is it necessary?

NO → Consider alternative solutions or deferring

YES → USE EMERGENCY FUND

Common Examples
✓ Urgent medical care
✓ Essential car repairs
✓ Emergency home repairs
✓ Unexpected job loss
✓ Essential travel for family

UNDERSTANDING PROTECTION LAYERS

Emergency funds provide multiple levels of financial security. The first layer handles minor emergencies; car repairs, urgent home maintenance, or unexpected medical costs. Deeper layers protect against more significant disruptions like job loss, major medical issues, or extended income reduction.

The relationship between emergency funds and insurance coverage is important. Emergency savings often cover insurance deductibles and out-of-pocket maximums, making these costs crucial factors in determining appropriate fund size. Understanding how emergency savings complement insurance protection helps you create comprehensive financial security.

PSYCHOLOGICAL BENEFITS

The emotional security provided by emergency funds is as valuable as financial protection. Knowing you can handle unexpected expenses without creating debt or disrupting long-term financial goals creates significant stress reduction. This psychological benefit contributes to overall family financial stability. Essential factors in emergency fund sizing include:

- Monthly essential expenses
- Income stability assessment
- Insurance deductible amounts
- Family size and needs
- Career field considerations

CREATING FUND ACCESSIBILITY

Emergency fund accessibility requires careful balance. Funds must remain readily available for genuine emergencies while being separate enough from regular accounts to prevent casual access. Take the time to understand different account options and access methods as you work to create an appropriate emergency fund structure.

The timing of emergency access matters. Some emergencies require immediate access to funds, while others allow several days for fund transfer. Creating tiered access; keeping some funds immediately available while maintaining higher yields on deeper reserves; provides optimal balance.

Remember: Emergency funds serve multiple protective purposes beyond covering unexpected expenses. Focus on creating comprehensive protection that addresses both financial and emotional security needs. Effective emergency funds combine immediate accessibility with broader financial stability support.

BUILDING EMERGENCY SAVINGS

KEY PRINCIPLE
Successful emergency fund building requires systematic progress rather than waiting for "extra" money.

During my early recovery from bankruptcy, I initially thought my tight consultant income prevented emergency fund building. "I'll start saving when I land a bigger contract," I told myself repeatedly. Then came my breakthrough moment; realizing that transferring just $25 weekly from my irregular income would gradually build protection.

This small, consistent action proved more effective than waiting for large payments that rarely materialized as expected. Within six months, this humble habit had created my first $500 safety net since bankruptcy.

CREATING SAVING SYSTEMS

Automatic savings systems are key successful emergency fund building. Setting up automatic transfers, even for lesser amounts, creates consistent growth while removing decision fatigue. These systems work best when aligned with paycheck timing and normal bill payment schedules.

Regular savings require psychological preparation as much as financial planning. Understanding that small, consistent contributions often outperform irregular larger deposits helps maintain motivation. Tracking progress through manageable milestones rather than focusing solely on final goals supports consistent saving behavior. Emergency savings typically develop through distinct stages:

- Starter fund ($500-1,000)
- Basic security (1 month expenses)
- Core protection (3-6 months)
- Extended security (6-12 months)
- Comprehensive coverage (12+ months)

MANAGING GROWTH PHASES

As you build your initial emergency fund building, maintaining momentum is key. The first $500-1,000 you stash away provides crucial protection against minor emergencies while building saving habits. This starter fund helps you prevent debt accumulation from small, unexpected expenses, supporting continued financial progress.

As you transition from basic to comprehensive emergency savings, you'll want to adjust your strategy. While initial savings might come from simple expense reduction, building larger reserves often requires income increases, systematic saving from bonuses, or creative funding sources.

BALANCING COMPETING PRIORITIES

Emergency fund building must balance against other financial needs. Understanding how emergency savings fit within broader financial goals helps you maintain appropriate focus. While emergency funds provide crucial protection, over-saving in emergency accounts could stall your progress toward other important financial objectives.

The relationship between emergency savings and debt repayment requires careful consideration. While maintaining basic emergency savings during debt repayment proves crucial, building extensive reserves while carrying high-interest debt might prove counterproductive. Finding an appropriate balance between protection and debt elimination is required for optimal financial progress.

MAXIMIZING FUND EFFICIENCY

Account selection significantly affects emergency fund effectiveness. High-yield savings accounts, money market accounts, or carefully structured CD ladders can increase returns while maintaining appropriate accessibility. Understanding different account options helps you optimize emergency fund growth while preserving necessary liquidity.

Remember: Emergency fund building requires consistent effort rather than sporadic attention. Focus on creating sustainable saving systems while maintaining appropriate balance with other financial goals. Successful emergency savings grow through regular small contributions rather than irregular large deposits.

Balancing Access and Growth

Strategic placement of emergency funds

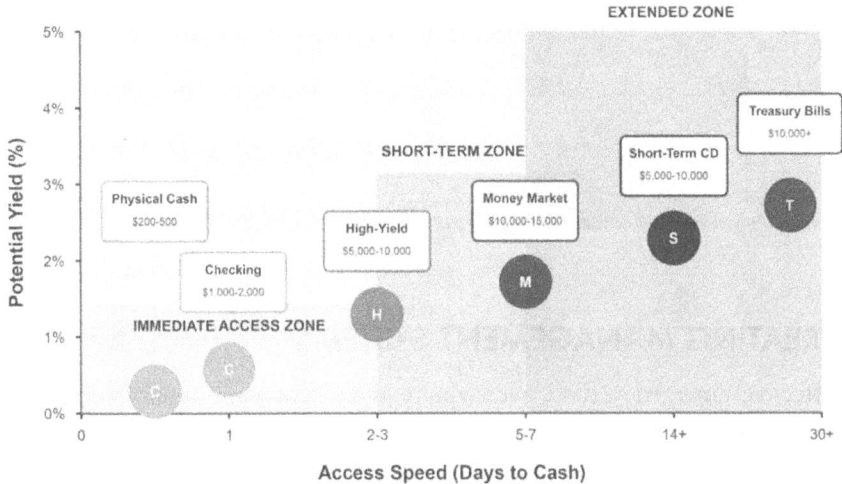

MANAGING EMERGENCY FUNDS

> **KEY PRINCIPLE**
> Emergency fund management requires active oversight rather than passive storage.

Managing emergency funds resembles maintaining critical equipment; regular checks and adjustments ensure reliability when needed. Many people adopt a "set and forget" approach after building emergency savings, missing opportunities to optimize protection while risking fund inadequacy when emergencies arise.

After building a modest $2,000 fund post-bankruptcy, I needed to withdraw $800 for an unexpected car repair. When assessing my remaining balance, I realized I'd been keeping it in a zero-interest checking account while inflation steadily eroded its value. "I've been protecting the dollars but losing their purchasing power," I noted in my financial journal that evening. This experience taught me that emergency funds need regular attention and optimization; not just accumulation; to maintain their protective power.

Your Protection Path

Sample timeline for building complete emergency coverage

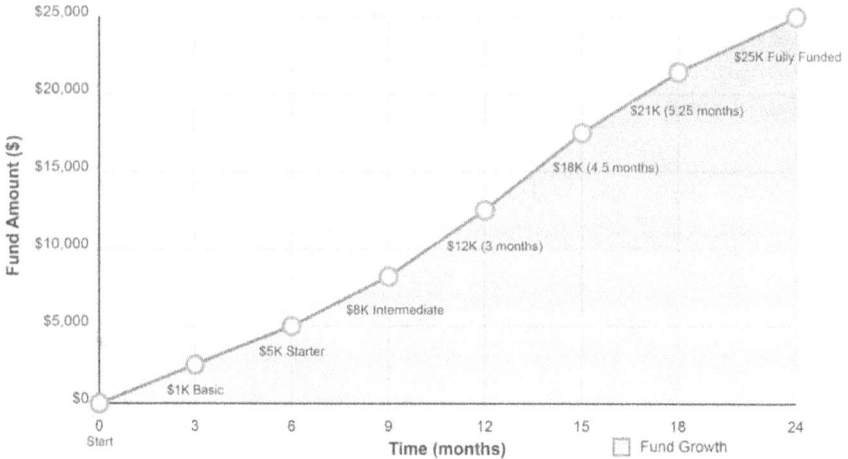

$25K Fully Funded
$21K (5.25 months)
$18K (4.5 months)
$12K (3 months)
$8K Intermediate
$5K Starter
$1K Basic

Fund Amount ($): $0, $5,000, $10,000, $15,000, $20,000, $25,000

Time (months): 0 Start, 3, 6, 9, 12, 15, 18, 24

☐ Fund Growth

CREATING MANAGEMENT SYSTEMS

Effective emergency fund oversight requires systematic review processes. Monthly assessments help ensure fund adequacy while quarterly deep reviews evaluate protection levels against changing life circumstances. These reviews should consider both fund size and structure while assessing potential adjustments needed.

Regular rebalancing helps you maintain appropriate emergency protection. Life changes; income increases, family additions, or new responsibilities; often require emergency fund adjustments. Key factors requiring regular evaluation:

- Current monthly expenses
- Family size changes
- Career stability shifts
- Insurance coverage updates
- Economic condition impacts

EMERGENCY FUND CALCULATION EXAMPLE

Let's calculate appropriate emergency fund targets for three households:

SCENARIO 1: Single professional, stable job, renting

Expense	Amount
Rent:	$1,800
Utilities:	$200
Food:	$500
Transportation:	$300
Insurance:	$200
Minimum debt payments:	$500
Monthly essential expenses:	**$3,500**

Emergency Fund Target	
- Initial (3 months):	$10,500
- Full (6 months):	$21,000

SCENARIO 2: Family of four, single income, homeowners

Expense	Amount
Rent:	$2,200
Utilities:	$400
Food:	$1,000
Transportation:	$500
Insurance:	$400
Minimum debt payments:	$800
Monthly essential expenses:	**$5,300**

Emergency Fund Target	
- Initial (3 months):	$15,900
- Full (6 months):	$31,800

SCENARIO 3: Self-employed consultant, variable income

Expense	Amount
Rent:	$2,500
Utilities:	$300
Food:	$600
Transportation:	$400
Insurance:	$500
Minimum debt payments:	$700
Monthly essential expenses:	**$5,000**

Emergency Fund Target	
- Initial (6 months):	$30,000
- Full (9 months):	$45,000

Note how emergency fund targets vary significantly.

OPTIMIZING FUND STRUCTURE

Emergency fund structure requires periodic optimization. Different life stages and circumstances might require adjusting the balance between immediate accessibility and potential returns. Understanding how to structure funds across multiple accounts often provides optimal protection while maintaining appropriate growth.

The relationship between emergency funds and other financial accounts needs regular review. While you should keep emergency savings separate from regular spending accounts, opportunities for improved returns or better accessibility might emerge through account restructuring.

INFLATION PROTECTION

Maintaining emergency fund purchasing power requires specific attention. Inflation can significantly erode emergency fund value over time, particularly in low-interest saving environments. Understanding how to protect against inflation while maintaining necessary liquidity helps preserve emergency fund effectiveness.

Account yield optimization becomes increasingly important as emergency funds grow. While maintaining appropriate accessibility remains crucial, larger emergency funds might benefit from carefully structured tiers providing better returns on deeper reserves while keeping immediate-need funds readily available.

USAGE AND REPLENISHMENT

Clear protocols for emergency fund usage help you maintain long-term effectiveness. Establish specific criteria for accessing emergency savings to prevent casual withdrawal. This also ensures that funds remain available for genuine emergencies. These protocols should include both access guidelines and replenishment requirements.

Emergency fund replenishment requires particular attention after usage. Create specific plans for rebuilding emergency savings after withdrawals ahead of time. This way, you'll maintain continuous protection even during unexpected bumps in the road. Understanding how quickly different emergency fund levels need restoration helps you prioritize replenishment efforts.

Remember: Emergency fund management requires regular attention and adjustment. Focus on maintaining both fund adequacy and accessibility while optimizing structure for changing circumstances. The most effective emergency funds often combine consistent oversight with strategic adjustment to changing needs.

LONG-TERM EMERGENCY FUND STRATEGY

KEY PRINCIPLE
Sustainable emergency protection requires evolving strategies rather than static savings targets.

Long-term emergency fund planning resembles developing a comprehensive insurance strategy; protection needs change as assets grow and life circumstances evolve. Many people maintain the same emergency fund approach throughout their financial journey, missing opportunities to create more sophisticated protection as their situation changes.

My perspective on emergency protection transformed completely after rebuilding my career at Big Tech. The initial, simple three-month expense fund that I established during my recovery had to evolve as my assets and income grew substantially. Managing RSUs, rental properties, and increased responsibilities meant my potential financial emergencies had grown in both size and complexity.

We now needed protection for both our lifestyle and our investments. Simple cash reserves weren't enough anymore.

DEVELOPING COMPREHENSIVE PROTECTION

Long-term emergency planning extends beyond basic cash reserves. Different assets and income sources require different protection strategies. Understanding how various financial tools work together creates more complete protection.

The relationship between emergency funds and wealth building requires a careful balance. While maintaining appropriate cash reserves remains important, opportunity costs increase with substantial emergency funds. Creating strategic approaches that provide protection while minimizing drag on long-term wealth building becomes increasingly important. Advanced emergency protection often includes multiple components:

- Primary cash reserves
- Strategic credit lines
- Investment buffers
- Insurance integration
- Business continuity planning

INVESTMENT INTEGRATION

Your emergency fund strategy should become more sophisticated as your wealth grows. While maintaining appropriate cash reserves, think about how to incorporate investment components. This will provide you with additional protection while supporting your long-term growth. Understanding how to balance liquidity needs with investment opportunities helps you optimize emergency protection.

The role of conservative investments in emergency planning is important. Bond ladders, stable value funds, or other conservative investments might provide additional emergency protection while offering better long-term returns than cash reserves. Understanding how to incorporate these tools while maintaining necessary accessibility creates more efficient protection.

BUSINESS CONSIDERATION

Self-employed individuals and business owners need particularly sophisticated emergency planning. Personal and business emergency funds often require careful coordination while maintaining appropriate separation. Understanding how different business structures and revenue patterns affect emergency planning helps create appropriate protection strategies.

RISK MANAGEMENT INTEGRATION

Comprehensive emergency planning requires integration with broader risk management strategies. Insurance coverage, legal protection, and asset structure all affect emergency fund requirements. Understanding how different risk management tools work together helps you optimize overall financial protection.

LEGACY PLANNING

Long-term emergency strategies must consider family and legacy implications. Emergency funds might need to protect multiple generations or support wealth transfer objectives. Understanding how emergency protection fits within estate planning helps you create lasting financial security.

CHAPTER SUMMARY AND KEY TAKEAWAYS

Through my journey from bankruptcy to financial stability, I've learned that effective emergency protection combines systematic saving with strategic planning. The lessons from both personal experience and helping others show that emergency funds require active management rather than passive accumulation.

CORE EMERGENCY FUND PRINCIPLES:

Protection Over Perfection: During my recovery, I discovered that creating appropriate protection matters more than reaching specific dollar amounts. One contractor's experience reinforced this; by developing comprehensive protection strategies rather than focusing solely on cash reserves, he created stronger financial security that matched his evolving needs.

Systems Over Windfalls: Working with others showed how systematic saving creates better protection than waiting for large deposits. A dental hygienist's experience demonstrated this when her small regular contributions built more reliable protection than occasional larger amounts. The most successful emergency funds often grow through consistent small actions rather than dramatic gestures.

Evolution Over Stasis: Through both success and failure, I've learned that emergency protection needs change with life circumstances. Recent experiences helping families navigate financial transitions showed how adaptive protection strategies create better outcomes than static savings targets. Success comes from growing emergency protection alongside personal financial evolution.

ACTION PLAN

First 30 Days: Foundation Building
- Assess current emergency protection
- Calculate essential monthly expenses
- Establish automatic saving systems
- Create fund accessibility protocols
- Begin protection planning

60-Day Implementation
- Build systematic saving habits
- Develop fund management processes
- Strengthen protection layers
- Create usage guidelines
- Establish review schedules

90-Day Establishment
- Evaluate protection adequacy
- Deepen emergency reserves
- Plan future adaptations
- Build long-term strategy
- Maintain regular assessment

FINAL THOUGHTS

Remember: Emergency fund success isn't about reaching a perfect number; it's about creating appropriate protection for your specific situation. Proper emergency planning provides both financial security and peace of mind.

YOUR NEXT STEP

If you don't have an emergency fund, open a separate savings account today and set up a $25 automatic weekly transfer. That's it. Don't overthink the amount; start the habit.

If you already have emergency savings, ask yourself: Is it truly accessible in 24 hours? Is it protected from your own impulse to "borrow" from it? The best emergency fund is one you forget exists until you need it.

CHAPTER 5
STUDENT LOANS

LEARNING OBJECTIVES

- Understand how different types of student loans affect your future
- Learn to navigate repayment options effectively
- Master loan forgiveness and management strategies
- Develop sustainable approaches to education debt
- Create long-term plans for loan management

OPENING STORY

The financial aid office made it sound so simple: sign here, attend classes, get an MBA, pay later. At twenty-five, I didn't fully grasp that those signatures would follow me through career changes, a failed business, and even bankruptcy; when a judge discharged my credit cards, medical bills, and business debts but looked at me and said, "Your student loans remain your responsibility." That moment crystallized something I now share with everyone navigating education debt: student loans play by different rules than any other financial obligation, and understanding those rules can mean the difference between decades of burden and a strategic path to freedom.

INTRODUCTION

Student loans represent more than just debt; they're often an investment in future earning potential. Yet for many Americans, education debt has become a burden that affects everything from career choices to homeownership dreams. Understanding how to manage these loans effectively can transform your student loan debt from a lifetime burden into a manageable part of your financial picture.

Managing student loans resembles navigating a complex transportation system; you need to understand different routes, transfer points, and potential shortcuts to reach your destination efficiently. Many borrowers focus solely on making payments, missing opportunities for loan forgiveness, income-driven repayment, or strategic prepayment.

The most successful student loan management strategies combine understanding loan types with creating appropriate repayment strategies. Like planning a long journey, knowing your options, and choosing the right path can significantly affect both your immediate comfort and how quickly you reach your destination.

UNDERSTANDING MODERN STUDENT LOANS

KEY PRINCIPLE
Different types of student loans carry distinct terms, protections, and management options that significantly affect your financial future.

Student loan management resembles understanding different types of mortgages; each loan type comes with its own rules, benefits, and limitations. Many borrowers treat all student loans the same, missing crucial differences between federal and private loans that could affect their repayment options. Understanding these differences helps create more effective management strategies.

During my bankruptcy, I discovered that not all debts are created equal. While most obligations could be discharged, my student loans remained firmly in place. This unavoidable truth taught me that student loan management requires a different approach than other forms of debt. Despite my MBA and financial certifications, I hadn't fully understood the unique protections and limitations of federal student loans. This lesson helps me guide others through understanding that different types of debt need different management strategies.

FEDERAL VS. PRIVATE LOAN FUNDAMENTALS

Federal student loans offer unique benefits and protections that private loans don't provide. Direct Subsidized loans, where the government pays interest during school and deferment periods, prove particularly valuable for undergraduate students with financial need. Unsubsidized loans, while accruing interest from disbursement, still offer flexible repayment options and potential forgiveness opportunities.

The following graphic highlights the difference between federal and private student loans.

Federal vs. Private Student Loans

Understanding Fundamental Differences

	Federal Loans	Private Loans
Interest Rates	Fixed rates (currently 4.99-7.54%)	Variable rates (3-13%)
Repayment Options	• Income-driven plans • SAVE • PAYE • IBR • Extended options	• Standard fixed plans • Limited flexibility • Fewer hardship options
Forgiveness	• Public Service Loan Forgiveness • Teacher Loan Forgiveness • Disability Discharge	• No standard forgiveness • Some rare hardship options
Borrower Protections	• Deferment • Forbearance • No credit check • No cosigner required	• Limited hardship options • Credit check required • Often needs cosigner

Private student loans function more like traditional consumer debt. Credit-based approval and pricing mean rates can vary significantly between borrowers. Limited repayment flexibility and few forgiveness options make private loans generally less favorable than federal options. Understanding these limitations before borrowing helps you make better financing decisions.

REPAYMENT FLEXIBILITY DIFFERENCES

Income-driven repayment options represent a crucial advantage of federal loans. These plans can limit monthly payments to a percentage of discretionary income, providing valuable protection during career starts or financial challenges. Private loans rarely offer similar flexibility, often requiring full payments regardless of income.

Deferment and forbearance options provide important safety nets for federal loan borrowers. While interest may still accrue, the ability to temporarily pause payments during financial hardship helps prevent default. Private loans typically offer more limited payment postponement options, if any.

CONSOLIDATION AND REFINANCING DISTINCTIONS

Loan consolidation and refinancing opportunities differ significantly between loan types. Federal consolidation maintains government benefits while potentially simplifying repayment. Private refinancing might lower interest rates but it comes at a cost. Once you refinance via a private loan company, this permanently removes federal benefits and protections. Understanding these trade-offs helps you make appropriate refinancing decisions.

FORGIVENESS AND DISCHARGE OPPORTUNITIES

Public Service Loan Forgiveness and other forgiveness programs apply only to federal loans. These programs can provide substantial benefits for qualifying borrowers but require careful attention to program requirements. Private loans generally offer no forgiveness options outside of disability or death discharge.

Default consequences and resolution options vary between loan types. Federal loans offer multiple paths for those who have missed or late payments, including rehabilitation and consolidation. Private loan default often leads directly to collections and legal action, with fewer options for resolution.

BORROWING CONSIDERATIONS

There are future borrowing implications that you need to carefully consider. Federal loan limits ensure some protection against over-borrowing, while private loans often allow borrowing up to the full cost of attendance. Understanding these differences helps you make better decisions about education financing.

Remember: Understanding student loan types creates the foundation for effective management. Focus on knowing your loan types and their specific features before making repayment decisions. Successful student loan management starts with understanding loan characteristics rather than focusing solely on payment amounts.

DEVELOPING YOUR REPAYMENT STRATEGY

KEY PRINCIPLE

Effective loan repayment requires a strategy that matches your life circumstances rather than following generic advice.

Creating a student loan repayment strategy resembles developing a financial GPS route; you need to know both your destination and potential paths before choosing the best way forward. Many borrowers automatically choose standard repayment plans or focus solely on paying as much as possible, missing opportunities to align repayment with their broader financial goals and life circumstances.

My experience with student loan repayment options took a difficult shift during my financial recovery. After bankruptcy, I struggled with my remaining student loan payments under the standard repayment plan. Once I thoroughly researched income-driven options, my payments dropped from $650 monthly to $175 under an income-based plan, creating crucial breathing room while I rebuilt my consulting business. "Understanding all my options changed everything," I explained to Lacey. "I could finally build emergency savings while still making progress on my loans instead of feeling trapped in an unsustainable payment cycle."

The chart below outlines how different repayment plans lead to different monthly payments. Importantly, it also demonstrates the trade-off between lower payments and overall higher interest paid over the life of the loan.

| Loan Amount: | $35,000 | Interest Rate: | 5.5% |
| Repayment Term: | 10 Years | Total Cost Comparison | With $35,000 Loan |

Repayment Plan	Monthly Payment	Total Interest Paid
Standard Plan Fixed payments over 10 years	$378	$10,390
Graduated Plan Payments increase every 2 years	$225 - $525	$12,750
Extended Plan Up to 25-year repayment term	$303	$16,360
SAVE Plan Income-based payments	$125	$18,750*

* Potential loan forgiveness after 20-25 years

INCOME-DRIVEN REPAYMENT PLANS

Income-driven repayment plans offer crucial flexibility for federal loan borrowers. The new SAVE Plan calculates payments based on discretionary income, defined as earnings above 225% of the federal poverty level. This more generous calculation often results in lower payments than previous plans, while maintaining progress toward potential forgiveness.

Key Income-Driven Plans Include:
- **SAVE Plan (Saving on a Valuable Education):** Newest and most generous plan for most borrowers
- **PAYE (Pay as You Earn):** Caps payments at 10% of discretionary income
- **REPAYE (Revised Pay as You Earn):** Similar to PAYE but with different interest subsidies
- **IBR (Income-Based Repayment):** Available to borrowers before newer plans were created

- **ICR (Income-Contingent Repayment):** Higher percentage of income but accepts Parent PLUS loans via consolidation

STRATEGIC LOAN ALLOCATION

Strategic loan allocation is crucial when you're managing multiple loans. Targeting extra payments toward higher-interest loans while maintaining minimum payments on others often saves you substantial money over time. Understanding how different loans accrue interest is important for you to properly optimize payment allocation.

CAREER-BASED REPAYMENT CONSIDERATIONS

Career-based repayment options deserve careful consideration. Public Service Loan Forgiveness can provide substantial benefits for government and non-profit employees, while other professions might benefit more from aggressive repayment strategies. Understanding how career choices affect repayment options helps you make better professional decisions.

PAYMENT OPTIMIZATION TECHNIQUES

Payment timing and automation can significantly impact loan management success. Automatic payments often provide interest rate reductions while ensuring consistent progress. Understanding payment processing and interest calculation methods helps you optimize payment timing.

REFINANCING EVALUATION FRAMEWORK

Refinancing decisions require careful analysis of both benefits and drawbacks. While private refinancing might lower interest rates, it permanently removes federal benefits and protections. Understanding the long-term implications of refinancing helps you prevent costly mistakes. Look for and consider:
- Current and potential interest rate difference
- Remaining loan term
- Need for income-driven options in the future
- Public service forgiveness eligibility
- Current and projected career stability
- Emergency fund status

HARDSHIP OPTIONS

Economic hardship options provide important safety nets but require careful use. While deferment and forbearance can help during genuine financial difficulties, excessive use increases overall loan costs as you'll ultimately accrue more interest. Understanding these options helps you maintain them as emergency tools rather than regular solutions.

TAX CONSIDERATIONS

You need to consider the tax implications of different repayment strategies. Student loan interest deductions, forgiveness tax consequences, and income-driven repayment calculations all affect overall financial planning. Understanding these tax effects allows you to create more effective repayment strategies.

Remember: Successful repayment requires matching your strategy to your personal circumstances. Focus on creating sustainable approaches that support both loan repayment and broader financial goals. The most effective repayment strategies often combine multiple approaches rather than relying on single solutions.

MANAGING MULTIPLE LOANS

KEY PRINCIPLE
Successfully managing multiple loans requires coordination and strategy rather than treating each loan in isolation.

Many borrowers handle each loan separately, missing opportunities to create comprehensive strategies that could improve overall outcomes. Understanding how different loans interact helps you develop more effective management approaches.

My confusion about handling various student loans reflected a common struggle during my early career. Managing both federal and private student loans from undergraduate and MBA programs, I initially paid whatever I could toward each loan. "I was making payments everywhere but not seeing progress anywhere," I admitted during financial counseling.

After developing a coordinated strategy that prioritized my highest-interest private loans while maintaining minimum payments on federal loans, my progress became both visible and motivating. This strategic approach accelerated my path to complete repayment despite limited resources.

CREATING A COMPREHENSIVE LOAN INVENTORY

Loan consolidation decisions require careful consideration of both benefits and drawbacks. Federal consolidation can simplify management by combining multiple loans into one payment but may affect interest rates and forgiveness eligibility. Private consolidation through refinancing might lower rates but it also removes federal benefits permanently. Essential components include:

- Loan servicer information and contact details
- Current balance and interest rate for each loan
- Loan type (federal subsidized, unsubsidized, private, etc.)
- Monthly payment amount and due date
- Repayment plan and remaining term
- Special features (forgiveness eligibility, rate reduction options)

STRATEGIC PAYMENT PRIORITIZATION

Interest rate variations between loans can provide you with opportunities to maximize your payments. Targeting extra payments toward higher-rate loans while maintaining minimum payments on others often provides the best financial return. However, some borrowers might prioritize paying off private loans first to eliminate less flexible debt, even if interest rates are lower. Prioritize in different ways:

- Highest Interest First (Avalanche): Minimizes total interest paid
- Smallest Balance First (Snowball): Creates motivating quick wins
- Least Flexible First: Eliminates private loans before federal
- Hybrid Approach: Combines elements based on personal situation

PAYMENT MANAGEMENT SYSTEMS

Tracking all your payments is important when you work with multiple loans. Different servicers, due dates, and payment requirements can create confusion if you don't properly organize. Developing systematic tracking methods helps you prevent missed payments and optimize payment allocation:

- Dedicated calendar reminders for each loan payment
- Automated payment systems with manual verification
- Spreadsheet tracking all loan details and payment history
- Loan management apps that integrate multiple servicers
- Regular servicer website account reviews

SERVICER COMMUNICATION STRATEGIES

Loan servicer communications should be managed carefully when dealing with multiple loans. Different servicers may have varying requirements, processing times, and communication methods. Understanding how to effectively interact with each servicer can prevent payment problems and helps you maximize repayment options.

UNDERSTANDING FORGIVENESS ELIGIBILITY VARIATIONS

Forgiveness program eligibility often varies between loans. Some federal loans may qualify for specific forgiveness programs while others don't. Understanding these differences helps you create appropriate strategies for different loan types. Common forgiveness eligibility criteria include:

- Public Service Loan Forgiveness qualification varies by loan type
- Parent PLUS loans have limited income-driven options
- Older FFEL program loans require consolidation for certain benefits
- Perkins loans have their own forgiveness programs
- Private loans generally have no forgiveness options

FINANCIAL HARDSHIP PLANNING

Financial hardship options differ between loan types and servicers. Federal loans generally offer more flexible hardship options than private loans, but requirements and application processes vary. Understanding available options for each loan helps you maintain progress during difficult times.

INVESTMENT DECISION FRAMEWORK

Investment decisions become more complex when you're contending with multiple loans. Balancing loan repayment with other financial goals requires that you understand the full impact of different payment strategies. Some borrowers might benefit from maintaining minimum payments while investing excess funds, while others might prioritize debt elimination.

Remember: Multiple loan management requires comprehensive strategy development. Focus on understanding how different loans interact while creating coordinated repayment approaches. The most successful multiple loan management often involves strategic prioritization rather than treating all loans equally.

FORGIVENESS AND DISCHARGE OPTIONS

KEY PRINCIPLE
Understanding loan forgiveness programs requires knowing both eligibility requirements and long-term implications rather than assuming qualification.

Loan forgiveness resembles qualifying for a complex tax deduction; specific requirements must be met, documentation maintained, and timing carefully considered. Many borrowers assume forgiveness programs offer easy solutions, missing crucial requirements that could affect their eligibility. Understanding how different forgiveness programs work lets you create realistic paths toward debt elimination.

During my time at Raytheon, I assumed I'd automatically qualify for certain loan benefits through their education assistance program. "I didn't realize that only certain payment types and loan structures would qualify," I explained to a colleague facing similar confusion. "Missing these details nearly cost me thousands in potential benefits."

After understanding the specific requirements, I adjusted my repayment approach to ensure my payments counted toward potential forgiveness, creating substantial long-term savings despite short-term payment increases.

The chart below gives you a snapshot of the different requirements you need to fulfill in order to qualify for loan forgiveness.

The Path to Loan Forgiveness

Qualifying for PSLF and IDR Forgiveness

Public Service Loan Forgiveness (PSLF)	Income-Driven Repayment (IDR) Forgiveness
Full-time employment in qualifying public service	Enroll in income-driven repayment plan
Make 120 qualifying payments (10 years)	Make payments based on income
Submit PSLF form annually	20-25 years of qualifying payments
Remaining balance forgiven tax-free	Remaining balance forgiven (taxable)

PUBLIC SERVICE LOAN FORGIVENESS (PSLF)

Public Service Loan Forgiveness represents one of the most significant forgiveness opportunities, though it requires careful attention to specific elements:

PSLF Essential Requirements:
- Qualifying employment in government or non-profit organizations
- Direct Loans in eligible repayment plans
- 120 qualifying payments while working full-time
- Annual certification of employment
- Proper loan consolidation if needed

Common PSLF Pitfalls
- Working for a non-qualifying employer despite public service work
- Making payments under ineligible repayment plans

- Not certifying employment regularly
- Having non-Direct federal loans that weren't consolidated
- Working less than 30 hours per week

INCOME-DRIVEN REPAYMENT FORGIVENESS

Income-driven repayment forgiveness operates differently from PSLF, requiring longer periods but offering broader eligibility. Understanding the tax implications of forgiveness under these plans proves crucial, as forgiven amounts may be taxable unlike PSLF forgiveness. Key programs include:

- SAVE Plan: 20-25 years depending on loan type
- PAYE: 20 years
- REPAYE: 20 years for undergraduate, 25 for graduate loans
- IBR: 20-25 years depending on when you borrowed
- ICR: 25 years

PROFESSION-SPECIFIC FORGIVENESS OPTIONS

Teacher loan forgiveness provides another option for educators but cannot be earned simultaneously with PSLF for the same period of service. Understanding the interaction between different forgiveness programs helps you choose the most beneficial option. Additional profession-based programs include:

- Nurse Corps Loan Repayment Program
- National Health Service Corps
- Attorney Loan Repayment Assistance Programs
- Military Service Loan Forgiveness
- State-specific professional forgiveness programs

DISABILITY AND DEATH DISCHARGE

Disability discharge requires meeting specific medical criteria and documentation requirements. Permanent disability must be demonstrated according to program standards, with ongoing verification requirements in many cases.

Death discharge provides important protection for families, but requirements vary between federal and private loans. Some private loans may still hold co-signers responsible, making this consideration important during loan selection.

SCHOOL-RELATED DISCHARGES

Closed school discharge helps students affected by school closures, but timing requirements apply. Understanding eligibility windows and application procedures helps affected students pursue appropriate relief.

Borrower defense discharge addresses fraudulent school practices, requiring substantial documentation of misconduct. Success often depends on demonstrating specific misrepresentations that affected enrollment decisions.

False certification discharge helps students whose eligibility was misrepresented by schools. Understanding qualifying circumstances helps identify when this option might apply.

DOCUMENTATION REQUIREMENTS

Each forgiveness program requires specific documentation and verification. Maintaining organized records of employment, payments, and program eligibility is crucial for successful forgiveness applications. Essential documentation practices:

- Save all correspondence with loan servicers
- Keep employment certification records
- Maintain copies of repayment plan requests
- Track all payments made
- Document all interactions regarding forgiveness programs

Remember: Forgiveness programs require careful attention to specific requirements and documentation. Focus on understanding program details while maintaining records of eligibility. Successful forgiveness strategies involve long-term planning rather than assuming automatic qualification.

MANAGING LOANS DURING CAREER CHANGES

KEY PRINCIPLE

Career changes require strategic loan management as opposed to keeping loan payments on autopilot.

The impact of career transitions on student loan management became evident during my shift from corporate employment to consulting after my restaurant failure. After five years of consistent student loan payments while at Raytheon, my income suddenly became irregular and unpredictable.

I needed to understand exactly how this career move would affect my loans. The salary decrease meant potential qualification for income-driven plans, but the self-employment documentation requirements created new complications that required careful navigation during an already challenging transition period.

INCOME TRANSITION PLANNING

Income changes significantly affect repayment options and strategies. Higher income might enable accelerated repayment, while income reductions might necessitate adjusting payment plans. Understanding how different income levels affect various repayment options helps you maintain sustainable payments during transitions. Income change considerations:

- Recalculating income-driven payment amounts
- Evaluating standard vs. income-driven plans at new income level
- Assessing potential for increased payments with higher income
- Understanding qualification changes for certain programs
- Planning for tax consequences of payment changes

EMPLOYEE BENEFITS EVALUATION

Employment benefits often include loan repayment assistance, requiring careful evaluation during job changes. Some employers offer substantial loan payment contributions, making total compensation more valuable than salary alone. Common employer assistance programs:

- Direct payment toward student loans
- Matching contributions to both loans and retirement
- Education stipends for continuing education
- Tuition reimbursement for advanced degrees
- Professional development funding

SELF-EMPLOYMENT CONSIDERATIONS

Self-employment transitions create unique loan management challenges. Income variability affects your payment calculations, while tax treatment of business income can impact income-driven repayment amounts. Understanding these effects helps self-employed borrowers maintain appropriate payment levels. Self-employment loan management strategies:

- Using prior-year tax returns for initial IDR calculations
- Building loan payment reserves during higher income periods
- Understanding how business deductions affect IDR calculations
- Planning for estimated tax payments and loan obligations
- Documenting income changes for mid-year payment adjustments

INDUSTRY-SPECIFIC OPPORTUNITIES

Industry changes may affect forgiveness eligibility beyond just PSLF. Some industries offer specific loan repayment programs or forgiveness options, making industry transitions significant for loan management.

GEOGRAPHIC RELOCATION IMPACTS

Geographic relocations can affect loan management through cost-of-living changes. Higher living costs might necessitate payment adjustments, while lower costs might enable increased loan payments. Some location factors that effect loans:

- State income tax differences affecting take-home pay
- Housing cost variations impacting disposable income
- Regional salary differences for similar positions
- State-specific loan assistance programs
- Cost-of-living adjustments to discretionary income

PROFESSIONAL DEVELOPMENT DECISIONS

Professional development decisions often involve additional education and potentially more loans. Understanding how existing loans affect eligibility for additional education funding helps make informed decisions about further education.

WORK STATUS CHANGES

Work-status changes between full-time, part-time, or contract work affect both payment ability and forgiveness eligibility. Understanding these impacts helps maintain appropriate loan management during work arrangement changes. Employment status considerations:

- Minimum hours required for certain forgiveness programs
- Income verification differences for variable schedules
- Maintaining eligibility during temporary work reductions
- Documentation needs for changing employment types
- Special considerations for seasonal or irregular employment

Remember: Career transitions require careful consideration of loan management implications. Focus on understanding how different career choices affect loan repayment and forgiveness options. Successful loan management during transitions often involves proactive planning rather than reactive adjustments.

LONG-TERM LOAN MANAGEMENT SUCCESS

KEY PRINCIPLE
Sustainable loan management requires adapting strategies as your financial situation evolves rather than maintaining fixed approaches.

My student loan management approach evolved dramatically over fifteen years; from taking on debt during my MBA program, to aggressive payments during my Raytheon success years, to seeking forbearance during restaurant failure, to strategic repayment during recovery.

"My loan management strategy today looks nothing like what it was during my financial collapse," I explained during a financial education seminar, "but the basic principles of understanding loan terms and aligning payments with current financial reality have remained constant." This evolution taught me that effective student loan management requires regular strategy adjustments as circumstances change rather than a set-and-forget approach.

LIFE STAGE ADJUSTMENT STRATEGIES

Life stage changes significantly affect optimal loan management strategies. Early in your career, your priorities will likely often focus on establishing manageable payments, while mid-career compensation allows for accelerated repayments. Understanding how different life stages affect loan management helps create appropriate strategies.

- **Early Career:** Focus on affordable payments and building emergency funds
- **Career Establishment:** Begin accelerating payments as income stabilizes
- **Mid-Career:** Potentially refinance or increase payments substantially
- **Family Formation:** Balance loan payments with other family financial needs
- **Pre-Retirement:** Ensure loans will be eliminated before retirement

FINANCIAL PRIORITY INTEGRATION

Financial priority shifts require loan strategy adjustments. Marriage, home purchase, or family planning often requires balancing loan repayment with other financial goals. Understanding how loans fit into your broader financial plans helps you maintain appropriate focus. Priority balancing strategies include:

- Creating weighted financial goals that include loan repayment

- Developing minimum/maximum payment ranges for different life phases
- Establishing clear timelines for loan elimination alongside other goals
- Reassessing loan strategies during major life transitions
- Building decision frameworks for competing financial priorities

INVESTMENT AND DEBT BALANCE

Investment decisions become increasingly important as your income grows. Balancing loan repayment with retirement saving and other investments requires understanding opportunity costs and return potential. Some borrowers benefit from maintaining minimum loan payments while maximizing investment contributions. Your investment-debt decisions should:

- Compare loan interest rates to potential investment returns
- Consider tax benefits of both loan payments and investments
- Evaluate psychological benefits of debt elimination versus investing
- Account for employer matches and other "guaranteed returns"
- Create hybrid approaches that address both simultaneously

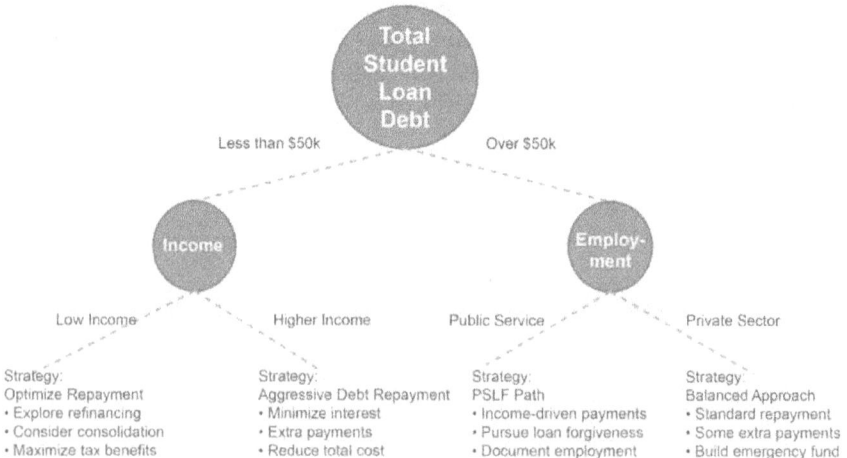

Total Student Loan Debt

Less than $50k   Over $50k

Income   Employment

Low Income   Higher Income   Public Service   Private Sector

Strategy: Optimize Repayment	Strategy: Aggressive Debt Repayment	Strategy: PSLF Path	Strategy: Balanced Approach
• Explore refinancing	• Minimize interest	• Income-driven payments	• Standard repayment
• Consider consolidation	• Extra payments	• Pursue loan forgiveness	• Some extra payments
• Maximize tax benefits	• Reduce total cost	• Document employment	• Build emergency fund

TAX STRATEGY INTEGRATION

As you develop your tax strategy, this affects optimization of your loan management approaches. Student loan interest deductions, retirement contribution impacts, and other tax considerations influence effective loan management. Understanding these interactions helps you create tax-efficient repayment strategies. Some tax optimization techniques include:

- Timing loan payments to maximize annual interest deductions

- Coordinating retirement contributions with student loan payments
- Understanding how income-driven plans affect adjusted gross income
- Planning for potential tax implications of loan forgiveness
- Leveraging education tax credits while managing loan obligations

ECONOMIC ADAPTATION STRATEGIES

Economic changes require adaptations to your strategy. Interest rate environments, inflation levels, and economic conditions affect optimal loan management approaches. Understanding these impacts helps you adjust strategies appropriately. Economic Responsiveness Approach:

- Reassess refinancing opportunities during interest rate changes
- Build additional payment reserves during economic uncertainty
- Understand how inflation affects real cost of fixed-rate loans
- Review income-driven plans during economic downturns
- Consider accelerated payments during strong economic periods

FAMILY PLANNING CONSIDERATIONS

Family planning considerations increasingly affect loan management decisions. Child education savings, insurance needs, and other family priorities interact with loan management strategies. Understanding these relationships helps you maintain appropriate balance. Family Integration Framework:

- Balance children's education funding with loan repayment
- Create contingency plans for family growth or changes
- Develop coordinated family financial plans that include loans
- Understand how changing family size affects income-driven payments
- Build financial literacy plans that include student loan lessons

CAREER DEVELOPMENT INTEGRATION

Career development opportunities might affect long-term loan management. Additional education, professional certifications, or career changes could impact loan management strategies. Understanding these implications helps you make informed professional development decisions. Career-Loan Coordination Strategy:

- Evaluate return on investment for additional education
- Consider employer education benefits and their impact on loans
- Assess timing of career transitions relative to loan forgiveness
- Create flexible career plans that accommodate loan obligations

- Leverage professional development to increase income and accelerate repayment

PERIODIC STRATEGY REVIEW PROCESS

Regular comprehensive loan strategy reviews ensure continued optimization. As financial circumstances and loan programs evolve, periodic reassessment helps maintain appropriate approaches. Strategic Review Framework:

- Quarterly assessment of current repayment strategy effectiveness
- Annual comprehensive loan management evaluation
- Systematic review after major life events or financial changes
- Regular monitoring of loan program changes and opportunities
- Periodic professional guidance for complex situations

CREATING A COMPLETION CELEBRATION PLAN

Planning for eventual loan elimination provides motivation and closure. Creating specific celebration plans and next financial steps helps you maintain focus through the final phases of repayment. Loan Completion Planning:

- Develop concrete plans for redirecting loan payments after completion
- Create meaningful celebration of debt elimination
- Establish clear next financial priorities
- Document lessons learned through the repayment journey
- Consider mentoring others facing similar student loan challenges

Remember: Long-term loan management success requires regular strategy review and adjustment. Focus on maintaining sustainable approaches that adapt to changing circumstances while supporting broader financial goals. The most successful loan management strategies evolve with changing life situations rather than remaining static.

CHAPTER SUMMARY AND KEY TAKEAWAYS

Through my journey from bankruptcy to financial stability, I've learned that effective student loan management combines understanding loan programs with adapting strategies to your personal situation. The lessons from both personal experience and helping others show that loan success requires active management rather than passive repayment.

CORE STUDENT LOAN MANAGEMENT PRINCIPLES:

Understanding Over Action: During my recovery, I discovered that understanding loan options matters more than making rushed payoff attempts. Experience showed that knowing how different decisions affect your loans leads to better choices than simply making minimum payments.

Strategy Over Speed: Working with others demonstrated how strategic approaches create better outcomes than rushing to pay off debt. Careful planning, especially with federal loans, leads to significantly better long-term results. One colleague's decision to pursue PSLF instead of aggressive repayment saved over $45,000 in loan payments.

Integration Over Isolation: Through both success and failure, I've learned that loan management works best when integrated with broader financial planning. Recent experiences helping families navigate education debt showed how balancing loan payments with other financial goals creates better long-term outcomes.

ACTION PLAN

First 30 Days: Foundation Building
- Review and organize all loan documentation
- Identify loan types and the status of each loan
- Understand available repayment options
- Calculate current loan payments and interest
- Create your loan management tracking system

60-Day Implementation
- Select appropriate repayment strategies
- Set up payment automation
- Establish documentation procedures
- Create forgiveness tracking (if applicable)
- Build emergency fund for loan payments

90-Day Establishment
- Review and adjust payment strategies
- Integrate with broader financial planning
- Create long-term loan management plan
- Set up a regular review schedule
- Document your future decision framework

FINAL THOUGHTS

Remember: Student loan success isn't about finding perfect solutions; it's about creating manageable strategies that align with your broader financial goals. Through bankruptcy and recovery, I learned that effective loan management requires understanding options and making informed choices rather than just focusing on quick payoff.

YOUR NEXT STEP

Log into your loan servicer's website this week. Verify every loan, every balance, every interest rate. Many borrowers discover errors or forgotten loans during this exercise. You can't manage what you don't accurately understand.

Student loans may feel like a life sentence, but they're not. They're a finite obligation with a definite end; whether through payoff, forgiveness, or strategic management. The path forward starts with clarity about where you stand today.

MOVING FORWARD

You've now built the foundation. You understand where your money goes, how to manage what you owe, where to keep what you have, and how to prepare for the unexpected. These aren't just concepts; they're the bedrock that everything else rests on.

But a foundation alone isn't enough. In my post-bankruptcy years, I learned that building wealth means nothing if you can't protect it. A single identity theft incident, an inadequate insurance policy, or a security breach can unravel years of careful progress.

Section II turns to protection: your credit reputation, your insurance safety nets, and the digital security that guards your financial life. The goal isn't paranoia; it's peace of mind that comes from knowing your foundation is defended.

SECTION II
PROTECTION & SECURITY

With your foundation in place, the next priority is protecting what you're building. This section focuses on the defensive aspects of financial planning; the elements that protect your assets and financial identity from various threats. Through my work in Big Tech, I've learned that security in the digital age requires more than simply good passwords or insurance policies; it demands a comprehensive approach to protection.

During my bankruptcy, I discovered how quickly financial security can crumble without proper protection. Now, managing substantial assets and complex digital financial tools, I understand how crucial these protective elements become at every wealth level. Whether you're rebuilding credit after setbacks or protecting significant assets, these chapters provide essential guidance for financial security.

Chapter 6: Credit explores building and maintaining strong credit. After bankruptcy destroyed my credit, rebuilding taught me that credit management involves more than just paying bills; it requires understanding how credit affects your entire financial life.

Chapter 7: Insurance addresses protecting what you build. Through both personal loss and professional experience, I've learned that proper insurance creates crucial protection against setbacks that could otherwise derail financial progress.

Chapter 8: Financial Technology Security covers protecting your digital financial life. As someone managing substantial assets across multiple platforms, I understand that digital security has become inseparable from financial security.

These chapters help you build your financial fortress, providing protection that grows with your wealth. Through my experiences, I've seen how proper protection enables confident wealth building while preventing devastating setbacks.

Whether you're establishing basic protection like I did during recovery, managing complex digital assets like I do now, or planning for early retirement like Lacey and I are, these chapters provide frameworks for building lasting financial security. Understanding and implementing these protective elements helps you build wealth with confidence while avoiding unnecessary risks.

CHAPTER 6
CREDIT

LEARNING OBJECTIVES

- Master the fundamental components of credit scoring
- Learn effective credit building and recovery strategies
- Understand how credit affects various life aspects
- Develop sustainable credit management habits
- Create long-term credit optimization plans

OPENING STORY

My first credit card offer after bankruptcy felt like a cruel joke; a $300 limit with a $200 annual fee already charged to the card and a 29.99% interest rate. Yet within two years, through careful management, my credit score rose from the low 400s to over 600. This experience taught me that credit building isn't about quick fixes; it's about understanding how credit works and making informed, consistent decisions.

INTRODUCTION

Credit scores function like a financial report card, but with rules that often seem mysterious and contradictory. Many people focus on the score itself without understanding the mechanisms that create it, missing opportunities for effective credit building.

Your credit profile affects more aspects of life than most people realize; from renting an apartment to getting a job, from insurance rates to mobile phone contracts. Understanding these widespread impacts helps motivate proper credit management.

The most successful approach to credit management combines technical knowledge with consistent positive habits. Like maintaining physical health, good credit requires both understanding of how the system works and daily habits that support long-term success.

Most importantly, you'll discover that good credit isn't about gaming the system; it's about demonstrating responsible fiscal management over time.

UNDERSTANDING CREDIT FUNDAMENTALS

> **KEY PRINCIPLE**
> Credit scores reflect patterns of behavior rather than just payment history.

Credit scoring is a complex algorithm that evaluates multiple aspects of your financial behavior simultaneously. Many people focus solely on making payments on time, missing the nuanced interplay of various factors that determine credit scores.

My credit revelation came during my first mortgage application after bankruptcy. Though I had missed no payments on my secured card for over a year, my score remained stuck at 640. This is because I consistently used 90% of my available credit.

"I thought being responsible meant using my card for everything and paying it off each month," I noted in my recovery journal. "Learning how credit utilization affected my score completely changed my approach." Once I began keeping my usage below 30%, my score jumped 45 points in just two months.

The graphic below breaks down how your credit score is calculated by the big consumer report agencies.

What Really Makes Up Your Credit Score

The five factors and their impact

FICO Score Ranges:
- Poor: 300-579
- Fair: 580-669
- Good: 670-739
- Very Good: 740-799
- Excellent: 800-850

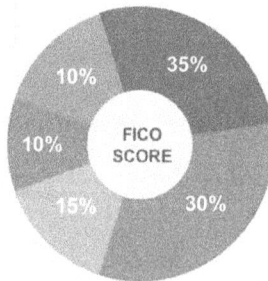

Payment History (35%)
- On-time payment streak
- Late payment severity
- Collections and charge-offs

Credit Utilization (30%)
- Overall utilization ratio
- Individual card utilization
- Number of cards with balances

Length of History (15%)
- Age of oldest account
- Average age of all accounts
- Time since most recent activity

New Credit (10%)
- Recent applications
- New account percentage

Credit Mix (10%)
- Variety of account types
- Installment vs. revolving accounts

UNDERSTANDING SCORE RANGES

FICO SCORE CLASSIFICATIONS

POOR	FAIR	GOOD	VERY GOOD	EXCELLENT
300–579	580–669	670–739	740–799	800–850
Highest rates	Higher rates	Reasonable terms	Near-best terms	Best rates
Secured cards only	Limited options	Likely approval	Strong approval	Auto approvals
Major restrictions	Basic cards	Standard cards	Quality cards	Premium access

Higher rates, limited access ← → Best rates, premium access

CREDIT REPORT COMPONENTS

SAMPLE CREDIT REPORT   Report Date: 03/15/2025

PERSONAL INFORMATION

Name: SARAH J SMITH

Current Address: 123 MAIN ST, ANYTOWN, ST 12345
Previous Address: 456 OAK AVE, OLDTOWN, ST 67890

CHECK FOR:
- Name variations
- Unknown addresses
- Inaccurate details
Red flags for identity theft

CREDIT SCORE

300 ————————○———— 850

721
GOOD

SCORE RANGES:
- 300-579: Poor
- 580-669: Fair
- 670-739: Good
- 740-799: Very Good
- 800-850: Excellent

CREDIT ACCOUNTS

MAJOR BANK CREDIT CARD
Account #: XXXX-XXXX-XXXX-1234 | Opened: 06/2022
Limit: $10,000 | Balance: $2,450 | Status: Current

NATIONAL MORTGAGE LENDER
Account #: 98765432 | Opened: 09/2021
Original Amount: $320,000 | Balance: $305,670 | Status: Current

HIGH IMPACT

REVIEW FOR:
- Accounts you don't recognize
- Incorrect balances
- Late payments
- Account status
- Credit utilization
- Payment history
The most important section

MEDIUM IMPACT

CREDIT INQUIRIES

AUTO FINANCING CO | 11/12/2024 | Hard Inquiry
PREAPPROVED CARD OFFER | 01/20/2025 | Soft Inquiry

INQUIRY TYPES:
- Hard: Affects score, stays 2 years
- Soft: No score impact, only visible to you

COLLECTIONS

No collection accounts reported

VERIFY:
- Collection validity
- Paid collections
- Statute of limitations

PUBLIC RECORDS

INCLUDES:
Bankruptcies, tax liens

BUILDING CREDIT STRATEGICALLY

> **KEY PRINCIPLE**
> Credit building requires systematic action rather than random good behavior.

After bankruptcy left me with a credit score in the low 400s, I approached rebuilding methodically rather than desperately accepting every subprime offer flooding my mailbox. Instead of grabbing anything I could get, I created a two-year recovery plan.

Starting with a secured card with a $300 limit, following specific steps including perfect payment history and utilization management, I reached 650 within two years; enough to qualify for my first post-bankruptcy apartment lease.

CREATING YOUR CREDIT FOUNDATION

Initial credit building requires careful first steps. Like laying a building's foundation, these early actions determine the stability of your future credit profile. Starting with a secured credit card or becoming an authorized user on a responsible person's account often provides better results than accepting high-fee subprime cards.

The relationship between initial credit actions and long-term success proves crucial. Small, consistent positive behaviors; like maintaining low balances and never missing payments; create stronger credit profiles than trying to build credit quickly through multiple new accounts.

DEVELOPING CREDIT MIX

Credit diversity develops naturally through proper planning. While credit mix affects only 10% of your score, strategic addition of different credit types demonstrates comprehensive credit management ability. However, opening new accounts should always serve genuine financial needs rather than just credit building. Important factors for ongoing credit building:

- Maintain utilization below 30% consistently
- Keep oldest accounts active and healthy
- Space new credit applications appropriately
- Monitor authorized user opportunities
- Build positive payment patterns

TIME-BASED STRATEGY DEVELOPMENT

Credit building requires different approaches at different stages. Initially, rebuilding credit should focus on establishing positive payment history and managing limited credit responsibly. As your profile strengthens, you'll be presented with opportunities for better terms and higher limits, which allows for more sophisticated credit optimization.

The patience required for credit building is challenging for those seeking quick results. Meaningful credit improvement typically takes 12-24 months of consistent positive behavior. Being aware of this helps you maintain realistic expectations and prevents discouraged abandonment of credit building efforts.

CREATING SUSTAINABLE HABITS

Long-term credit success requires establishing sustainable practices. Automatic payments, regular credit monitoring, and systematic credit utilization management create consistent positive credit behaviors. These habits are important during life transitions when credit management might otherwise suffer from reduced attention.

Remember: Credit building success comes from strategic action rather than hope. Focus on creating systematic positive credit behaviors and maintain patience for results. Effective credit building strategies combine careful planning with consistent execution over time.

MANAGING EXISTING CREDIT

KEY PRINCIPLE
Effective credit management requires active attention to your credit rather than passive bill paying.

Managing established credit resembles tending a valuable garden; regular maintenance and attention help you catch small issues that can otherwise grow into major problems. Many people with good credit scores adopt a passive approach, making payments but missing opportunities to optimize their credit profile and protect against potential issues.

The turning point about credit management came during a time when I had rebuilt my score to a respectable 720. After establishing a perfect payment history for three years post-bankruptcy, I was shocked when a single forgotten $18 payment on a rarely used store card dropped my score by 63 points. The payment; for a shirt I'd bought and forgotten about during a hectic work period; cost me more in credit damage than the actual item. I learned that good credit requires active management, not just avoiding major mistakes.

UNDERSTANDING CREDIT MONITORING

Regular credit review provides crucial insight into credit health. Monthly checks help you identify potential issues early, while quarterly deep dives allow thorough examination of credit patterns and opportunities for improvement. This regular attention helps you spot problems proactively and identify optimization opportunities before they affect major financial decisions.

Credit monitoring services offer convenience but they shouldn't replace personal attention. Understanding how to read and interpret your own credit reports helps you identify reporting errors, recognize improvement opportunities, and maintain long-term credit health. Personal monitoring also allows you to develop deeper understanding of how different actions affect your credit profile.

OPTIMIZING CREDIT UTILIZATION

The relationship between credit use and credit scores requires particular attention. Even with perfect payment history, high utilization can drop credit scores. Maintaining utilization below 30% overall and on individual cards helps maximize score potential, while consistently high utilization can mask other positive credit behaviors.

Payment timing affects credit scores more than many realize. Making payments before statement closing dates can help maintain lower reported utilization, even with regular card use. Understanding this timing helps you manage credit scores actively rather than reactively.

The graph illustrates the relationship between your credit utilization and overall credit score.

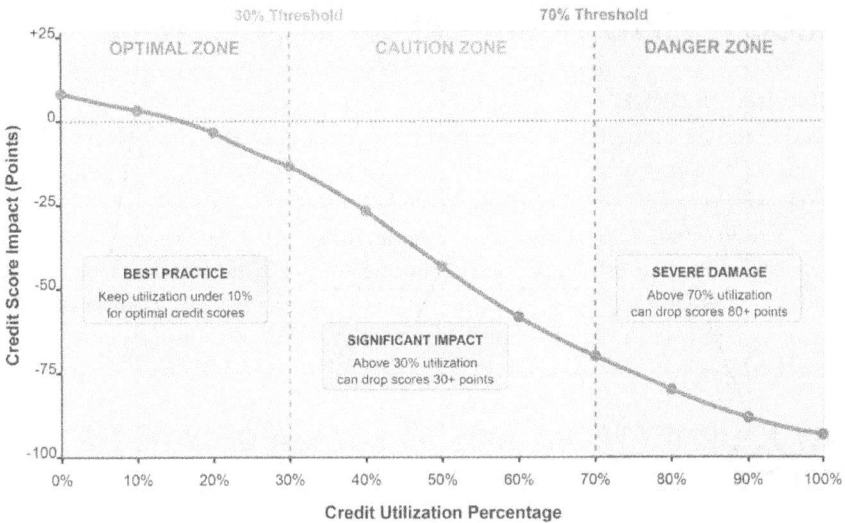

Credit Utilization Percentage

BUILDING LONG-TERM STRENGTH

Credit strength grows through consistent positive patterns. Maintaining older accounts, using credit regularly but responsibly, and avoiding unnecessary new credit applications all contribute to long-term credit health. These patterns demonstrate stability and reliability to potential lenders.

The balance between credit use and credit score optimization can challenge everyone, including financially sophisticated individuals. One must strike a balance between using credit enough to demonstrate active management and maintaining low utilization. Regular small purchases paid in full often prove more beneficial than avoiding credit use entirely.

PROTECTING CREDIT HEALTH

Credit protection requires proactive measures beyond fraud alerts. Regular review of your accounts, prompt investigation of unexpected changes, and thorough documentation of credit activities all help protect credit health. Understanding how different actions might affect your credit score helps you prevent unintended negative impacts.

Remember: Credit management success requires active attention rather than passive bill paying. Focus on creating systems that support both credit use and credit score optimization. Effective credit management combines regular monitoring with strategic use patterns.

RECOVERING FROM CREDIT CHALLENGES

> **KEY PRINCIPLE**
> Credit recovery requires patience and strategy rather than quick fixes or credit repair services.

Credit recovery resembles rehabilitating after an injury; progress requires consistent effort, proper technique, and realistic expectations. Many people seek immediate solutions through credit repair companies or aggressive new credit applications, often making their situations worse rather than better.

MY JOURNEY FROM 400S TO 800+: A DECADE OF CREDIT REBUILDING

My experiences illustrate that bankruptcy isn't a financial death sentence. When I filed for bankruptcy in 2015, my credit score plummeted to the low 400s; a number so dismal it seemed almost impossible to recover from.

I still remember receiving my first credit offer post-bankruptcy: a subprime card with a $300 limit, $200 of which was immediately consumed by annual fees, leaving me with just $100 of actual credit. The interest rate was a staggering 29.99%. Despite these terrible terms, I recognized it as a necessary first step back into the credit system.

"The rebuilding process isn't about getting the best terms initially," I explain to those facing similar challenges. "It's about demonstrating consistent positive behavior that gradually rebuilds creditor trust."

The Credit Rebuilding Road
Realistic timeline for score improvement

| POOR (300-579) | FAIR (580-669) | GOOD (670-739) | VERY GOOD (740-799) | EXCELLENT (800+) |

FIRST IMPROVEMENTS
- 3 months of on-time payments
- Keep utilization under 30%
- Become authorized user

(↑ 20-30 points possible)

DIVERSIFICATION
- Apply for unsecured card
- Develop credit mix
- Keep oldest accounts active

(↑ 30-50 points possible)

EXCELLENCE
- 3+ years perfect history
- Diverse, mature accounts
- Low utilization across cards

(↑ 10-30 points possible)

STARTING POINT
- Obtain credit reports
- Dispute inaccuracies
- Apply for secured card

START   3 MONTHS   6-12 MONTHS   1-2 YEARS   2-3 YEARS   3+ YEARS

BUILDING HISTORY
- 6-12 months perfect payment
- Request credit line increase
- Add credit-builder loan

(↑ 40-60 points possible)

OPTIMIZATION
- 2+ years perfect payment
- Keep utilization under 10%
- Strategic applications only

(↑ 20-40 points possible)

Note: Timeline represents typical progression with consistent positive actions. Individual results may vary.

My approach followed a methodical progression:

Year 1: Foundation Building (400s → 500s)

I used that first secured, high-fee card for small, essential purchases which I paid in full immediately. Every transaction was deliberate. After six months of perfect payment history, I applied for a second secured card with slightly better terms.

"The hardest part wasn't getting approved for credit," I often tell people. "It was resisting the temptation to use that credit for anything beyond the minimal transactions needed to build payment history."

Years 2-3: Strategic Expansion (500s → 600s)

By my second year post-bankruptcy, I qualified for a basic unsecured card. Rather than celebrating with increased spending, I maintained the same disciplined approach: small, planned transactions with immediate payment. When offered credit limit increases, I accepted them but didn't change my usage patterns.

During this phase, I discovered the power of credit utilization in score calculations. By keeping my reported balances below 10% of available credit; often by making payments before statement closing dates; I saw my score increase despite my recent bankruptcy.

Years 4-5: Product Improvement (600s → 700s)

As my score crossed the 650 score threshold, I began receiving offers for better credit products. I strategically applied for cards with no annual fees and modest rewards, always spacing applications at least six months apart to minimize inquiry impact.

When Lacey and I began our relationship, our open discussions about credit management accelerated my learning. "Have you considered how the age of your accounts affects your score?" she asked, introducing me to the concept of average account age as a scoring factor.

This insight led me to maintain all my initial rebuilding accounts, even after qualifying for better products. Despite their poor terms, those original accounts became valuable assets as they aged, contributing to my steadily improving score.

Years 6-7: Strategic Patience (Low 700s)

With my score now in the lower 700s, the temptation to accelerate the process through additional products was strong. Instead, I focused on patience; allowing time to heal my credit report as negative items became less impactful with age.

"The bankruptcy will fall off your report after 7-10 years," a credit counselor had advised me early in the process. "Sometimes the most powerful credit-building strategy is simply maintaining perfect behavior while waiting for time to pass."

During this phase, my credit management focused more on optimization than expansion. I timed payments to maintain optimal utilization, strategically used different cards to keep all accounts active, and carefully monitored my credit reports for inaccuracies.

Years 8-10: The Final Push (700s → 800+)

When my Chapter 7 bankruptcy finally fell off my credit report after 10 years, my score jumped nearly 50 points overnight. This boost, combined with years of positive history, pushed me into the high-700s. By continuing the same disciplined approach while gradually adding a diverse mix of credit types; including a mortgage for our home purchase; my score finally crossed the 800 threshold.

What this milestone represents is huge. My score, higher than it ever was even before my bankruptcy, reflects a fundamentally different relationship with credit than I had in my pre-bankruptcy life.

Before bankruptcy, I maintained a decent score while accumulating unsustainable debt. Today, my excellent score reflects actual financial health; low utilization, diverse credit types, perfect payment history, and zero concerning behaviors.

This decade-long journey taught me that credit recovery isn't just about restoring a number; it's about establishing entirely new financial habits. The score is merely a reflection of those improved behaviors.

For those beginning their own credit recovery journey, I offer this encouragement: the path from the 400s to 800+ is long but entirely possible. It requires consistency, patience, and strategic decision-making. But more than anything, it requires a fundamental shift from viewing credit as a spending tool to understanding it as a financial reputation that opens or closes doors throughout your life.

CREATING YOUR RECOVERY PLAN

Recovery begins with a clear understanding of your current situation. Take time to obtaining all three credit reports and analyze each negative item. This gives you direction on effective action to take. Any errors you spot provide immediate opportunities for improvement through proper disputes.

The emotional aspect of credit recovery often proves as challenging as the technical steps. Accepting past challenges while maintaining focus on future improvement helps create sustainable progress. Understanding that recovery takes time helps maintain motivation through the process.

ADDRESSING NEGATIVE ITEMS

Collection accounts require strategic handling based on their age and validity. Recent collections often allow negotiation for "pay for delete" arrangements, while older collections might best be left untouched if the statute of limitations has expired. Each situation requires individual evaluation rather than blanket approaches.

The impact that late payments have on your credit score diminishes over time. However, their effect can be further mitigated through proper action. Goodwill letters to creditors sometimes succeed in removing isolated late payments, particularly for customers with an otherwise strong payment history. Building recent positive payment patterns helps offset past negative marks.

BUILDING NEW POSITIVE HISTORY

While addressing negative items, creating new positive credit history is equally important. Secured credit cards, credit-builder loans, or being added as an authorized user on a responsible person's account can help you establish new positive patterns. These new accounts demonstrate current creditworthiness while older negative items fade.

The balance between addressing old issues and building new credit requires careful consideration. Open too many new accounts too quickly and you'll harm your recovery efforts. On the other hand, opening too few new accounts can slow your positive credit building efforts. Understanding proper timing and sequencing helps you optimize recovery progress. Credit recovery typically progresses through distinct phases:

- Initial stabilization (3-6 months)
- Active improvement (6-18 months)
- Score optimization (18-24 months)
- Long-term maintenance (ongoing)

Each phase requires different strategies and areas of focus. Early recovery emphasizes stopping negative patterns and establishing basic positive habits. Later phases focus more on optimization and long-term credit strength building.

LONG-TERM CREDIT SUCCESS

> **KEY PRINCIPLE**
> Lasting credit excellence requires developing sophisticated credit management rather than just maintaining good scores.

Long-term credit management resembles maintaining peak athletic performance; it requires ongoing attention, adaptation to changing circumstances, and prevention of potential issues before they arise. Many people relax after achieving a good score, missing opportunities for optimization and risking unexpected setbacks.

My perspective on credit management evolved dramatically after reaching my initial goal of 750, four years after bankruptcy. I assumed maintaining my score simply meant continuing my existing habits of on-time payments and low utilization. Then, my son's experience with identity theft taught me that even excellent credit needs vigilant protection and maintenance. "Now I understand that sophisticated credit management isn't just about maintaining scores; it's about creating opportunities," I explained during a family financial discussion. This transformed how I approach credit monitoring for my entire family.

CREATING CREDIT OPTIMIZATION SYSTEMS

Advanced credit management extends beyond basic good habits. Strategic decisions about credit utilization patterns, account aging, and new credit opportunities require regular analysis and adjustment. Understanding how different credit actions affect your profile helps you maintain optimal credit positioning.

Regular credit review sessions become increasingly important once you've established excellent credit. Monthly monitoring lets you maintain awareness, while quarterly deep dives allow for strategic planning and optimization. These reviews focus not just on maintaining scores but on positioning for future opportunities. Strong credit provides opportunities beyond basic approval and good rates:

- Negotiating power with lenders
- Access to premium credit products
- Higher credit limits and better terms
- Employment and business advantages
- Insurance rate optimization

PROTECTING CREDIT EXCELLENCE

Credit protection becomes increasingly important as your credit score rises. Higher scores often face greater drops from negative events, making prevention crucial. Understanding potential threats and maintaining proper documentation helps you protect the credit excellence that you've worked so hard to establish.

The relationship between credit use and credit maintenance requires careful balance. Using credit enough to demonstrate active management while maintaining optimal utilization patterns often challenges even sophisticated credit users. Regular small purchases with immediate payment often prove more beneficial than minimal credit use.

PLANNING FOR LIFE CHANGES

Major life events require credit strategy adjustment. Career changes, relocations, or family additions often affect credit needs and management approaches. Understanding how different life changes impact credit helps maintain excellence through transitions.

Credit excellence provides opportunities for helping others build credit as well. Adding responsible family members as authorized users or providing guidance on credit building helps create positive credit impact beyond personal benefit.

FUTURE CREDIT POSITIONING

For long-term credit planning, you need to think about emerging credit trends and opportunities. Changes in scoring models, new credit products, and evolving financial technologies can create opportunities and challenges alike. Staying informed about credit industry developments helps you maintain optimal credit positioning.

Remember: Credit excellence requires sophisticated management rather than simple maintenance. Focus on creating systems that optimize credit positioning while protecting against potential issues. Effective long-term credit success involves combining proactive management with strategic opportunity recognition.

CHAPTER SUMMARY AND KEY TAKEAWAYS

Through my journey, I've learned that successful credit management combines technical understanding with consistent positive habits. The lessons from personal experience and helping others show that lasting credit success requires active management rather than passive bill paying.

CORE CREDIT MANAGEMENT PRINCIPLES:

Understanding Over Action: During my recovery, I discovered that understanding credit mechanics matters more than making rushed credit moves. One client's experience reinforced this; by understanding how utilization affected her scores, she achieved better results than those who simply applied for every available card. Success comes from knowing how the credit system works rather than hoping for quick fixes.

Strategy Over Speed: Working with others showed how methodical approaches create better outcomes than rushing credit building. An accountant's experience demonstrated this when her systematic approach to credit recovery produced stronger, more lasting results than aggressive credit repair attempts. Successful credit improvement often comes from patient, strategic action.

Prevention Over Correction: Through both success and failure, I've learned that maintaining good credit requires less effort than repairing damaged credit. Recent experiences helping families navigate credit challenges showed how proactive management prevents issues that reactive approaches struggle to fix.

ACTION PLAN

First 30 Days: Foundation Building
- Pull and analyze all three credit reports
- Calculate current credit utilization
- Document all existing credit accounts
- Establish credit monitoring systems
- Create payment automation systems

60-Day Implementation
- Address any identified credit issues
- Optimize credit utilization patterns
- Establish regular review schedule
- Build positive payment history
- Create credit management systems

90-Day Establishment
- Asses your progress
- Adjust credit strategies as needed
- Plan for future credit development
- Build long-term credit goals
- Maintain ongoing monitoring

FINAL THOUGHTS

Remember: Credit success isn't about achieving perfect scores; it's about creating sustainable credit management that supports your financial goals. Through bankruptcy and recovery, I learned that effective credit management requires both knowledge and consistent positive habits. Your credit journey will be unique, whether you're:
- Rebuilding after setbacks
- Building credit for the first time
- Optimizing good credit
- Maintaining excellent scores

The principles remain consistent: understand the system, create sustainable habits, and maintain active management. With proper development, credit becomes a powerful tool for financial success rather than a source of stress or limitation.

Remember that credit needs change with life circumstances. Stay informed about credit developments, maintain proper management habits, and don't hesitate to adjust your approach as situations change. Your goal isn't perfect credit scores but effective credit management that supports your life goals while maintaining financial flexibility.

CHAPTER 7
INSURANCE

LEARNING OBJECTIVES

- Understand how different types of insurance work together
- Master effective coverage selection strategies
- Learn to balance protection with cost
- Develop comprehensive insurance planning
- Create lasting financial security through proper coverage

OPENING STORY

The true value of insurance became clear during my recovery period. A minor car accident that resulted in $4,200 in damage could have derailed my financial rebuilding completely. Instead, because I had maintained proper coverage despite tight finances, my $500 deductible preserved the stability I'd worked so hard to establish. This experience taught me that insurance isn't about minimal coverage; it's about creating appropriate protection for your specific situation.

INTRODUCTION

Insurance functions like a shield protecting your financial life from unexpected threats. Many people view insurance as an unnecessary expense until they need it, missing the crucial role it plays in preserving financial stability.

Understanding insurance goes beyond comparing premiums; it requires evaluating how different coverage types interact to protect your financial life. Many people focus solely on cost, missing opportunities to create more effective protection through strategic coverage selection.

Most importantly, you'll discover that effective insurance planning isn't about buying every possible policy. Researching and choosing insurance plans is about creating appropriate protection for your specific situation. The methods we'll discuss work whether you're starting basic coverage or protecting substantial assets.

UNDERSTANDING INSURANCE FUNDAMENTALS

KEY PRINCIPLE
Different types of insurance work together to create comprehensive protection rather than functioning in isolation.

Insurance protection resembles a financial immune system; different components work together to protect against various threats. Many people view each insurance type separately, missing opportunities to create more effective protection through coordinated coverage.

My insurance strategy evolved as my assets grew from bankruptcy to financial stability. During early recovery, a simple liability-only auto policy and basic renter's insurance were all I could afford. As my consulting business grew and I began acquiring rental properties, I discovered my traditional emergency fund no longer provided adequate protection against my expanded risks.

As my net worth rebuilt, I realized emergency planning needed to cover both personal financial needs and growing business liabilities.. Simple cash reserves now required complementary insurance protection to create truly comprehensive security.

CORE INSURANCE TYPES

- Homeowners/Renters Coverage
    - Structure protection
    - Personal property coverage
    - Liability protection
    - Additional living expenses
    - Natural disaster coverage
- Medical Coverage Components
    - Preventive care
    - Emergency services
    - Prescription coverage
    - Specialist care
    - Hospital services
- Personal/Professional Coverage
    - General liability
    - Professional liability
    - Umbrella policies
    - Auto liability
    - Property liability

UNDERSTANDING COVERAGE INTERACTION

Different insurance types create overlapping protection. Homeowners insurance might provide some liability coverage, while auto insurance often includes personal injury protection. Understanding these overlaps helps prevent coverage gaps while avoiding unnecessary duplication.

Life Stage	Health	Life	Disability	Property/ Auto	Liability/ Umbrella	Long-term Care
Young Single	High	Med	Low	High	Low	High
Young Family	High	High	Low	High	Low	Med
Mid-Career Family	High	High	High	High	Low	Low
Pre-Retirement	High	Med	Med	High	High	Low
Retirement	High	Med	Med	High	High	High

Medium Need   High Need   Low Need   Pink background = Common Coverage Gap

The relationship between deductibles and premiums requires careful consideration. Higher deductibles usually means lower premiums but require more substantial emergency savings. Finding an appropriate balance between out-of-pocket costs and monthly expenses helps create sustainable protection. Effective insurance planning starts with understanding personal risk factors:

- Asset exposure
- Income stability
- Family responsibilities
- Health considerations
- Lifestyle factors

COVERAGE LEVEL DETERMINATION

Insurance needs change with life circumstances. Major life events; marriage, children, property purchases, or business formation; often require coverage adjustments. Regularly reviewing your insurance options ensures that you maintain appropriate protection through all life changes.

SELECTING APPROPRIATE COVERAGE

> **KEY PRINCIPLE**
> Effective insurance selection requires understanding your specific risks rather than following generic coverage recommendations.

Your coverage must fit your specific situation and needs rather than following a one-size-fits-all approach. Previously, I'd simply selected whatever health plan my employer offered without much thought. Suddenly responsible for my own coverage, I discovered significant premium differences between seemingly similar plans.

"I nearly selected the most expensive option thinking it meant better protection," I confided to my mentor. After analyzing coverage details, I found a mid-tier plan that provided essential protection at half the cost, saving me over $400 monthly. These savings empowered me to rebuild my foundation.

HEALTH INSURANCE SELECTION

As you work to understand your health insurance options, you need to evaluate the following:
- Premium costs versus out-of-pocket expenses
- Network restrictions and provider access
- Prescription drug needs and coverage
- Anticipated medical services
- Family health considerations

Health plan selection often means balancing immediate costs against potential risks. While high-deductible plans offer lower premiums, they require sufficient savings to handle larger out-of-pocket expenses. Understanding your health needs and financial capacity helps you determine appropriate coverage.

PROPERTY INSURANCE DECISIONS

Property coverage needs vary significantly based on:
- Location and natural disaster risks
- Property value and replacement costs
- Personal property worth
- Liability exposure
- Additional structures or features

The gap between market value and replacement cost often surprises property owners. Standard coverage based on market value might prove insufficient for actual replacement needs, particularly in older homes.

LIFE INSURANCE CONSIDERATIONS

Life insurance needs depend heavily on personal circumstances such as:
- Family financial obligations
- Income replacement requirements
- Debt obligations
- Future education expenses
- Estate planning goals

Term versus permanent life insurance decisions require careful evaluation of long-term objectives. While term insurance provides affordable death benefit protection, permanent insurance can serve additional financial planning purposes when properly structured.

TERM LIFE INSURANCE

Coverage Period (10-30 years)

Protection for a specific time period

Key Features:
- Lower premiums
- Fixed payment amount
- No cash value component
- Expires at end of term

Typical Cost: $

Pros:
- Affordable coverage
- Simple to understand
- Higher death benefits for premium

Cons:
- Coverage ends when term expires
- No investment component

PERMANENT LIFE INSURANCE

Lifetime Coverage

Protection for your entire life with cash value

Main Types:

Whole Life	Universal Life
Fixed premiums	Flexible
Guaranteed cash value	premiums and death benefits

Typical Cost: $$$

Pros:
- Lifetime coverage
- Builds cash value
- Potential tax advantages

Cons:
- Significantly higher premiums
- Complex product features

BEST FIT BY LIFE STAGE

TERM IDEAL — CONSIDER BOTH — PERMANENT ADVANTAGES INCREASE

Young Family | Mid-Career | Established Career | Pre-Retirement | Retirement

TERM MAKES SENSE WHEN:
- You need maximum coverage at lowest cost
- Coverage is needed for specific time period
- Your budget is limited

PERMANENT MAKES SENSE WHEN:
- You want lifetime coverage
- Cash value and tax benefits are priorities
- Estate planning needs are important

159

LIABILITY PROTECTION STRATEGY

Comprehensive liability protection requires that you understand your levels of exposure. Think about the following factors as you consider the risks you and your family are exposed to:

- Professional activities
- Property ownership
- Personal activities
- Asset protection needs
- Future earning potential

Umbrella policies provide extended liability protection beyond standard coverage limits. These policies are valuable for individuals with substantial assets or high income potential.

MANAGING INSURANCE COSTS

KEY PRINCIPLE

Effective insurance cost management requires balancing protection with affordability rather than simply choosing the cheapest options.

My perspective on insurance costs transformed after a minor basement flood in my rented apartment. Just starting my financial recovery, I had selected the absolute cheapest renter's policy available; $8 monthly with a $1,000 deductible.

As I mentioned earlier, when a pipe burst and damaged some belongings, I realized my $1,000 deductible exceeded my emergency fund. "Saving six dollars monthly on premiums had left me exposed when I actually needed coverage," I wrote in my financial journal. This experience taught me that affordable insurance means finding the right balance, not just the lowest price.

UNDERSTANDING TRUE INSURANCE COSTS

The relationship between premiums, deductibles, and coverage limits creates the foundation for effective cost management. Lower premiums often mean higher out-of-pocket costs when claims occur. Understanding your financial capacity to handle different deductible levels helps determine appropriate premium levels.

Insurance costs extend beyond monthly premiums. Policy fees, deductibles, copayments, and coverage exclusions all affect the true cost of protection.

STRATEGIC COST MANAGEMENT

Effective insurance cost management often involves strategic choices about coverage levels and deductibles. For example, maintaining higher deductibles on property insurance while keeping lower deductibles on health coverage might better match your risk tolerance and financial resources. This tailored approach often provides better protection than applying the same cost-saving strategy across all insurance types.

Multi-policy discounts and loyalty programs can significantly reduce insurance costs without sacrificing coverage. However, these savings should support appropriate coverage decisions rather than driving them. The goal is to find the right protection at the best available price, not simply minimizing current expenses.

LONG-TERM COST CONSIDERATIONS

Insurance needs and costs evolve with life changes. Career advancement, family growth, or asset accumulation often require coverage adjustments. Regular review of insurance costs and coverage helps maintain appropriate protection while managing expenses effectively.

The impact of claims on future insurance costs requires careful consideration. While insurance exists to provide protection, frequent small claims can lead to higher premiums or even coverage cancellation. Understanding when to file claims versus handling expenses directly helps you maintain long-term cost effectiveness.

Remember: Insurance cost management success requires finding an appropriate balance between protection and expense. Focus on understanding total cost impact rather than just comparing premiums. Effective insurance cost management combines strategic coverage choices with appropriate deductible levels and available discounts.

MANAGING CLAIMS AND COVERAGE

KEY PRINCIPLE
Successful claims management requires preparation and prompt action rather than reactive responses during emergencies.

Managing insurance claims resembles preparing for a crucial presentation; success depends largely on preparation done before the actual event.

My claim experience highlighted the importance of preparation when my car was rear-ended six months into my financial recovery. Having organized my insurance documentation and understanding my coverage details was key during those stressful moments. Because I had photos of my vehicle's condition, understood my coverage limits, and knew exactly who to call, the entire claims process went smoothly despite my anxiety. This incident reinforced that preparation before emergencies significantly improves outcomes when they inevitably occur.

BEFORE THE CLAIM

Effective claims management starts long before any incident occurs. Understanding your coverage details, maintaining current documentation, and knowing proper response procedures creates the foundation for successful claims. Many people discover coverage limitations or documentation requirements only after losses occur, when it's too late to make adjustments.

Documentation becomes your most powerful tool during claims. Regular home inventories, maintenance records, and condition photographs provide crucial evidence for claims processing. Digital storage of these records ensures accessibility even if physical documents are damaged or destroyed during covered events.

DURING THE CLAIM

The first 24 hours after an incident are critical. Your actions during this time often determine claim success. Immediate damage mitigation, proper incident documentation, and prompt notification to insurance carriers can significantly affect claim outcomes. Understanding your responsibilities for damage prevention helps you avoid claim denials based on failure to protect property after initial damage.

Communication with insurance representatives requires careful attention. Maintaining detailed records of all conversations, including dates, names, and specific discussion points helps prevent misunderstandings and supports claim progress. Many successful claims rely as much on clear communication as on actual coverage terms.

AFTER THE CLAIM

Practice patient persistence as you wait for your claim to be resolved. Understanding typical processing timeframes and required documentation helps you maintain appropriate expectations while ensuring steady progress. Many people either passively wait for claim processing or become unnecessarily confrontational, neither of which are likely to produce results.

The impact of claims on future coverage deserves careful consideration. While insurance exists to provide protection, understanding how different types of claims affect future insurability and premiums helps inform your decisions about whether to file claims for smaller losses.

LONG-TERM COVERAGE MANAGEMENT

Regular coverage review becomes increasingly important after experiencing claims. Understanding how your coverage performed during actual incidents helps you identify necessary adjustments. Many people maintain unchanged coverage even after filing a claim reveals gaps or limitations in their protection.

The relationship between different insurance types often becomes clearer during claims. For example, auto accidents might involve health insurance, auto coverage, and potentially umbrella liability protection. Understanding these interactions helps you maintain appropriate coverage across all insurance types.

Remember: Claims management success requires preparation and understanding rather than reactive responses. Focus on maintaining appropriate documentation and understanding coverage details before incidents occur. The most effective claims handling often combines prompt action with patient persistence through resolution.

LONG-TERM INSURANCE STRATEGY

> **KEY PRINCIPLE**
> Effective long-term insurance planning requires evolving protection that grows with your changing life circumstances rather than static coverage.

Long-term insurance strategy resembles maintaining a living security system that adapts to changing threats and needs. Many people set their insurance coverage once and forget it, missing crucial opportunities to adjust protection as their lives and assets evolve.

Starting with basic renter's and health insurance during bankruptcy recovery, I initially thought insurance planning meant simply increasing coverage amounts as my income grew. It wasn't until sitting with our advisor before buying our Nashville home that I realized how fundamentally different my insurance needs had become. My risks and responsibilities had transformed; from protecting modest possessions to safeguarding a complex portfolio of primary residence, rental properties, and growing assets.

LIFE STAGE PROTECTION

Insurance needs shift dramatically through different life phases. Young professionals might focus primarily on health and disability coverage, while growing families require more comprehensive protection including life insurance and expanded liability coverage. Understanding how different life stages affect insurance needs is important. It enables you to maintain appropriate protection at each stage.

The relationship between personal and professional insurance requirements grows more complex as careers advance. Business ownership, professional liability exposure, and increased assets often require sophisticated insurance strategies. Many successful professionals discover their personal and professional insurance needs become increasingly intertwined.

WEALTH PROTECTION EVOLUTION

As assets grow, insurance strategies must evolve beyond basic protection. High-value homes, art collections, or luxury vehicles often require specialized coverage beyond standard policies. Understanding these specialized insurance needs helps prevent coverage gaps that could threaten accumulated wealth.

FUTURE PLANNING CONSIDERATIONS

Long-term care needs require particularly careful consideration in insurance planning. The potential impact of extended care requirements on personal and family finances makes this an increasingly important aspect of comprehensive protection. Understanding available options and appropriate timing for long-term care coverage helps create sustainable protection.

When insurance planning, you must also consider your evolving family needs. Children's transition to adulthood, aging parents' care requirements, or changes in family structure all affect insurance strategy. Regular review of how family circumstances affect insurance needs helps maintain appropriate protection.

CREATING SUSTAINABLE PROTECTION

Understanding how different coverage types interact helps you optimize protection while managing expenses. Many people maintain unnecessary coverage overlaps or gaps simply because they don't review their complete insurance picture regularly.

The balance between self-insurance and coverage purchase often shifts with increasing wealth. Higher deductibles or selective coverage elimination might make sense as assets grow, while other areas might require increased protection. Understanding when to self-insure versus maintain coverage helps you optimize long-term insurance strategy.

Remember: Your insurance strategy must evolve with your changing circumstances. Focus on maintaining protection that matches your current situation while planning for future needs. The most effective long-term insurance planning often combines regular strategy review with proactive coverage adjustment.

CHAPTER SUMMARY AND KEY TAKEAWAYS

Through my journey from bankruptcy to financial stability, I've learned that effective insurance planning combines comprehensive protection with strategic cost management. The lessons from both personal experience and helping others show that successful insurance strategy requires active management rather than passive policy renewal.

CORE INSURANCE PRINCIPLES:

Protection Over Price: During my recovery, I discovered that appropriate coverage matters more than finding the lowest premiums. One client's experience reinforced this; by focusing on proper protection rather than minimum coverage, she avoided financial devastation when facing multiple simultaneous claims. Success comes from understanding protection needs rather than simply minimizing costs.

Strategy Over Simplicity: Working with others showed how comprehensive insurance planning creates better outcomes than piecing together individual policies. A business owner's experience demonstrated this when his coordinated coverage protected him through a complex claim that crossed multiple insurance types. The most effective protection often comes from understanding how different coverage types work together.

Evolution Over Stasis: Through both success and failure, I've learned that insurance needs change with life circumstances. Static coverage often leaves crucial gaps in protection during major life transitions. Regular insurance strategy review and adjustment proves essential for maintaining appropriate coverage.

ACTION PLAN

First 30 Days: Coverage Review
- Evaluate current insurance policies
- Identify potential coverage gaps
- Document assets and risks
- Review deductibles and limits
- Create insurance inventory

60-Day Implementation
- Address immediate coverage needs

- Coordinate multiple policies
- Establish documentation systems
- Create claims response plans
- Set up a regular schedule for policy review

90-Day Establishment

- Develop your long-term strategy
- Build relationship with agents
- Create coverage adjustment plans
- Document protection strategies
- Plan future coverage needs

FINAL THOUGHTS

Remember: Insurance success isn't about having every possible policy; it's about creating appropriate protection for your specific situation. Through bankruptcy and recovery, I learned that effective insurance planning provides both financial security and peace of mind.

YOUR NEXT STEP

When did you last review your insurance policies? If it's been more than a year, schedule time this month to audit your coverage. Life changes; marriages, children, home purchases, income increases; all require insurance adjustments.

The goal isn't maximum coverage. It's appropriate coverage: enough protection to prevent catastrophe without paying for insurance you'll never need.

CHAPTER 8
TECHNOLOGY SECURITY

LEARNING OBJECTIVES

- Master essential digital financial security practices
- Understand modern financial threats and prevention
- Learn effective digital banking and payment safety
- Develop sustainable security habits
- Create lasting protection for your digital financial life

OPENING STORY

Working in technology taught me that security isn't just about strong passwords. A near-miss with identity theft during my recovery period drove this lesson home. When someone attempted to open credit cards using information from my bankruptcy filing, I realized that my financial security safeguards were not enough. Robust financial security in our digital age requires systematic protection, not just occasional caution. Your efforts to bolster digital financial security need to be as routine as locking your front door.

INTRODUCTION

Our financial lives now exist as much in the digital realm as in our physical wallets. From mobile banking and online shopping to payment apps and digital investments, technology has transformed how we handle money, creating new opportunities and new risks.

Digital financial security resembles maintaining a sophisticated home security system; different protective measures must work together while remaining practical for daily use. Many people either ignore basic security practices as inconvenient or create systems so complex they become impractical.

Digital protection extends beyond basic password practices and should encompass comprehensive security habits that protect your entire financial life. Like physical security, digital protection requires both proper tools and consistent habits.

Most importantly, you'll discover that effective digital security isn't about avoiding technology; it's about using it wisely and safely. The methods we'll discuss work whether you're just starting with online banking or managing complex digital finances.

UNDERSTANDING DIGITAL RISKS

KEY PRINCIPLE
Digital financial security requires understanding current threats rather than relying on outdated protection methods.

Digital financial risks evolve like sophisticated viruses, constantly adapting to bypass existing protections. Many people rely on outdated security practices, leaving themselves vulnerable to modern threats that exploit new technologies and behaviors.

When someone attempted to open credit cards using information from my bankruptcy filing, I began to understand the need for systematic protection. What appeared to be a legitimate email from my bank nearly tricked me into providing account credentials. Only my habit of calling my bank's official number instead of clicking links saved me from a fraud attempt that could have devastated my fragile financial rebuilding.

MODERN THREAT LANDSCAPE

Today's financial threats operate with unprecedented sophistication. Fraudsters combine social engineering with technology to create convincing deceptions. Modern attacks often mimic legitimate institutions so perfectly that even careful people can be deceived.

Social engineering attacks have evolved beyond obvious fraud attempts. Criminals now research potential victims through social media and public records, crafting highly personalized approaches that exploit specific circumstances and relationships. This targeted approach makes the traditional "if it seems too good to be true" warnings insufficient.

The Modern Financial Threat Landscape

Understanding digital vulnerabilities and attack vectors

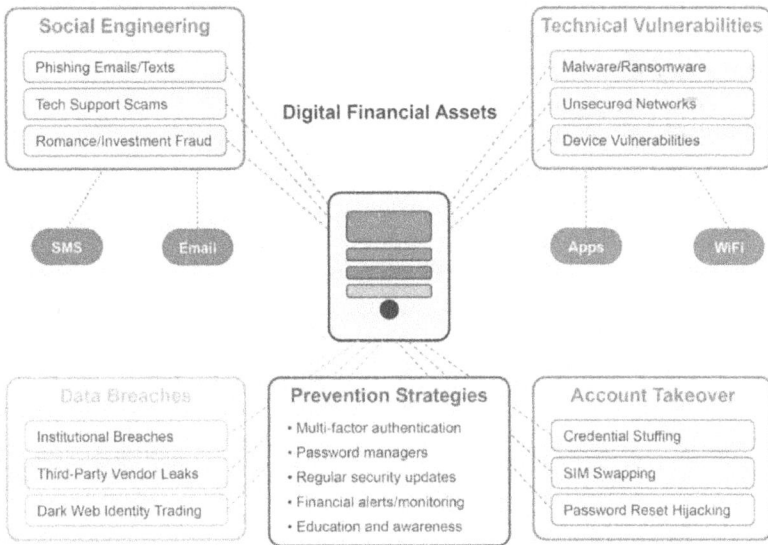

Social Engineering
- Phishing Emails/Texts
- Tech Support Scams
- Romance/Investment Fraud

Digital Financial Assets

Technical Vulnerabilities
- Malware/Ransomware
- Unsecured Networks
- Device Vulnerabilities

SMS   Email   Apps   WiFi

Data Breaches
- Institutional Breaches
- Third-Party Vendor Leaks
- Dark Web Identity Trading

Prevention Strategies
- Multi-factor authentication
- Password managers
- Regular security updates
- Financial alerts/monitoring
- Education and awareness

Account Takeover
- Credential Stuffing
- SIM Swapping
- Password Reset Hijacking

Common Attack Methods

Text and email phishing have evolved significantly. Modern attacks often:

- Reference recent legitimate transactions
- Include correct personal details
- Copy official communication styles
- Create artificial time pressure
- Use sophisticated spoofing techniques

Phone-based fraud has become particularly dangerous. Scammers now:

- Spoof legitimate business numbers
- Reference actual account details
- Use background noise from real call centers
- Follow official-sounding scripts
- Maintain professional demeanor

DIGITAL PAYMENT VULNERABILITIES

Payment app fraud represents a growing threat as more people use digital payment services. Unlike traditional banking, many payment apps offer limited fraud protection and may provide no recourse for scammed users. Understanding these limitations is important for ensuring safe digital payments.

Public Wi-Fi networks create heightened risks for financial activities. Even password-protected public networks can expose sensitive data to interception. Many people don't realize that conducting financial business on public Wi-Fi can compromise their security regardless of other protective measures. These basic digital hygiene practices provide essential protection:

- Regular password updates
- Multi-factor authentication
- Separate email for financial accounts
- Regular security review
- Careful app permission management

Remember: Digital security requires understanding and adapting to evolving threats. Focus on developing awareness of current risks while maintaining consistent protective habits. Effective digital protection often combines technical measures with behavioral awareness.

Password Protection Options

Finding your security solution

Solution Type	Key Features	Security Level	Best For	Cost
Browser-Based (Chrome, Firefox, etc.)	• Auto-fill functionality • Built-in convenience • Sync across devices	Moderate	Casual internet users with few accounts	Free
Cloud Password (LastPass, Bitwarden)	• Cross-platform support • Password generation • Secure sharing options	High	Most users needing cross-device access	$0-40/yr
Local Password (KeePass, Password Safe)	• Complete offline control • No third-party exposure • Manual sync options	Very High	Privacy-focused users with technical skills	Free
Hardware-Based (YubiKey, Titan Key)	• Physical authentication • Phishing-resistant • Works with other solutions	Highest	High-security needs financial professionals	$25-60
Manual Methods (Password notebook)	• No digital exposure • No technical requirements • Complete control	Low-Moderate	Tech-averse users with few accounts	$5-20

Note: Best security comes from combining multiple approaches (e.g., password manager + hardware key)

CREATING YOUR SECURITY SYSTEM

KEY PRINCIPLE

Effective digital protection requires building systematic habits rather than relying on random security measures.

Creating digital financial security resembles establishing a morning routine; it must be both thorough and sustainable enough to maintain consistently.

Though I worked in technology, I had focused on complex security measures while overlooking basic daily habits.

When explaining what happened to Lacey, I admitted, "I've been teaching complex security practices but neglecting the simple daily habits that matter most." This experience transformed my approach; I focus on creating security routines people can maintain consistently rather than sophisticated systems they'll eventually abandon from fatigue.

BUILDING YOUR SECURITY FOUNDATION

Digital security starts with establishing core protective practices. Just like how physical security begins with locking doors, digital security begins with establishing fundamental habits that you should automate. These basics tools and practices form the foundation that lets you build more advanced protection.

Password management tools are a convenient way for you to protect your accounts. Rather than trying to remember dozens of complex passwords, a password manager lets you easily maintain unique, strong passwords for every account. This single tool can dramatically improve security while adding convenience.

ESSENTIAL DAILY PRACTICES

Regular account monitoring should be a part of your regular digital security practices. Checking accounts daily, even briefly, helps you spot unauthorized activity quickly. Without regular account review, many successful fraud attempts can go undetected for days or weeks.

Transaction alerts serve as an early warning system. Setting up notifications for all account activity might seem overwhelming at first. Once established, transaction alerts quickly become a natural way to maintain awareness of your financial activity. These alerts often provide the first indication of compromise.

CREATING SECURE ACCESS METHODS

Implement multi-factor authentication in your accounts to immediately improve their security. While receiving codes via text message provides basic protection, using dedicated authentication apps offers stronger security. Research different authentication options to best assess which methods work best for your different accounts.

Biometric security features like fingerprint or face recognition can enhance protection when properly implemented. However, it's important to maintain backup access methods in case of a lockout. Many biometric systems will automatically lock you out of your account after a set number of failed attempts. Balance security and accessibility when setting up your biometric options to create sustainable protection.

FAMILY SECURITY INTEGRATION

Family financial security requires teaching good habits to all members. Children need age-appropriate guidance about digital security, while elderly family members often need patient support adopting new security practices. Creating family security habits helps protect everyone's financial well-being.

Conduct regular family security discussions to maintain awareness and update practices across family members as needed. During monthly family meetings, you can review recent scam attempts, discuss security concerns, and reinforce good habits. These conversations help create a culture of security awareness.

EMERGENCY ACCESS PLANNING

When implementing security systems, you must include plans for emergency account access. Trusted family members need appropriate access information in case of incapacity or death. However, this information must be secured against unauthorized access while remaining available when needed.

Documentation proves crucial for emergency access. Take steps to ensure family members can handle financial matters during emergencies without compromising security. Maintain secured records of account access methods, contact information, and the steps for running through security recovery procedures.

Remember: Security success requires developing sustainable habits rather than implementing random measures. Focus on creating practices you can maintain consistently while building more sophisticated protection over time. Effective security often comes from simple habits performed reliably rather than complex systems used sporadically.

Reference this graphic as you build out the various components of your digital security systems.

Your Digital Financial Shield

Building comprehensive protection

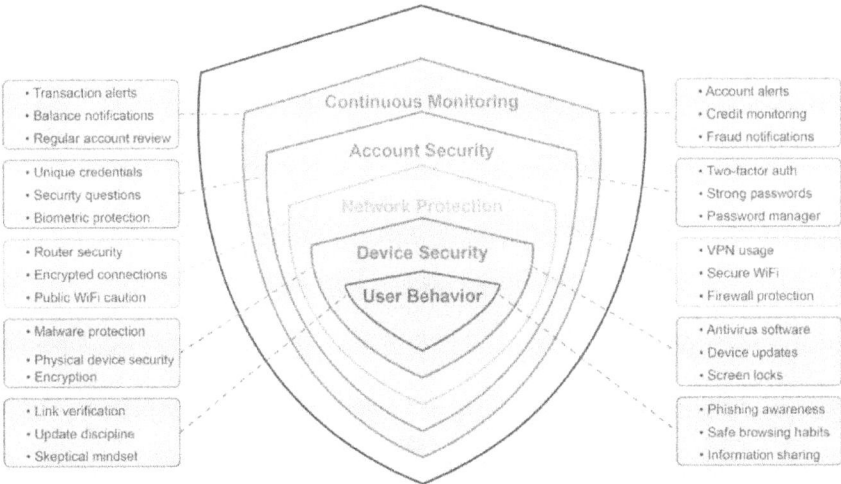

- Transaction alerts
- Balance notifications
- Regular account review

- Unique credentials
- Security questions
- Biometric protection

- Router security
- Encrypted connections
- Public WiFi caution

- Malware protection
- Physical device security
- Encryption

- Link verification
- Update discipline
- Skeptical mindset

Continuous Monitoring

Account Security

Network Protection

Device Security

User Behavior

- Account alerts
- Credit monitoring
- Fraud notifications

- Two-factor auth
- Strong passwords
- Password manager

- VPN usage
- Secure WiFi
- Firewall protection

- Antivirus software
- Device updates
- Screen locks

- Phishing awareness
- Safe browsing habits
- Information sharing

Note: Effective digital security requires all five layers working together to provide comprehensive protection.

SECURE BANKING PRACTICES

> **KEY PRINCIPLE**
> Safe online banking requires active security measures rather than passive trust in bank systems.

Digital banking security resembles maintaining a high-security vault; multiple protective layers working together provide better protection than any single strong measure. Many people rely solely on their bank's security systems, missing opportunities to create additional protection through their own practices.

My experience with an attempted account breach changed my perspective on banking security forever. Despite using a strong password, someone nearly accessed my rebuilding emergency fund through a compromised email address I'd used for password recovery. The attempt came during my financial recovery when a loss of savings would have been devastating.

"I thought the bank's security was enough," I explained during a family financial education session. "Now I understand that my own security practices matter just as much as the bank's protections." This close call changed how I approach all digital financial activities.

CREATING SECURE BANKING FOUNDATIONS

Secure online banking starts with establishing proper account access methods. When accessing online banking, you should always use dedicated devices and secure networks. Many security compromises occur through simple exposure on unsecured networks or shared devices.

Email security proves particularly crucial for banking protection. Since email often serves as a password recovery method, compromised email accounts can bypass other security measures. Maintaining separate, secured email accounts for financial services helps you prevent unauthorized access.

Mobile Banking Protection

Mobile banking requires specific security considerations. While banking apps generally provide better security than mobile browsers, they need proper configuration and protection. Follow these online banking best practices when setting up and using your online baking apps:

- Enable all available security features
- Maintain current app versions
- Use device security features

Device protection becomes crucial with mobile banking. Lost or stolen phones could give another person access to your financial accounts if they are not properly secured. Understanding how to remotely lock or wipe devices adds essential protection for mobile banking users.

TRANSACTION SECURITY

Payment verification systems can further bolster your protection when making banking transactions. While verification codes might seem inconvenient, they can prevent unauthorized transfers. Understanding different verification options helps you choose appropriate security levels for different types of transactions.

Regular transaction monitoring helps you identify unauthorized activity quickly. Setting appropriate alert thresholds for different account activities lets you maintain awareness without creating alert fatigue. Find the right balance between monitoring and convenience to uphold effective, sustained security practices.

ACCOUNT RECOVERY PREPARATION

Account recovery procedures require advance preparation. Take the time to understand how to regain account access if security measures fail. Many people discover too late that they lack necessary recovery information or documentation during critical moments.

Regularly update all security contact information. Maintaining current phone numbers, email addresses, and alternate contact methods ensures you can recover account access when needed. Regularly review your recovery options to lack of access during emergencies.

Remember: Banking security requires active participation rather than passive reliance on bank systems. Focus on creating multiple security layers while maintaining practical access methods. Effective banking protection often combines bank security systems with personal security practices.

PAYMENT AND SHOPPING SECURITY

> **KEY PRINCIPLE**
> Safe digital payments require different protection levels for different types of transactions rather than the same security approach to all purchases.

My lesson about payment security came the hard way during early financial recovery when my debit card information was compromised from an online purchase. "I used my debit card because the purchase was only fifty dollars," I explained to my financial accountability partner. "That small transaction gave thieves direct access to my checking account, causing a cascade of rejected payments when I could least afford it."

This painful experience taught me that payment method matters more than transaction size; now I use credit cards with fraud protection for all online purchases regardless of amount.

STRATEGIC PAYMENT METHODS

Different payment types offer varying levels of protection Credit cards typically provide the strongest fraud protection, creating a buffer between merchants and your bank account. Many people avoid credit cards fearing debt, missing their value as security tools when paid in full monthly.

DIGITAL WALLET SECURITY

Digital wallets add security through tokenization, replacing actual card numbers with temporary codes. This protection is valuable for online shopping and recurring payments. However, proper digital wallet setup and maintenance is required for effective protection.

Choosing which payment app to send or receive money with requires careful consideration. While convenient across the board, different payment apps offer varying security features and fraud protection. Understanding these differences helps you choose appropriate apps for different payment needs.

Safe online shopping requires specific security practices. Apply the following precautions when shopping online:

- Verify website security before entering payment information
- Use dedicated payment methods for online purchases
- Monitor transaction notifications immediately
- Save confirmation information securely
- Review recurring payment arrangements regularly

MERCHANT ASSESSMENT

Evaluating merchant security is increasingly important as online shopping rises in popularity. Large, established retailers typically maintain better security than smaller websites. While this shouldn't prevent you from supporting smaller businesses, it's important to be aware of some of the added risks. Using more secure payment methods with less established merchants can provide additional protection to offset any unnecessary exposure.

SUBSCRIPTION MANAGEMENT

Recurring payment security requires particular attention. Many people lose track of active subscriptions and automatic payments, creating ongoing security exposure. Regular review of recurring charges helps you maintain payment security while preventing unwanted charges.

Remember: Payment security requires matching protection levels to transaction types. Focus on using appropriate payment methods while maintaining awareness of different security needs. Effective payment protection often combines convenient everyday methods with enhanced security for higher-risk transactions.

LONG-TERM SECURITY MAINTENANCE

KEY PRINCIPLE
Digital security requires regular updates and adaptation rather than one-time solutions.

Long-term digital security resembles maintaining a modern car; regular updates, preventive maintenance, and adaptation to new conditions ensure continued protection. Many people implement security measures once and consider themselves protected, missing the evolving nature of digital threats.

My perspective about digital security shifted when my supposedly "strong" password appeared in a major data breach. As a technology professional who had used the same complex password for years, I thought

I was protected. The breach notification arrived during my financial recovery period when I was particularly vulnerable.

"I discovered that what qualified as secure five years ago provides little protection today. This incident taught me that security requires constant evolution, not just initial setup; a lesson that now shapes how I protect all my financial accounts.

Take time to set up a financial early warning system. The graph below illustrates the different types of alerts you should implement as part of this system.

Your Financial Early Warning System

Setting effective alerts and monitoring

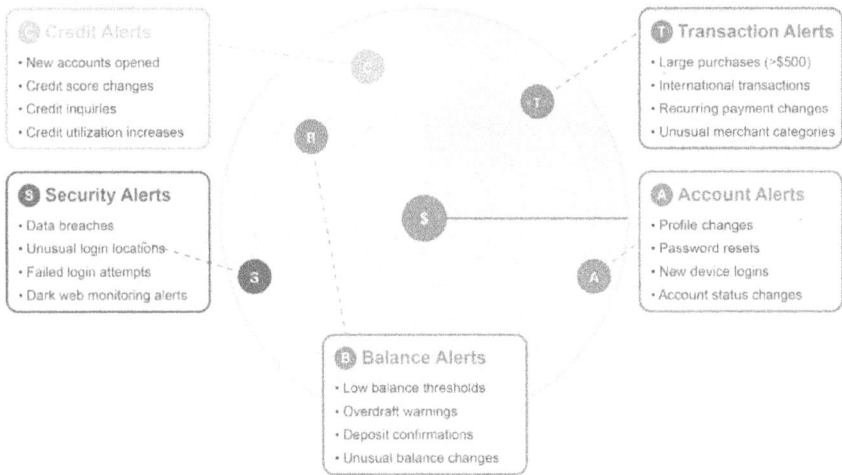

C Credit Alerts
- New accounts opened
- Credit score changes
- Credit inquiries
- Credit utilization increases

T Transaction Alerts
- Large purchases (>$500)
- International transactions
- Recurring payment changes
- Unusual merchant categories

S Security Alerts
- Data breaches
- Unusual login locations
- Failed login attempts
- Dark web monitoring alerts

A Account Alerts
- Profile changes
- Password resets
- New device logins
- Account status changes

B Balance Alerts
- Low balance thresholds
- Overdraft warnings
- Deposit confirmations
- Unusual balance changes

Regular Security Review

Establish a systematic security review process to maintain protection. These checks should include:

- Monthly security check-ups
- Quarterly password updates
- Semi-annual security feature reviews
- Annual comprehensive protection assessment
- Ongoing threat awareness

ADAPTING TO NEW TECHNOLOGY

Financial technology constantly evolves and it's important to adapt to these changes. Mobile payment systems, cryptocurrency, and digital banking features create new opportunities but also pose new security risks. Understanding emerging technologies helps you maintain appropriate protection without missing beneficial innovations.

It's important for you to regularly assess your balance between security and convenience. For example, while biometric authentication and automated systems offer both, their proper implementation needs ongoing attention. Many people either resist helpful security advances or adopt new features without understanding their limitations.

FAMILY SECURITY EVOLUTION

Your family security needs will always change as technology evolves. Children's increasing digital independence requires adjusted protection strategies, while aging parents might need simplified security approaches. Conduct regular family security discussions where you can cover these issues. Having these discussions help your family maintain appropriate protection for everyone.

Teaching sustainable security habits is important. Rather than implementing rigid rules, help family members understand security principles. This enables them to make good decisions independently. Preparation in this area proves particularly valuable as digital financial services expand.

EMERGENCY PLANNING UPDATES

Emergency access plans need regular updates as digital services change. Contact information, access methods, and recovery procedures require periodic review. Many people discover during emergencies that their carefully crafted access plans have become outdated.

Your documentation must evolve with changing security measures. Maintain current records of security features, access methods, and recovery procedures to ensure continued accessibility and protection. Regularly conduct reviews to keep your documentation from becoming obsolete.

FUTURE SECURITY PREPARATION

Understanding emerging security trends helps you prepare for future needs. While specific threats change, fundamental security principles remain relevant. Focusing on these principles while adapting specific practices helps maintain effective protection.

CHAPTER SUMMARY AND KEY TAKEAWAYS

Through my journey from basic digital banking to managing complex financial technology, I've learned that effective digital security combines fundamental practices with adaptive protection. The lessons from both personal experience and helping others show that digital financial security requires active management rather than passive reliance on technology.

CORE SECURITY PRINCIPLES:

Prevention Over Recovery: During my recovery period, I discovered that preventing security breaches matters more than having recovery plans. One colleague's experience reinforced this; by implementing proper security practices, she prevented fraud attempts that might have succeeded despite having recovery options. Success comes from proactive protection rather than reactive measures.

Habits Over Tools: Working with others showed how consistent security habits create better protection than relying solely on security tools. A family member's experience demonstrated this when her regular account monitoring caught unauthorized activity that automated systems missed. The most effective security often comes from combining good habits with appropriate tools.

Evolution Over Stasis: I've learned that security needs constantly change with technology. Recent experiences helping others navigate digital fraud attempts showed how static security measures become vulnerable over time. Regular security updates and adaptations prove essential for maintaining protection.

ACTION PLAN

First 30 Days: Security Foundation
- Review all financial account security settings
- Enable multi-factor authentication
- Update critical passwords
- Set up account alerts
- Create secure password management system

60-Day Implementation
- Establish regular monitoring habits
- Develop family security practices
- Create emergency access plans
- Build documentation systems
- Set up security review schedule

90-Day Establishment
- Review and adjust security measures
- Update protection strategies
- Strengthen weak security areas

- Plan future security needs
- Maintain security awareness

FINAL THOUGHTS

Remember: Digital security success isn't about having the most sophisticated tools; it's about maintaining consistent protection through both basic practices and adaptive measures. Through managing increasingly complex financial technology, I've learned that effective security requires both vigilance and adaptability.

YOUR NEXT STEP

Check one thing right now: Is two-factor authentication enabled on your primary email account? If not, stop reading and enable it. Your email is the master key to your financial life; password resets, account notifications, and sensitive documents all flow through it.

Digital security isn't about becoming paranoid. It's about making yourself a harder target than the next person. Most financial fraud targets the path of least resistance. Don't be that path.

MOVING FORWARD

With your foundation established and your defenses in place, you're ready for what most people want to jump to first: building wealth.

I understand the impulse. During my recovery, I was eager to start investing again, to feel like I was moving forward rather than just treading water. But I'm grateful I took time to secure my foundation first. When I finally did begin rebuilding wealth; starting with just $25 weekly; I did so from a position of stability rather than desperation.

Section III explores the paths to growing your money: traditional investing, real estate, and the strategic decisions that compound over time. Whether you're starting small like I once did or managing significant assets, the principles remain the same. The difference now is that you're building on solid ground.

SECTION III
WEALTH BUILDING

You've built your foundation. You've established protection. Now comes the part most people want to skip to first: making your money grow.

I understand the impulse; I felt it too. But there's a reason this section comes third, not first. Wealth building without foundation is speculation. Wealth building without protection is reckless. Wealth building *with* both is how lasting prosperity happens.

The strategies in this section work at any scale. The same principles that guided my first $25 weekly investment during recovery now inform how I manage substantial equity compensation and rental properties. The math scales; the mindset doesn't change.

Chapter 9: Investing covers long-term wealth building through market participation. You'll learn why consistency matters more than timing, why simplicity often beats complexity, and how to build an investment approach you can actually maintain through market cycles.

Chapter 10: Real Estate addresses building wealth through property ownership. Real estate can be a powerful wealth-building tool; or an expensive lesson in emotional decision-making. This chapter helps ensure it's the former.

Two chapters. Two major wealth-building vehicles. Everything you need to start growing what you've built.

CHAPTER 9
INVESTING

LEARNING OBJECTIVES

- Master fundamental investment principles and strategies
- Learn to balance risk and potential returns effectively
- Understand different investment vehicles and their roles
- Develop sustainable investment habits
- Create lasting wealth-building practices

OPENING STORY

The irony of my first post-bankruptcy investment wasn't lost on me. After years of managing multi-million-dollar projects and studying complex financial models in my MBA program, I started rebuilding my investment portfolio with $25 weekly deposits into a simple index fund. This humble restart taught me something crucial: successful investing isn't about complex strategies or large sums; it's about consistent action and sound principles.

INTRODUCTION

Money works differently when you understand how to make it grow. Whether you're saving your first hundred dollars or managing substantial assets, the fundamental principles of investing remain remarkably consistent.

Building wealth through investing resembles growing a garden; it requires proper planning, consistent attention, and patience for results. Many people seek quick returns through complex strategies, missing the power of simple, consistent investment practices.

Understanding investment basics proves crucial for long-term financial success. Like learning any new skill, investing becomes clearer and more manageable when you grasp the fundamental principles before attempting advanced techniques.

Most importantly, you'll discover that successful investing isn't about getting rich quick; it's about making informed choices consistently over time.

UNDERSTANDING INVESTMENT FUNDAMENTALS

KEY PRINCIPLE

Investment success requires understanding basic principles rather than chasing trends or following hot tips.

Investing fundamentals resemble the laws of physics; while strategies may vary, certain principles remain constant. Many people jump into investing focused on picking winning stocks or timing markets, missing the foundational concepts that drive long-term success.

As I learned during my post-bankruptcy restart, successful investing isn't about complex strategies or large sums; it's about consistent action and sound principles. Despite the modest beginning, these disciplined contributions established the foundation that would eventually grow into a substantial investment portfolio spanning multiple asset classes.

THE POWER OF COMPOUND GROWTH

Compound growth creates the foundation for investment success. Like a snowball growing as it rolls downhill, investment returns build upon themselves over time. Understanding this concept helps you maintain long-term perspective when markets fluctuate.

Consider two different investors: Jennifer starts investing $200 monthly at age 25, while Michael waits until 35 to invest $400 monthly. Despite investing twice as much monthly, Michael's later start means that by age 65, Jennifer's portfolio will likely be substantially larger, demonstrating the power of time in investing.

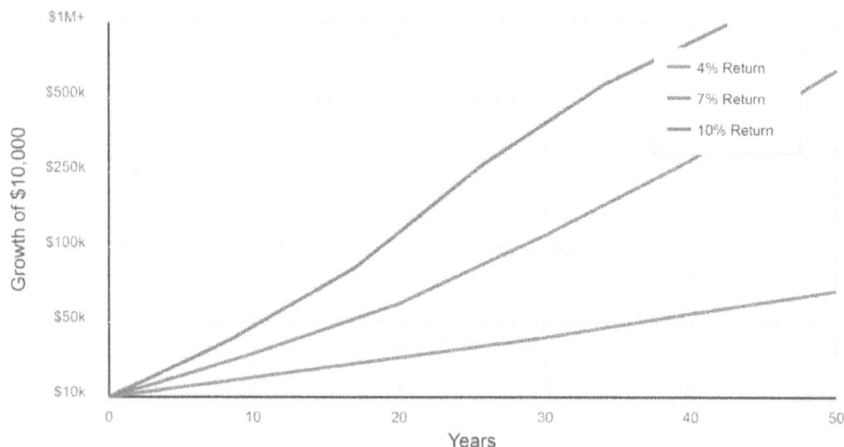

UNDERSTANDING RISK AND RETURN

The relationship between risk and return requires careful consideration. Higher potential returns generally accompany higher risk levels, but this relationship isn't always linear. Many new investors either avoid risk entirely, limiting their growth potential, or take unnecessary risks seeking quick gains.

Different investment types serve different purposes:
- Stocks provide growth potential and inflation protection
- Bonds offer stability and income
- Cash provides security and flexibility
- Real estate combines growth with income
- Index funds offer diversified market exposure

Investment Calculation Example: The Power of Different Returns

Let's examine how different investment approaches affect a $10,000 initial investment over 30 years:

Conservative Approach (4% average annual return):
$10,000 \times (1.04)^{30} = \$32,434$

Moderate Approach (7% average annual return):
$10,000 \times (1.07)^{30} = \$76,123$

Aggressive Approach (10% average annual return):
$10,000 \times (1.10)^{30} = \$174,494$

This $142,060 difference between conservative and aggressive approaches demonstrates why understanding your time horizon is crucial. For long-term goals like retirement, the higher volatility of growth-oriented investments often becomes less significant than their return potential.

Understanding Risk and Return

The relationship between potential growth and volatility

Emerging Markets
International Stocks
Small Cap Stocks
Large Cap Stocks
Balanced Funds
Bonds
Cash

Potential Return

High

Low

Low

High

Risk (Volatility)

THE MARKET REALITY

Markets move in cycles, not straight lines. Understanding this prevents emotional reactions to market movements. Many investors harm their long-term results by reacting to short-term market changes, either selling during downturns or buying during excitement.

Successful investing requires accepting market volatility while maintaining focus on long-term goals. Like ocean waves, daily market movements matter less than the overall tide of long-term growth. Keeping this perspective in mind helps you maintain consistent investment behavior through market cycles.

INVESTMENT COSTS MATTER

Investment costs can significantly hurt long-term results. Small differences in fees compound over time, potentially reducing returns by hundreds of thousands of dollars over decades. It pays to understand investment costs. Minimizing these costs helps you maximize long-term growth.

Remember: Investment success comes from understanding and applying fundamental principles rather than finding "secret" strategies. Focus on building knowledge while maintaining consistent investment practices. The most successful investors often follow simple, well-understood principles rather than complex trading strategies.

BUILDING YOUR INVESTMENT STRATEGY

> **KEY PRINCIPLE**
> Effective investing requires a clear plan aligned with your goals rather than chasing returns or following trends.

One of the most pivotal moments in our investing journey came when Lacey and I first combined our investment approaches. Despite our over ten-year age gap, we needed to create a unified strategy that respected both our different time horizons and risk tolerances.

"I'm not comfortable with aggressive growth stocks," Lacey admitted during one of our early investment discussions. In her late twenties, she theoretically had the time horizon for higher risk, but her natural conservatism made her hesitant. "I know the math says I should be more aggressive at my age, but watching my parents struggle during the 2008 recession made me wary of market volatility."

Meanwhile, at forty, I should have been moving toward more conservative investments according to traditional wisdom. Yet my experience rebuilding from bankruptcy made me comfortable with calculated risks when backed by solid research.

We decided to start with $25 weekly investments into three different funds; a total market index fund, a growth-oriented technology fund, and a more conservative dividend fund. Rather than rigidly allocating based on age-based formulas, we carefully monitored our emotional responses to market fluctuations during the first six months.

"I noticed something interesting," Lacey said during our quarterly review. "I don't mind the volatility in the index fund because I understand what it represents, but the technology fund's swings make me anxious even though I believe in the companies."

This observation led us to develop what we call our "comfort-adjusted allocation"; a portfolio that balances mathematical optimization with psychological sustainability. Instead of following standard age-based advice, we built a portfolio where we both felt comfortable maintaining course during market declines.

Our current allocation is more aggressive than typical recommendations for my age and more conservative than standard advice for Lacey's age, but it perfectly fits our combined risk tolerance. This approach has allowed us to stay invested through market volatility without the emotional reactions that could lead to poor timing decisions.

The lesson we learned transcends specific allocation percentages: the mathematically "optimal" portfolio that you can't stick with during market turbulence is actually inferior to a "suboptimal" portfolio that you'll maintain through all market conditions.

STARTING WITH PURPOSE

Every successful investment strategy begins with a clear understanding of your goals. Different objectives; retirement, college funding, or financial independence; require different approaches. Understanding your time horizon and risk tolerance helps you create appropriate investment allocations.

Long-term investing differs fundamentally from short-term trading. While markets fluctuate daily, building wealth requires focusing on years or decades rather than days or months. This perspective helps you maintain consistent behavior through market volatility.

ASSET ALLOCATION FUNDAMENTALS

Your investment mix creates the foundation for long-term success. Like a well-balanced diet, proper investment allocation provides necessary nutrients for financial growth while managing risk. Understanding how different assets work together helps create resilient portfolios. A basic but effective allocation often includes:

- Growth assets (stocks) for long-term appreciation
- Stability assets (bonds) for income and protection
- Security assets (cash) for opportunities and emergencies
- Real assets (property, commodities) for inflation protection

IMPLEMENTATION APPROACHES

Simple often proves more effective than complex. Index funds provide broad market exposure with minimal costs, while individual stock picking requires substantial time and expertise. Many successful investors build significant wealth through straightforward, low-cost investment approaches.

Regular investment provides better results than timing attempts. Setting up automatic investments removes emotion from the process while taking advantage of dollar-cost averaging. This systematic approach often outperforms attempts to time market entry points.

RISK MANAGEMENT

Understanding your risk capacity differs from emotional risk tolerance. While someone might feel comfortable with high risk, their financial situation might require more conservative approaches. Balancing these factors helps you create sustainable investment strategies.

Regularly rebalance your investments to maintain appropriate risk levels. As different investments perform differently, portfolio allocations drift from targets. Systematic rebalancing helps you maintain intended risk levels while potentially improving returns through disciplined buying and selling.

MANAGING YOUR INVESTMENTS

KEY PRINCIPLE
Successful investment management requires patient monitoring rather than constant trading or adjustments.

Managing investments resembles tending a garden; most of the work involves patient observation and occasional pruning rather than constant interference. Many investors damage their results through excessive trading or frequent strategy changes, missing the power of disciplined, long-term management.

My experience illustrates this principle. During my early financial rebuilding, I initially checked my investments daily during my financial rebuilding, making frequent adjustments based on market news and economic reports. This constant tinkering created both emotional stress and suboptimal returns.

I was exhausting myself trying to optimize everything. When I finally stepped back and focused on quarterly reviews instead of daily trades, both my returns and my peace of mind improved dramatically. This lesson in patience became a cornerstone of our investment approach.

CREATING YOUR MANAGEMENT SYSTEM

Effective investment management requires clear processes rather than reactive decisions. Establishing regular review periods; monthly for monitoring, quarterly for minor adjustments, and annually for major strategy reviews; helps you maintain discipline while avoiding emotional decisions.

Documentation is crucial for long-term success. Maintain clear records of your investment decisions, including the reasoning behind them. Use these documents to evaluate your strategies more effectively and prevent reactive changes during market volatility.

PORTFOLIO MONITORING

Regular monitoring differs from constant watching. Effective investment monitoring means looking for significant issues while ignoring daily fluctuations. Monitor these key areas of your portfolio on a regular basis:

- Asset allocation drift
- Investment performance versus appropriate benchmarks
- Cost and fee impacts
- Tax implications
- Progress toward goals

REBALANCING STRATEGIES

Regular rebalancing maintains your intended investment strategy. When different investments perform differently, your portfolio naturally drifts from its target allocation. Systematic rebalancing helps maintain appropriate risk levels while potentially improving returns through disciplined buying and selling.

TAX MANAGEMENT

Tax implications significantly affect long-term results. Understanding how different accounts (traditional IRAs, Roth IRAs, taxable accounts) and various investment types are taxed allows you to optimize after-tax returns. Many investors focus solely on pre-tax returns, missing opportunities for tax-efficient investing.

Strategic tax loss harvesting during market declines can improve after-tax returns while maintaining investment strategy. However, tax decisions should support rather than drive investment strategy.

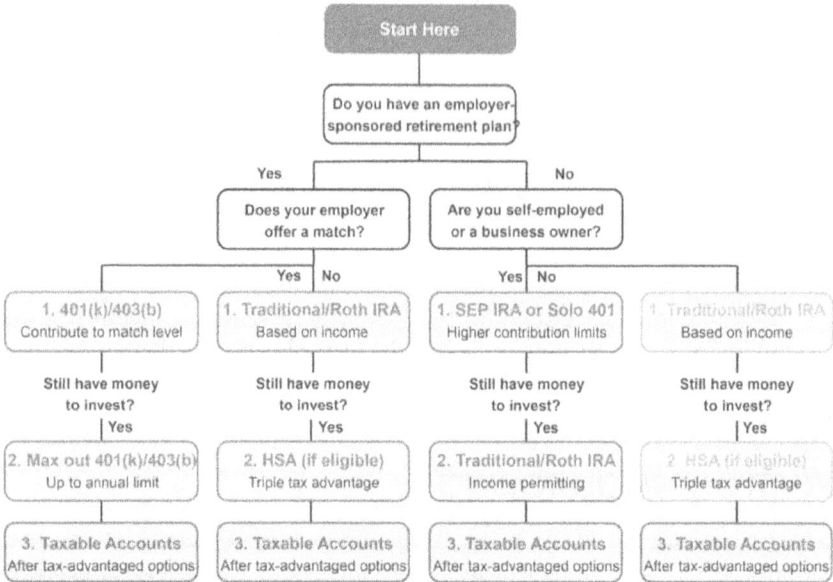

```
                          ┌─────────────────┐
                          │   Start Here    │
                          └─────────────────┘
                                   │
                          ┌─────────────────────┐
                          │ Do you have an       │
                          │ employer-sponsored   │
                          │ retirement plan?     │
                          └─────────────────────┘
                    Yes                           No
        ┌──────────────────────┐      ┌──────────────────────┐
        │ Does your employer    │      │ Are you self-employed │
        │ offer a match?        │      │ or a business owner?  │
        └──────────────────────┘      └──────────────────────┘
         Yes          No                Yes          No
```

1. 401(k)/403(b) Contribute to match level	1. Traditional/Roth IRA Based on income	1. SEP IRA or Solo 401 Higher contribution limits	1. Traditional/Roth IRA Based on income
Still have money to invest? | Yes	Still have money to invest? | Yes	Still have money to invest? | Yes	Still have money to invest? | Yes
2. Max out 401(k)/403(b) Up to annual limit	2. HSA (if eligible) Triple tax advantage	2. Traditional/Roth IRA Income permitting	2. HSA (if eligible) Triple tax advantage
3. Taxable Accounts After tax-advantaged options	3. Taxable Accounts After tax-advantaged options	3. Taxable Accounts After tax-advantaged options	3. Taxable Accounts After tax-advantaged options

COST CONTROL

Investment costs compound over time like returns. Regular review of investment expenses, including mutual fund fees, transaction costs, and advisory fees, helps maximize long-term results. Even small fee reductions can significantly impact wealth accumulation over decades.

LONG-TERM INVESTMENT SUCCESS

KEY PRINCIPLE
Lasting investment success requires maintaining perspective through market cycles rather than reacting to short-term events.

Long-term investing resembles ocean navigation; while daily waves and weather matter, maintaining your chosen course through changing conditions determines ultimate success. Many investors let short-term market movements or economic news divert them from well-planned strategies, missing the power of consistent, long-term execution.

My thirty-year journey from Marine Corps service through bankruptcy to financial recovery captures this principle. Having invested through the

2008 financial crisis before my bankruptcy, and then rebuilding afterward through the pandemic crash of 2020, I witnessed multiple market cycles. "What I learned through each downturn," I explained to my son when helping with his first investments, "wasn't just about surviving market drops, but understanding that maintaining my strategy during difficult times created the most significant gains when markets recovered." This perspective now helps me maintain calm during market volatility while others panic.

Let's talk about how consistent investments typically outpace large, one-time investments due to the decrease in risk.

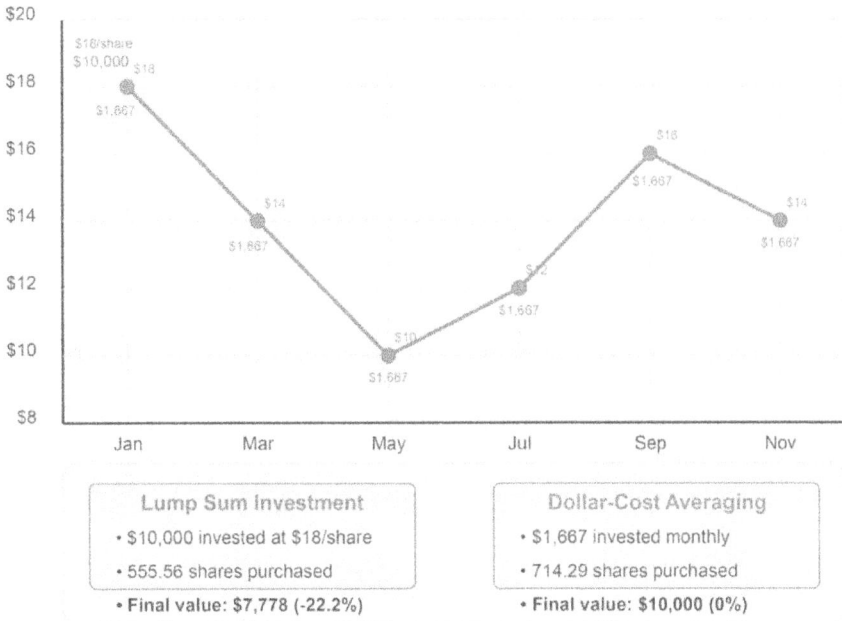

Lump Sum Investment	Dollar-Cost Averaging
• $10,000 invested at $18/share	• $1,667 invested monthly
• 555.56 shares purchased	• 714.29 shares purchased
• Final value: $7,778 (-22.2%)	• Final value: $10,000 (0%)

BUILDING LASTING SUCCESS

Adopting a long-term perspective is a crucial advantage for an investor. Understanding market history helps you maintain confidence during inevitable downturns. While each market crisis feels unique and permanent during the experience, history shows markets consistently recover and reach new highs over time.

Market volatility creates opportunity rather than just risk. Regular investment during market declines often provides better long-term results than waiting for "safe" times to invest. This counter-intuitive truth challenges emotional responses but rewards disciplined investors.

ADAPTING THROUGH LIFE STAGES

Investment strategies must evolve with changing life circumstances. Young investors can often accept more risk and volatility, while those near retirement typically need more stability. Understanding how different life stages affect investment needs helps maintain appropriate strategies.

Major life transitions require careful strategy adjustment. Think about how these changes require a shift in your investment strategy

- Career changes affecting income
- Family additions changing financial needs
- Housing decisions impacting available capital
- Retirement planning affecting risk tolerance
- Health issues influencing investment timeframes

Investment Allocation by Life Stage

Sample portfolios for different goals and time horizons

Aggressive Growth	Balanced Growth	Conservative
Early Career, 20-35 years	Mid-Career, 35-50 years	Near/In Retirement, 50+ years

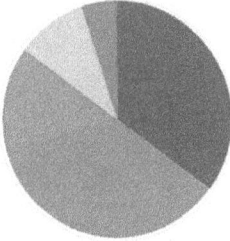

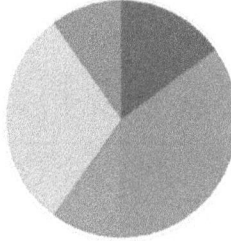

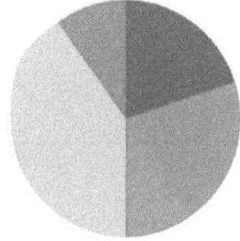

US Stocks

International Stocks

Bonds

Cash

Alternative Investments

Risk Level:

Higher Risk ←⎯ →⎯ Lower Risk

Note: These are sample allocations only. Your personal situation may require different allocations.

CREATING SUSTAINABLE PRACTICES

Successful long-term investing requires sustainable habits. Like maintaining physical health, investment success comes from consistent positive practices rather than occasional intense efforts. Creating manageable investment routines helps maintain long-term focus.

Regular investment review sessions help you maintain strategy alignment. Here are some ways you can ensure your investments are on the right track:

- Monthly monitoring for basic oversight
- Quarterly reviews for minor adjustments
- Annual deep dives for major strategy evaluation
- Regular goal progress assessment

MANAGING MARKET CHALLENGES

Market declines test every investor's resolve. Having clear processes for handling market volatility helps you maintain strategic focus during difficult periods. Many investors make their most costly mistakes during market stress, either selling at lows or making aggressive changes to long-term strategies. Understanding your personal response to market stress helps you create appropriate coping strategies. These can include:

- Regular review of investment principles
- Maintaining historical perspective
- Following established processes
- Consulting trusted advisors
- Focusing on long-term goals

CHAPTER SUMMARY AND KEY TAKEAWAYS

Through my journey from bankruptcy to building substantial wealth, I've learned that successful investing combines fundamental principles with consistent execution. My experiences taught me that investment success requires patience and discipline rather than complex strategies or market timing.

CORE INVESTMENT PRINCIPLES:

Process Over Prediction: During my recovery, I discovered that following consistent investment processes matters more than trying to predict market movements. One colleague's experience reinforced this; by maintaining regular investment through market declines, she achieved better results than those who tried timing market entries. Success comes from systematic investing rather than market forecasting.

Simplicity Over Complexity: Working with others showed how straightforward investment approaches often create better outcomes than complex strategies. A fellow investor's experience demonstrated this when his simple index fund portfolio outperformed his previous attempts at sophisticated trading. Achieving consistent success when investing often involves relying on basic principles that you apply consistently.

Patience Over Action: Through both success and failure, I've learned that investment returns reward patience more than frequent activity. Recent experiences helping families navigate market volatility showed how maintaining strategy through difficult periods leads to better outcomes than reactive changes.

ACTION PLAN

First 30 Days: Foundation Building
- Assess current investment situation
- Define clear investment goals
- Establish basic asset allocation
- Set up automatic investments
- Create investment monitoring system

60-Day Implementation
- Build regular investment habits
- Develop review processes
- Create rebalancing strategy
- Establish cost controls
- Document investment decisions

90-Day Establishment
- Review initial progress
- Adjust strategies as needed
- Strengthen weak areas
- Plan for market challenges
- Maintain long-term focus

FINAL THOUGHTS

Remember: Investment success isn't about finding perfect opportunities; it's about consistently executing sound principles over time. My journey taught me that effective investing requires discipline and patience more than special knowledge or timing skill. Your investment journey will be unique, whether you're:
- Starting with small amounts
- Rebuilding after setbacks
- Managing substantial assets
- Planning for retirement

The principles remain consistent: understand fundamental concepts, maintain disciplined processes, and focus on long-term results. With preparation and a proper approach, investing becomes a powerful tool for building wealth rather than a source of stress or uncertainty.

Remember that markets move in cycles. Stay focused on your long-term goals, maintain consistent investment practices, and don't let short-term events derail your strategy. Your success depends more on maintaining appropriate strategy through market cycles than on picking perfect investments or timing markets perfectly.

CHAPTER 10
REAL ESTATE

LEARNING OBJECTIVES

- Master fundamental real estate investment principles
- Learn effective property evaluation and selection
- Understand financing and management strategies
- Develop sustainable property investment practices
- Create lasting real estate wealth

OPENING STORY

My journey from homeowner to bankruptcy, then to renter, and finally to successful real estate investor taught me crucial lessons about property ownership. The most important lesson wasn't about finding the perfect property; it was about understanding how real estate truly works as a wealth-building tool.

INTRODUCTION

Real estate represents more than just a place to live; it can be a powerful vehicle for building wealth. Whether you're considering your first home purchase or looking to invest in rental properties, understanding the fundamentals of real estate can transform your financial future.

When investing in property, success comes from strategic thinking and careful planning rather than luck or timing. Many people approach real estate emotionally or impulsively, missing opportunities for effective wealth building through proper analysis and management.

Understanding real estate fundamentals is key for successful property investment. Like any complex system, real estate becomes more manageable when you understand its basic principles before attempting advanced strategies. Most importantly, you'll discover that successful real estate investing isn't about finding perfect properties; it's about making informed decisions based on solid principles. The methods we'll discuss work whether you're buying your first home or building a property portfolio.

UNDERSTANDING REAL ESTATE FUNDAMENTALS

KEY PRINCIPLE

Real estate success requires understanding value drivers rather than following market hype or emotional impulses.

Real estate fundamentals resemble the foundation of a building: while styles and features may vary, certain elements remain essential for lasting success. Many people focus on surface appeal or market trends, missing the fundamental factors that determine long-term property value and investment success.

After rebuilding my finances and securing stable income at Honeywell, I was eager to re-enter the market. "I focused entirely on purchase price rather than analyzing neighborhood trends, employment patterns, and property condition," I admitted to Lacey when discussing my previous failures. That expensive lesson taught me that understanding fundamentals matters more than finding 'deals.'

UNDERSTANDING VALUE DRIVERS

Property value depends on multiple interconnected factors. Like a complex equation, each element contributes to the final result. Understanding these relationships helps you evaluate properties effectively while avoiding costly mistakes. Location fundamentals remain crucial for property success. These key components include factors such as:

- Employment trends and stability
- Population growth or decline
- Infrastructure development
- School quality trends
- Transportation access

PROPERTY ECONOMICS

Real estate returns come from multiple sources:

- Appreciation potential
- Rental income
- Tax advantages
- Leverage benefits
- Inflation protection

MARKET ANALYSIS

Local market conditions significantly affect property success. Understanding market cycles, supply-demand dynamics, and demographic trends helps you identify opportunities while avoiding overvalued markets. Many investors follow general market headlines without analyzing specific local conditions that ultimately determine property success.

The Property Value Assessment Matrix

Looking beyond purchase price

Category	Criteria	Score (1-5)
Location	School quality, crime rate, amenities	
Market Trends	Property value growth, rental demand	
Property Condition	Age, maintenance, major systems	
Cash Flow	Rent-to-price ratio, monthly income	
Operating Expenses	Taxes, insurance, maintenance costs	
Appreciation Potential	Development plans, infrastructure	
Financing Terms	Interest rate, loan terms, closing costs	
Exit Strategy	Resale potential, buyer pool size	
Risk Assessment	Vacancy rates, tenant quality, regulations	
Overall Score	Add all category scores (min: 10, max: 50)	37/50

Score Legend: 1 (Poor) 2 (Below Average) 3 (Average) 4 (Good) 5 (Excellent)

Note: Properties scoring 35+ typically represent strong investment opportunities

PROPERTY CONDITION REALITY

Physical property characteristics affect both value and investment returns. Understanding construction quality, maintenance requirements, and improvement potential helps you evaluate true ownership costs. Many investors underestimate property condition impacts, leading to unexpected expenses that diminish returns.

Remember: Real estate success comes from understanding fundamental value drivers rather than following market excitement. Focus on analyzing essential factors while maintaining emotional discipline. The most successful real estate investors combine thorough analysis with patient execution.

SELECTING AND EVALUATING PROPERTIES

> **KEY PRINCIPLE**
> Effective property selection requires systematic analysis rather than emotional or intuitive decisions.

Our current approach to real estate investing stands in stark contrast to my first homebuying experience that ended in foreclosure. When Lacey and I decided to purchase our first investment property in 2022, the scars from my past financial collapse informed every decision we made.

"We're not buying based on what we can qualify for," I insisted during our initial property search. "We're buying based on conservative cash flow projections with substantial buffers."

Lacey, with her natural financial prudence, had already created detailed spreadsheets analyzing potential properties. "I want to see positive cash flow even if we have 25% vacancy and need a major repair," she explained, showing me calculations that included maintenance reserves, property management costs, and tax considerations.

This methodical approach led us to a modest single-family home that hardly seemed exciting on the surface; a departure from the emotionally-driven, status-focused property purchases of my pre-bankruptcy days. But the numbers told the story that mattered:

True Rental Cash Flow
Calculating your actual returns after all expenses

Property Details
Purchase Price: $225,000
Down Payment: $56,250 (25%)
Loan Amount: $168,750

Monthly Income

Rental Income	$1,850
Additional Income (laundry, storage, etc.)	$0
Total Monthly Income	**$1,850**

Monthly Expenses

Mortgage (Principal & Interest)	Base Cost	$820
Property Taxes	Part of PITI	$150
Insurance	Part of PITI	$80
Property Management	*Often Forgotten Expenses* 10% of Rent	$185
Maintenance Reserve	8% of Rent	$148
Vacancy Reserve	6% of Rent	$111
Total Monthly Expenses		**$1,494**

NET MONTHLY CASH FLOW	**$356**

Note: Cash-on-Cash Return = (Annual Cash Flow ÷ Total Cash Invested) × 100

Cash-on-Cash Return: ($356 × 12) ÷ $56,250 = 7.60%

With over \$350 monthly positive cash flow even after conservative reserves, the property represented something my previous real estate ventures never had; mathematical sustainability. "What I love about this approach," Lacey noted as we signed the closing documents, "is that we're making money on day one, not hoping for appreciation to save us."

The contrast with my previous real estate experience couldn't be more pronounced. My first home purchase had been guided by status considerations and stretched my finances to the breaking point. This investment property, while less impressive at first glance, was acquired through dispassionate analysis and built-in safety margins.

Perhaps most importantly, we structured our real estate investments separately from our primary residence and other assets; creating financial firewalls that would prevent property challenges from affecting our broader financial health. This compartmentalization strategy, something I painfully learned through bankruptcy, became a cornerstone of our approach to building wealth without excessive risk.

CREATING YOUR EVALUATION SYSTEM

Systematic property analysis requires clear criteria and consistent processes. A proper evaluation system helps ensure you consider all crucial factors while maintaining objectivity. Essential evaluation categories include:
- Financial metrics (cap rate, cash flow potential, ROI)
- Physical condition assessment
- Location analysis
- Market position

FINANCIAL ANALYSIS FUNDAMENTALS

Property numbers tell important stories beyond purchase price. Understanding key financial metrics helps you evaluate true investment potential:

Net Operating Income (NOI) = Total Income - Operating Expenses
- Include all potential income sources
- Account for vacancy rates
- Calculate realistic operating costs
- Consider maintenance reserves
- Factor property management

Cap Rate = NOI / Purchase Price
- Helps compare different properties
- Indicates market positioning
- Suggests potential risk levels
- Reflects market conditions

PHYSICAL PROPERTY ASSESSMENT

The physical condition of a property affects your investment returns. Professional inspections provide crucial information and you should always include them in your property assessments. That said, understanding what to look for helps you identify potential issues early:

- Structural integrity and physical condition of the property
- System conditions (HVAC, plumbing, electrical)
- Maintenance requirements
- Improvement potential
- Code compliance

LOCATION EVALUATION

Location analysis extends beyond general neighborhood appeal. Understanding current conditions and future trends helps you predict property potential. The factors that should go into your location evaluation include:

- Employment trends
- Development patterns
- Infrastructure plans
- Demographic shifts
- Market evolution

Remember: Property selection success requires systematic analysis rather than emotional decisions. Focus on thorough evaluation while maintaining objective perspective. The most successful property investments often result from careful analysis rather than quick decisions.

FINANCING AND MANAGING PROPERTIES

KEY PRINCIPLE
Successful property investment requires understanding both financials and operational management rather than focusing solely on purchase details.

Many investors focus exclusively on purchase financing, missing the crucial relationship between financing structures and long-term management success. My journey from single-family homeowner to real estate investor illustrates this principle perfectly.

"I initially thought securing the mortgage was the hard part," I shared during a family financial education session. "Then I discovered that matching financing terms with management realities determined actual profitability."

After acquiring our first investment property in, I learned that seemingly small details often determined whether a property generated reliable income or became a financial drain.

UNDERSTANDING FINANCING OPTIONS

Financing Type	Pros	Cons	Best For
Conventional Mortgage	• Lowest interest rates • Longest terms (30 years) • Widely available	• Stricter qualifying criteria • Typically limited to 10 loans • Higher down payment (20-25%)	Beginners
VA Loans (Author's Experience)	• No down payment required • No PMI requirement • Competitive interest rates	• Limited to veterans/military • VA funding fee • Primary residence focused	Veterans
Portfolio Loans	• No limit on number of properties • Flexible qualifying criteria • Can finance non-standard properties	• Higher interest rates • Shorter terms (15-25 years) • Larger down payments (25-30%)	Scaling
DSCR Loans	• Based on property income, not borrower income • No personal income verification	• Higher interest rates (1-2% above conventional) • Requires positive cash flow	Investors
Private/Creative Financing	• Highly flexible terms • Can finance unusual situations	• Requires strong relationships • Often shorter terms	Advanced

MANAGEMENT FUNDAMENTALS

Property management success requires systematic approaches to the following tasks and challenges.

Tenant Management:
- Screening processes
- Lease structures
- Communication systems
- Maintenance responses
- Collection procedures

Financial Management:
- Income/expense
- Reserve management
- Tax planning
- Cash flow monitoring

CREATING SUSTAINABLE SYSTEMS

Long-term success requires developing reliable management systems. These systems should include:
- Regular property inspections
- Preventive maintenance schedules
- Financial reporting processes
- Vendor relationships
- Emergency response plans

COST CONTROL STRATEGIES

Expense management significantly affects investment returns:
- Maintenance optimization
- Utility management
- Insurance cost control
- Tax planning
- Service contract optimization

Property expenses fall into several categories:
- Fixed costs (mortgage, taxes, insurance)
- Variable costs (utilities, maintenance)
- Replacement reserves
- Management expenses
- Marketing costs

Remember: Real estate success requires effective management systems as much as good acquisition decisions. Focus on creating sustainable operational processes while maintaining appropriate financing structures. The most successful property investors often combine strategic financing with efficient management practices.

BUILDING A REAL ESTATE PORTFOLIO

> **KEY PRINCIPLE**
> Growing a property portfolio requires strategic planning rather than simply acquiring more properties.

Building a real estate portfolio resembles constructing a pyramid; each level must be solid before you add the next, and the entire structure needs careful balance. Many investors rush to acquire multiple properties without creating proper foundations, risking the stability of their entire portfolio.

My real estate portfolio evolution captures this principle. Starting with our first modest single-family rental in Nashville, Lacey and I waited until it performed consistently for a full year before considering our next purchase. My previous experience with overextension had taught me patience. By thoroughly understanding one property's operations before adding another, we built stability while others we knew struggled with properties they acquired too quickly. This methodical strategy created the foundation for our growing real estate holdings.

STRATEGIC GROWTH PLANNING

Portfolio development requires clear vision and patience. Like a chess master thinking several moves ahead, successful portfolio builders consider how each property acquisition affects their overall strategy. Understanding how different properties work together helps create sustainable growth.

Property sequencing significantly affects portfolio success. Starting with smaller, manageable properties helps you develop experience and systems before tackling more complex investments. Many investors jump into complicated properties too soon, learning expensive lessons that could have been avoided through gradual progression.

FINANCIAL STRUCTURE EVOLUTION

Portfolio financing becomes increasingly complex with growth. Early properties often use conventional financing, but larger portfolios require more sophisticated approaches. Understanding how different financing methods work together helps you maintain portfolio stability while enabling continued growth.

Equity management is an important part of portfolio development. Strategic use of property equity through refinancing or lines of credit can fuel growth but requires careful balance. Many investors either overlook equity utilization opportunities or leverage too aggressively, missing the sweet spot of sustainable expansion.

MANAGEMENT SCALE DEVELOPMENT

Property management needs evolve with portfolio growth. Systems that work for one or two properties often prove inadequate for larger portfolios. Successful investors develop scalable management approaches that grow with their portfolios while maintaining efficiency.

The transition from self-management to professional management often determines portfolio success. Understanding when and how to make this transition helps you maintain property performance while enabling continued growth. Many investors hold onto direct management too long, limiting their ability to expand effectively.

RISK MANAGEMENT EVOLUTION

Portfolio growth requires sophisticated risk management techniques. You need a good combination of geographic diversification, property type variation, and tenant market diversity. Accounting for these factors leads to resilient portfolios. Understanding how different properties respond to market changes helps you maintain stability through economic cycles.

CHAPTER SUMMARY AND KEY TAKEAWAYS

Through my journey from foreclosure to successful real estate investing, I've learned that property success combines fundamental understanding with patient execution. The lessons from both personal experience and helping others show that real estate wealth requires strategic thinking rather than emotional decisions or market timing.

CORE REAL ESTATE PRINCIPLES:

Analysis Over Emotion: During my recovery, I discovered that thorough property analysis matters more than emotional reactions to properties. One investor's experience reinforced this; by maintaining strict evaluation criteria rather than following market excitement, she built a profitable portfolio while others chased losing "opportunities." Success comes from systematic evaluation rather than intuitive decisions.

Systems Over Speed: Working with others showed how developing proper management systems creates better outcomes than rapid acquisition. A fellow investor's experience demonstrated this when his carefully managed small portfolio generated better returns than those struggling with numerous poorly managed properties. The most successful real estate investors often focus on quality over quantity.

Strategy Over Opportunity: Through both success and failure, I've learned that strategic planning matters more than reacting to seemingly good deals. Recent experiences helping families build real estate portfolios showed how planned growth leads to better outcomes than opportunistic purchases.

ACTION PLAN

First 30 Days: Foundation Building
- Study local real estate markets
- Develop property evaluation criteria
- Create financial analysis systems
- Build professional network

- Establish investment goals

60-Day Implementation
- Begin property analysis practice
- Develop management systems
- Create financing relationships
- Build contractor networks
- Establish legal frameworks

90-Day Establishment
- Refine evaluation criteria
- Strengthen market knowledge
- Build operational systems
- Plan growth strategy
- Maintain learning focus

FINAL THOUGHTS

Remember: Real estate success isn't about finding perfect properties; it's about making informed decisions based on sound principles. Through foreclosure and recovery, I learned that effective real estate investing requires systematic approaches more than market timing or luck.

YOUR NEXT STEP

Before your next real estate decision; whether buying, selling, or investing; run the numbers without emotion. What does the math say? Real estate builds wealth when the fundamentals work, not when hope or excitement drives the decision. I lost a home to bankruptcy because I bought with my ego instead of my calculator. The house I own now was chosen differently.

MOVING FORWARD

Investing and real estate provide paths to grow your wealth; but they require fuel. For most of us, that fuel comes from our careers.

Your earning power is likely your greatest financial asset. The difference between optimizing it and letting it drift can mean hundreds of thousands of dollars over a working lifetime. And what you keep matters as much as what you earn; which is where tax strategy enters the picture.

Section IV addresses the income side of the equation: maximizing your career's financial potential and keeping more of what you make. From navigating modern compensation packages to strategic tax planning, these chapters help ensure your hard work translates into lasting wealth.

SECTION IV
CAREER & INCOME

Your career is probably your largest asset; larger than your home, larger than your investment accounts, larger than anything else on your balance sheet. Yet most people spend more time planning vacations than optimizing their earning potential.

This section addresses two interconnected realities: making more money and keeping more of what you make.

Chapter 11: Career Financial Planning goes beyond generic career advice. You'll learn to think about your career as an economic asset; one that can be developed, leveraged, and strategically managed. Whether you're navigating your first job or your fifth career transition, understanding career economics changes how you approach professional decisions.

Chapter 12: Taxes tackles the topic most people avoid until April. Tax strategy isn't about finding loopholes; it's about making informed decisions throughout the year so you don't give away money unnecessarily. As income grows, tax awareness becomes increasingly valuable.

Two chapters that work together: earn more, keep more. The combination is how real wealth accumulates.

CHAPTER 11
CAREER FINANCIAL PLANNING

LEARNING OBJECTIVES

- Understand how career choices affect financial outcomes
- Learn effective career development strategies
- Master compensation optimization techniques
- Develop career risk management skills
- Create sustainable long-term career success

OPENING STORY

The job offer sat open on my laptop screen, and for the first time in my career, I didn't immediately reach for a calculator. A Big Tech company had just offered me a senior leadership role at $160,000 base salary, a significant reduction from my Genpact compensation at the time. My pre-bankruptcy self would have dismissed it instantly. But sitting at our kitchen table that evening, Lacey and I approached the decision differently. "Walk me through the full picture," she said, pulling out a notepad.

The lower base was offset by substantial sign-on bonuses and RSU grants vesting over four years. Even if the stock dropped 50%, total compensation would equal my current package. With normal performance, it could deliver 80% more. But it wasn't just about math. We evaluated life integration; remote work, reduced travel.

A decade earlier, I would have chased the highest immediate compensation regardless of other factors. That approach contributed to decisions that ended in bankruptcy. We accepted the offer. Within three years, that "pay cut" transformed into compensation exceeding $600,000 annually. This chapter is about the framework that helped us recognize the opportunity; and make a decision that aligned financial success with the life we wanted to build together.

INTRODUCTION

Your career represents your most valuable financial asset, capable of generating millions in lifetime earnings. Yet many people spend more time researching a new phone purchase than they do planning their career trajectory. Understanding how career decisions affect your financial future can transform both your earning potential and long-term security.

Career financial planning resembles developing an investment portfolio; different choices create different returns, and strategic decisions compound over time. Like successful investors, those who understand how to maximize their career value often achieve better long-term results than those who simply focus on immediate earnings.

Successful career planning combines understanding current market value with developing future opportunities. Similar to building wealth through diversified investments, building career success requires balancing immediate returns with long-term growth potential. Whether you're starting your first job or planning a major transition, understanding career economics helps create better outcomes.

Most importantly, you'll discover that career success isn't about finding perfect opportunities; it's about making informed decisions that align with both your financial goals and personal values. The methods we'll discuss work whether you're earning minimum wage or managing substantial income, because they focus on fundamental principles that apply at every career stage.

UNDERSTANDING CAREER ECONOMICS

KEY PRINCIPLE

Career success requires understanding how different roles and industries affect financial outcomes rather than focusing solely on immediate salary.

Career economics functions like a complex market system; different skills, industries, and roles carry different values. Understanding these relationships helps you make better career decisions. Many people focus exclusively on base salary, overlooking various compensation elements and growth opportunities which affect long-term financial success.

The relationship between career choices and financial success became clear during my transition from military service to Raytheon. While evaluating different roles within the company, I initially focused only on base salary differences. After analyzing total compensation, including potential bonuses, stock options, and advancement tracks, I discovered that technical leadership positions offered better long-term value than slightly higher-paying individual contributor roles.

"I learned that base pay tells only part of the story," I explained to a mentee years later. This insight fundamentally shaped my approach to every subsequent career move.

The Financial Journey of Career Growth

How Advancement Impacts Wealth Building

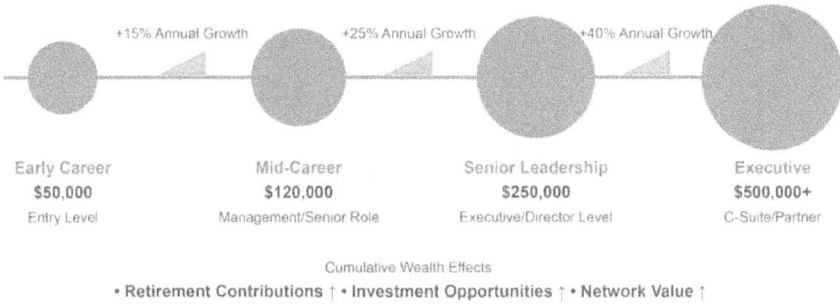

Early Career	Mid-Career	Senior Leadership	Executive
$50,000	$120,000	$250,000	$500,000+
Entry Level	Management/Senior Role	Executive/Director Level	C-Suite/Partner

+15% Annual Growth   +25% Annual Growth   +40% Annual Growth

Cumulative Wealth Effects
• Retirement Contributions ↑ • Investment Opportunities ↑ • Network Value ↑

UNDERSTANDING COMPENSATION COMPONENTS

Base compensation provides foundation but requires careful evaluation within broader context. Regular salary creates predictable income but may limit upside potential. Commission-based roles might offer lower guarantees but higher earning ceilings. Understanding how different compensation structures affect both immediate income and long-term potential helps make better career choices. Compensation Elements to Evaluate:

- Base salary/hourly wage
- Performance bonuses and commissions
- Profit sharing opportunities
- Equity compensation (stock options, RSUs)
- Certification and credential premiums
- Overtime and differential pay structures
- Sign-on and retention bonuses

Industry differences significantly affect career value. Some industries offer higher starting salaries but limited growth, while others provide lower initial compensation but better long-term opportunities. Healthcare, education, skilled trades, and technology each present unique compensation patterns and advancement paths.

Use the following graph to help you evaluate the different compensation components of your given career path.

Beyond Salary

Evaluating Total Career Value

Career Attribute	Value Score	Impact Description
Base Salary	8/10	Primary financial foundation, direct income potential
Bonus/Commission	6/10	Performance-linked income,upside earning potential
Equity/Stock Options	9/10	Long-term wealth building,potential exponential growth
Benefits Package	7/10	Healthcare, retirement matching,additional financial security
Professional Growth	8/10	Skill enhancement, future earning potential
Work-Life Harmony	7/10	Flexible schedules, reduced stress, sustained performance

Individual experiences may vary; holistic evaluation is key

GEOGRAPHIC IMPACT ASSESSMENT

Geographic factors play a major role on the real compensation value of a career. Cost of living differences, state tax variations, and local market conditions affect how far your earnings stretch. A higher salary in an expensive city might provide less actual wealth building potential than moderate income in an affordable area.

BENEFITS PACKAGE VALUATION

Benefits packages often represent significant hidden value. Health insurance quality, retirement matching, professional development support, and other benefits can substantially affect the value of your total compensation. Some positions offering moderate salaries provide exceptional benefits that increase total value significantly. Benefits value assessment to review:

- Health insurance premium coverage and quality
- Retirement contribution matching
- Professional development funding
- Tuition reimbursement programs
- Flexible work arrangements
- Paid time off policies
- Wellness programs and additional perks

CAREER PROGRESSION POTENTIAL

Career progression opportunities affect long-term earning potential more than starting compensation. Research the typical advancement paths, skill development opportunities, and industry growth patterns of your chosen career path. This lets you evaluate positions beyond immediate earnings. Some roles offering modest initial compensation provide valuable experience that creates substantial future opportunities.

ECONOMIC STABILITY ASSESSMENT

Market demand patterns influence career value stability. Essential services like healthcare, education, and skilled trades often provide more stable income than cyclical industries. Understanding how economic changes affect different careers enables you to build more resilient career plans.

NETWORK DEVELOPMENT VALUE

Leverage professional network development to create additional career value. Industry connections, professional relationships, and reputation often affect long-term success more than technical skills alone. Building strong professional networks while maintaining technical expertise creates more career opportunities and stability.

Remember: Career economics involves understanding both immediate compensation and long-term value creation potential. Focus on evaluating complete career value rather than just salary numbers. The most successful career decisions often result from understanding how different choices affect total lifetime earning potential rather than maximizing immediate income.

MANAGING CAREER RISK

> **KEY PRINCIPLE**
> Career stability requires understanding and actively managing different types of professional risks rather than assuming job security.

Many professionals focus solely on performing their current role well, missing how industry changes, skill obsolescence, or market shifts could affect their career stability.

My experience with skill evolution highlighted this principle during my consulting recovery period. After years focusing on project management methodologies, I discovered cloud technologies were rapidly transforming the industry. "I almost became obsolete without realizing it," I admitted to Lacey when discussing my career rebuilding strategy.

I dedicated evenings and weekends to learning Azure fundamentals alongside my existing skills in order to open opportunities I hadn't imagined. I was also able to mitigate career decline this way. My proactive approach to skill development transformed a potential career threat into advancement opportunities that eventually led to my Big Tech role.

TECHNOLOGICAL DISRUPTION PLANNING

Technical evolution creates constant career risk in most fields. Healthcare professionals face new treatment protocols and technology, educators encounter changing teaching methods and tools, and trades workers deal with evolving building codes and materials. Understanding how industry changes affect career requirements helps you maintain professional relevance.

ECONOMIC VULNERABILITY ASSESSMENT

Economic shifts affect career stability across industries. Economic downturns, industry consolidation, or changing consumer preferences can transform stable careers into vulnerable positions. Developing skills valued across multiple sectors helps you create career resilience against economic changes.

NETWORK DIVERSIFICATION STRATEGY

Professional network limitations create often-overlooked career risk. Maintaining connections only within current employers or narrow industry segments leaves professionals vulnerable during changes. Building broad professional relationships while maintaining strong industry connections provides better career protection.

INCOME CONCENTRATION MITIGATION

Relying entirely on single employers or income sources creates vulnerability to organizational changes or other disruptions. Developing multiple income streams through skills, certifications, or side work provides better financial stability.

Geographic limitations can create career risk in changing markets. Some regions experience industry decline while others see growth. Understanding how location affects career opportunities helps make better decisions about geographic mobility.

CERTIFICATION AND LICENSING MANAGEMENT

Certification and licensing changes affect many careers significantly. Healthcare, education, financial services, and other regulated fields face evolving requirements. Maintaining awareness of changing professional requirements helps you prevent career interruption.

KNOWLEDGE GAP PREVENTION

All professionals naturally develop knowledge gaps over the course of their careers. When left unaddressed, these gaps can place your career at risk. Regular professional development, continuing education, and skill updates are important for maintaining career relevance. Understanding which knowledge areas will affect your career value helps you prioritize learning efforts.

Remember: Career risk management requires active attention to changing professional landscapes. Focus on developing diverse skills and connections while maintaining core expertise. The most successful career protection practices combine strong current performance with continuous preparation for future changes.

BUILDING PROFESSIONAL VALUE

> **KEY PRINCIPLE**
> Career growth requires continuous value development rather than relying on past achievements or current expertise.

Building professional value resembles cultivating a garden; consistent attention and regular investment produce better results than sporadic effort. Many professionals become complacent after achieving certain positions or expertise levels, missing opportunities to develop new capabilities that could enhance their career value.

My career journey from Marine Corps service through corporate advancement to consulting to Big Tech leadership illustrates effective value building. I realized every position taught skills I could build upon. My military leadership experience created the foundation for project management roles, which developed into broader business skills, eventually enabling consulting opportunities.

These experiences collectively prepared me for technology leadership positions that wouldn't have been possible following a linear path. Success came from seeing each role as a building block rather than just a job, as illustrated in the image below

High-Value Skill Development

Connecting capabilities to compensation

Node Size: ● ● ●
Market Value   Low   Medium   High

Skill Category:
● Core Skills ● Technical ● Business ● Leadership ● Industry

Growth:
☆ High Growth

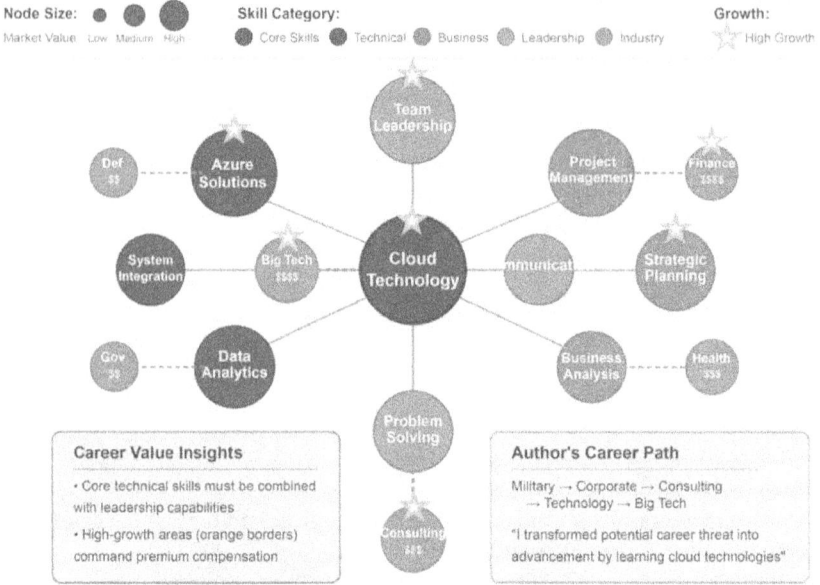

Career Value Insights

• Core technical skills must be combined with leadership capabilities

• High-growth areas (orange borders) command premium compensation

Author's Career Path

Military → Corporate → Consulting → Technology → Big Tech

"I transformed potential career threat into advancement by learning cloud technologies"

STRATEGIC SKILL DEVELOPMENT

Skill development requires strategic focus beyond current job requirements. Understanding which capabilities create future opportunities helps you prioritize learning efforts. Some skills, like project management, communication, and problem-solving, create value across multiple industries and roles.

INDUSTRY EXPERTISE BUILDING

People develop their industry expertise through both formal and informal learning. Professional certifications, hands-on experience, and specialized knowledge all contribute to career value. Understanding how different types of expertise affect career opportunities helps you guide development efforts.

LEADERSHIP CAPABILITY DEVELOPMENT

Leadership capabilities often determine advancement potential. Many professionals excel technically but struggle to develop team leadership skills. Understanding how management responsibilities affect career progression helps you prepare for advancement opportunities.

Communication skills increasingly affect career value across all fields. The ability to explain complex ideas, write effectively, and present

218

professionally creates opportunities beyond technical expertise. Developing strong communication capabilities while maintaining technical skills creates better career options.

PROBLEM-SOLVING FRAMEWORK DEVELOPMENT

Problem-solving abilities create substantial career value. Organizations increasingly value professionals who can identify issues, develop solutions, and implement improvements. Building strong analytical and problem-solving capabilities helps create advancement opportunities.

Relationship building affects career success significantly. Strong professional relationships often lead to opportunities regardless of industry or role. Understanding how to develop and maintain professional connections while delivering strong performance creates better career outcomes.

VISIBILITY ENHANCEMENT APPROACH

Industry visibility contributes to professional value development. Speaking at conferences, writing articles, or leading professional groups creates recognition beyond current employers. Building professional reputation while maintaining strong performance helps create new opportunities.

Remember: Professional value grows through consistent development rather than occasional effort. Focus on building capabilities that create future opportunities while maintaining current expertise. Successful career growth paths often combine strong current performance with continuous capability development.

NAVIGATING CAREER TRANSITIONS

> **KEY PRINCIPLE**
> Successful career transitions require strategic planning and execution rather than reactive job changes.

After experiencing my financial collapse, I transformed a challenging situation into opportunity by analyzing how my experience could create new value. "Instead of just looking for another corporate job, I analyzed how my blend of technical knowledge and business experience could serve state agencies," I shared with my son during his career planning. This strategic approach to career transition created better outcomes than a reactive job search would have. By focusing on the unique value I could provide, I rebuilt my career from ground zero.

FINANCIAL PREPARATION STRATEGY

Financial preparation significantly affects transition success. Career changes often involve temporary income reduction or additional training costs. Understanding financial requirements and building appropriate reserves helps you support successful transitions. Some transitions require substantial preparation time to build necessary resources.

SKILL TRANSFERABILITY ANALYSIS

Conducting a skill transfer analysis helps you identify valuable capabilities you can leverage to further your career. Most professionals develop skills that apply beyond their current roles. Understanding how existing capabilities create value in new positions helps you identify promising transition opportunities. Some skills, like project management or team leadership, transfer effectively across industries.

NETWORK ACTIVATION PROCESS

Professional network activation plays crucial roles in transitions. Industry connections often provide opportunities and insights beyond public job postings. Building and maintaining professional relationships while employed lets you create better transition options when needed. Some valuable opportunities never appear in formal job listings.

TRANSITION TIMING OPTIMIZATION

Timing decisions significantly affect transition success. Market conditions, personal circumstances, and professional opportunities all influence optimal transition timing. Understanding how different factors affect transition potential helps you identify appropriate timing.

EDUCATIONAL INVESTMENT PLANNING

As you plan your next career move, carefully evaluate all applicable education and certification requirements. Some transitions require specific credentials or qualifications. Understanding requirements early helps you create realistic transition timelines and preparation plans.

INDUSTRY KNOWLEDGE ACQUISITION

Industry knowledge development supports successful transitions. Understanding new industry environments, expectations, and opportunities helps you create better outcomes. Reading industry publications, attending events, and building relevant connections helps you prepare for transitions. Some industries require significant learning before successful entry.

PERCEPTION MANAGEMENT STRATEGY

Employer perception management affects how successfully you transition to your next career move. How current and potential employers view career changes influences the opportunities available to you. Understanding how to present transitions positively while maintaining professional relationships is important to create better outcomes. Some transitions benefit from careful communication planning.

Remember: Career transitions succeed through strategic planning rather than reactive changes. Focus on preparing thoroughly while maintaining current performance. The most successful transitions often combine careful preparation with appropriate timing and execution.

CREATING LONG-TERM CAREER SUCCESS

KEY PRINCIPLE
Lasting career success requires aligning professional choices with personal values rather than pursuing advancement for its own sake.

Building long-term career success resembles creating a masterpiece; it requires vision, patience, and consistent effort guided by personal values. Many professionals chase promotions or salary increases without considering how their choices align with their broader life goals, often achieving financial success at the cost of personal fulfillment.

My journey from military service to corporate work illustrates this principle. After fifteen years in progressive technology roles, I realized my passion for solving complex problems could create more satisfaction through multiple avenues. "Success isn't just about earning more," I explained to Lacey during our career planning sessions. "It's about building something that matters while supporting the life you want to live."

My definition of success evolved to combine financial stability with family time, location flexibility, and meaningful work; a balanced approach that has proven more sustainable than my earlier career's single-minded focus on advancement.

WORK-LIFE INTEGRATION FRAMEWORK

Work-life integration affects long-term career sustainability. Roles that conflict with personal values or family needs often prove unsustainable regardless of compensation. Understanding how your career choices may impact your overall life quality helps you create better long-term decisions. Some high-paying positions actually reduce life satisfaction through stress or time demands.

PERSONAL GROWTH OPPORTUNITY CULTIVATION

Personal growth opportunities contribute to lasting satisfaction. Careers that provide continuous learning and development often create more fulfillment than static roles. Understanding how different paths support personal growth helps you maintain long-term engagement. Some careers offer better opportunities for continuous development.

Impact potential can also play a role in long-term career satisfaction. Many professionals find fulfillment through meaningful contribution to others or society. Understanding how different roles create positive impact can help you align career choices with personal values. Some careers offer better opportunities for meaningful contributions.

FINANCIAL SECURITY PLANNING

Financial security needs balance with personal fulfillment. Career choices that create financial stress rarely support long-term success regardless of other benefits. Understanding personal financial requirements helps you evaluate opportunities appropriately. Some career paths require careful financial planning to maintain stability.

RELATIONSHIP QUALITY DEVELOPMENT

Professional relationship quality influences career satisfaction. Working with respected colleagues and mentors often creates more fulfillment than isolated roles. Understanding how different environments affect relationship development helps create better career decisions. Some careers offer better opportunities for meaningful professional relationships.

GEOGRAPHIC FLEXIBILITY UTILIZATION

Geographic flexibility has become increasingly important in expanding career possibilities. Remote work options and changing industry patterns create new opportunity considerations. Understanding how location requirements will affect your career choices helps you create better long-term planning. Some careers offer better geographic flexibility than others.

LEGACY POTENTIAL CREATION

Legacy potential matters for many professionals. Creating lasting positive impact through work often provides deep satisfaction. Understanding how different paths create legacy opportunities helps you align choices with personal values. Some careers offer better opportunities for creating lasting impact.

CHAPTER SUMMARY AND KEY TAKEAWAYS

Through my journey from military service through bankruptcy to career rebuilding, I've learned that successful career financial planning combines understanding market value with personal values. The lessons from both personal experience and helping others show that career success requires active management rather than passive progression.

CORE CAREER PRINCIPLES:

Strategy Over Opportunity: During my recovery, I discovered that strategic career development matters more than chasing immediate opportunities. Success comes from understanding how different choices affect long-term potential rather than focusing solely on current compensation. Many professionals miss valuable opportunities by pursuing short-term gains at the expense of long-term growth.

Development Over Stability: Working with others showed how continuous learning creates better outcomes than maintaining comfortable expertise. A colleague's experience demonstrated this when their ongoing skill development created new opportunities while others in their field faced obsolescence. The most successful professionals constantly expand their capabilities while maintaining core expertise.

Integration Over Isolation: Through both success and failure, I've learned that career decisions affect every aspect of life. Recent experiences helping others navigate transitions showed how aligning career choices with personal values creates better long-term outcomes than pursuing advancement alone.

ACTION PLAN

First 30 Days: Career Assessment
- Review current market value
- Identify skill gaps
- Evaluate growth opportunities

- Analyze risk factors
- Document professional goals

60-Day Implementation
- Begin skill development
- Expand professional network
- Create value-building plan
- Establish learning routines
- Build financial reserves

90-Day Establishment
- Review progress metrics
- Adjust development plans
- Strengthen professional relationships
- Create long-term career vision
- Build transition preparation

FINAL THOUGHTS

Remember: Career success isn't about climbing the ladder fastest; it's about building sustainable growth that supports your life goals. Through bankruptcy and recovery, I learned that effective career management considers both professional advancement and personal fulfillment.

YOUR NEXT STEP

Write down your current total compensation; not just salary, but benefits, equity, retirement contributions, everything. Now ask: Do you actually understand what you're earning? Most professionals can't accurately state their total compensation within 10%.

Your career is likely your largest asset. Manage it like one.

CHAPTER 12
TAXES

LEARNING OBJECTIVES

- Understand how different types of income affect your tax liability
- Master effective tax planning methods for various income sources
- Learn to navigate complex equity compensation taxation
- Develop sustainable tax documentation and compliance systems
- Create long-term tax optimization strategies that evolve with your career

OPENING STORY

The complexity of taxes became clear during my consulting recovery period. After submitting what I thought was a complete tax return, I received an IRS notice about unreported self-employment income and faced significant penalties. This experience taught me that tax management requires understanding not just rates but how different types of income affect your total tax picture. Now, helping others navigate their tax obligations, I see how crucial this knowledge becomes at every income level.

INTRODUCTION

Taxes represent more than just annual payments to the government; they affect every financial decision you make throughout the year. Whether you're earning regular wages, running a small business, or managing investments, understanding how taxes impact your decisions can significantly improve your financial outcomes.

Tax planning resembles playing chess; each move you make has consequences, and thinking several steps ahead improves your results. Many people focus solely on the April 15th deadline, missing optimization opportunities throughout the year that could significantly reduce their tax burden.

Successful tax management combines understanding current obligations with planning for future implications. Like strategic game play, knowing both immediate tax impacts and long-term consequences of financial decisions helps you create better outcomes.

Most importantly, you'll discover that effective tax management isn't about aggressive avoidance; it's about making informed decisions that legally optimize your tax situation. The methods we'll discuss work whether you're managing a modest income or substantial wealth, because they focus on fundamental principles that apply at every level.

UNDERSTANDING TAX FUNDAMENTALS

> **KEY PRINCIPLE**
> Tax management requires understanding how different types of income affect your total tax situation rather than focusing solely on tax rates.

The complexity of taxes became apparent when I received my IRS notice about unreported self-employment income, which carried significant penalties. Despite having CFP education coursework, I had misunderstood how my consulting income needed to be reported differently than my previous W-2 earnings. This experience taught me that tax management requires understanding not just rates but how different types of income affect your total tax picture.

Not All Income Is Created Equal

How Different Income Sources Are Taxed

Income Type	Tax Rate	Key Characteristics
Wages (W-2)	Ordinary Income	10-37% based on tax bracket Fully taxable Subject to payroll taxes
Qualified Dividends	0-20%	Lower rates for long-term investors Held >1 yearSpecial tax treatment
Long-Term Capital Gains	0-20%	Preferential rates Assets held >1 year Can offset gains/losses
Rental Income	Ordinary Income	Offset by expenses Depreciation benefits Investment property rules

TAX BRACKET REALITY

2025 Federal Tax Brackets (Married Filing Jointly):
- 10% on income up to $23,850
- 12% on income from $23,851 to $96,950
- 22% on income from $96,951 to $206,700
- 24% on income from $206,701 to $394,600
- 32% on income from $394,601 to $501,050
- 35% on income from $501,051 to $751,600
- 37% on income over $751,600

*Tax brackets are adjusted annually for inflation. Verify current rates at IRS.gov.

UNDERSTANDING PROGRESSIVE TAXATION

There are many misconceptions about how the progressive tax system works, especially as people increase their earnings over time. Here's how the tax system actually works as you break into higher income brackets:
- Only income within each bracket is taxed at that rate
- Moving into a higher bracket doesn't affect tax on lower amounts
- Effective tax rate is usually lower than highest bracket rate
- Tax planning can help manage bracket positioning
- Different income types may have different bracket treatments

How Tax Brackets Really Work

Understanding Marginal vs. Effective Rates

Tax Rate	For Single Filers	For Married Filing Joint	For Heads of Households
10%	$0 to $11,925	$0 to $23,850	$0 to $17,000
12%	$11,925 to $48,475	$23,850 to $96,950	$17,000 to $64,850
22%	$48,475 to $103,350	$96,950 to $206,700	$64,850 to $103,350
24%	$103,350 to $197,300	$206,700 to $394,600	$103,350 to $197,300
32%	$197,300 to $250,525	$394,600 to $501,050	$197,300 to $250,500
35%	$250,525 to $626,350	$501,050 to $751,600	$250,500 to $626,350
37%	$626,350 or more	$751,600 or more	$626,350 or more

Sample Calculation for $75,000 Income, Single Filer:
10% on first $11,925 = $1,192 12% on next $36,550 = $4,386 22% on remaining $26,525 = $5,835
Total Tax: $11,413 (Effective Rate: 15.2%)

Tax Bracket Calculation Example:

Let's examine how marginal tax brackets work for a married couple filing jointly with $125,000 in taxable income in 2025:

- First $23,850 taxed at 10% = $2,385
- Next $73,100 ($23,851 to $96,950) taxed at 12% = $8,772
- Final $28,050 ($96,951 to $125,000) taxed at 22% = $6,171

Total federal income tax: $17,328

Effective tax rate: 13.9% ($17,328 ÷ $125,000)

This couple's marginal tax rate is 22% (their highest bracket), but they pay only 13.9% of their total income in federal income tax.

Now, consider how an additional $10,000 in income affects their taxes:

- Additional $10,000 taxed at 22% = $2,200
- New total federal income tax: $19,528
- New effective tax rate: 14.4% ($19,528 ÷ $135,000)

This demonstrates why understanding your marginal tax bracket is crucial for tax-efficient decision making.

FICA TAXES

Social Security:
- 6.2% employee contribution
- 6.2% employer contribution
- Income cap ($176,100 for 2025)
- Self-employed pay both portions

Medicare:
- 1.45% employee contribution
- 1.45% employer contribution
- No income cap
- Additional 0.9% on income over $200,000 (single) or $250,000 (married)

ALTERNATIVE MINIMUM TAX (AMT)

Key AMT Considerations:
- Parallel tax system with different calculations
- Affects certain high-income earners
- Common triggers include:
  - Large, itemized deductions
  - Incentive stock options
  - Private activity bond interest
  - Certain tax credits

Remember: Understanding income types and their tax treatment creates the foundation for effective tax management. Focus on learning how different income sources affect your total tax picture. The most successful tax planning often starts with a clear understanding of income classification and its implications.

TAX PLANNING STRATEGIES

KEY PRINCIPLE

Effective tax planning requires year-round attention and strategic decisions rather than year-end reactions.

Tax planning took on new urgency during my transition from bankruptcy to consulting work. Previously, I had only thought about taxes during filing season, but self-employment income demanded year-round attention. "I used to get surprised by my tax bill every April," I admitted to Lacey early in our relationship. "Learning to plan ahead with estimated quarterly payments and tracking my business expenses transformed tax season from stressful to manageable."

Setting aside a percentage of each client payment for taxes and maintaining meticulous records of deductible expenses created both tax savings and peace of mind during this critical rebuilding period.

Tax Saving Opportunities

Finding Strategies for Your Income Level

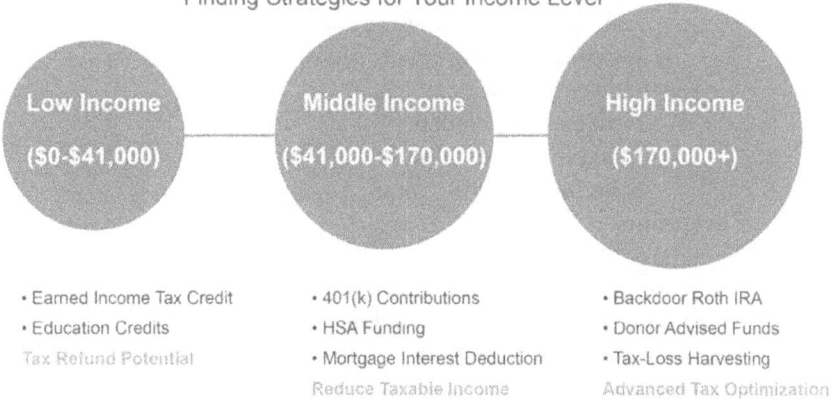

Low Income ($0-$41,000)	Middle Income ($41,000-$170,000)	High Income ($170,000+)
• Earned Income Tax Credit	• 401(k) Contributions	• Backdoor Roth IRA
• Education Credits	• HSA Funding	• Donor Advised Funds
Tax Refund Potential	• Mortgage Interest Deduction	• Tax-Loss Harvesting
	Reduce Taxable Income	Advanced Tax Optimization

Key Insights:
• Tax strategies evolve with income
• Proactive planning reduces tax burden
• Consult tax professional for personalized advice

INCOME TIMING STRATEGIES

Retirement Contributions:
- Traditional 401(k) or IRA reduces current taxable income
- Contribution limits for 2025:
    - 401(k): $23,500 ($7,500 catch-up over 50)
    - IRA: $7,000 ($1,000 catch-up over 50)
    - SEP IRA: Up to 25% of compensation
    - SIMPLE IRA: $16,000 ($3,500 catch-up over 50)

Deduction Bunching:
- Concentrate deductible expenses in alternating years
- Examples include:
    - Medical expenses
    - Charitable contributions
    - Property taxes
    - Professional development costs

TAX CREDIT OPTIMIZATION

Common Tax Credits:
- Child Tax Credit: Up to $2,000 per qualifying child
- Child Care Credit: Up to $3,000 (one child) or $6,000 (two or more)
- Education Credits:
    - American Opportunity Credit: Up to $2,500
    - Lifetime Learning Credit: Up to $2,000
- Energy Efficiency Credits:
    - Home improvements
    - Electric vehicles
    - Solar installations

Credit Phase-outs:
- Income limits vary by credit
- Phase-out ranges affect credit amount
- Planning can help maximize eligibility
- Documentation requirements vary
- Some credits are refundable

BUSINESS OWNER STRATEGIES

Self-Employed Considerations:
- Home office deduction
- Vehicle expenses
- Equipment depreciation
- Healthcare premium deduction

- Retirement plan options

Quarterly Estimated Payments:
- Due dates: April 15, June 15, September 15, January 15
- Calculate your quarterly estimated payment based on:
  - Prior year tax liability
  - Current year projected income
  - Safe harbor requirements
- Penalties apply for underpayment

INVESTMENT TAX MANAGEMENT

Investment Strategies:
- Tax-loss harvesting
- Long-term vs. short-term gains
- Qualified dividend income
- Municipal bond interest
- Investment expense tracking

Asset Location:
- Tax-deferred accounts (Traditional IRA/401(k))
- Tax-free accounts (Roth IRA/401(k))
- Taxable accounts
- Strategic asset placement
- Withdrawal planning

Remember: Tax planning success comes from consistent attention and strategic decisions throughout the year. Focus on understanding how different choices affect your tax situation before making financial decisions. Effective tax management combines regular planning with informed decision-making.

ADVANCED TAX PLANNING

KEY PRINCIPLE
Complex financial situations require sophisticated tax planning that integrates multiple strategies and long-term considerations.

Advanced tax planning resembles playing three-dimensional chess; moves affect multiple levels simultaneously, and long-term strategy becomes crucial. Many high-income earners focus on single strategies, missing opportunities for integrated approaches that could provide better overall results.

Tax planning became considerably more complex when I joined Big Tech with a compensation package heavily weighted toward RSUs. Lacey and I quickly realized that our previous approaches to tax management would need significant refinement. "This first vesting event is going to create a major tax bill," I explained one evening, showing Lacey the projected RSU schedule. "The withholding will cover some, but not all of what we'll owe."

Rather than seeing this as a problem, we created what we now call our "tax timeline"; a year-long calendar mapping income events, estimated tax payments, and planning opportunities that has transformed our approach to tax management.

Strategic Asset Location

Placing Investments for Tax Efficiency

Tax-Deferred Accounts	Roth Accounts	Taxable Accounts
• Bonds	• Growth Stocks	• Municipal Bonds
• High-Yield Investments	• International Stocks	• Index Funds
• Real Estate Investment Trusts	• Emerging Market Funds	• Low-Turnover ETFs
Tax-Deferred Growth	Tax-Free Growth	Tax-Efficient Investments

Key Strategies:
• Match investment tax efficiency
• Optimize for long-term growth
• Regularly rebalance

RETIREMENT ACCOUNT OPTIMIZATION

Traditional vs. Roth Strategy:
- Current vs. future tax rates
- Required Minimum Distributions (RMDs)
- Estate planning implications
- Social Security taxation
- Medicare premium impacts

Advanced Contribution Strategies:
- Backdoor Roth IRA
- Mega Backdoor Roth 401(k)
- After-tax 401(k) conversions
- SIMPLE/SEP IRA coordination
- Multiple employer plan options

BUSINESS STRUCTURE PLANNING

Entity Selection Implications:
- Sole Proprietorship
  - Schedule C reporting
  - Self-employment tax exposure

- o Personal liability risk
- S-Corporation
  - o Reasonable salary requirements
  - o Pass-through taxation
  - o Payroll tax planning
- C-Corporation
  - o Double taxation consideration
  - o Fringe benefit opportunities
  - o Accumulated earnings issues

REAL ESTATE TAX STRATEGIES

Property Investment Planning:
- Cost segregation studies
- 1031 exchange opportunities
- Passive activity rules
- Qualified Business Income deduction
- Depreciation recapture planning

Rental Property Considerations:
- Material participation tests
- Real estate professional status
- Grouping elections
- Loss limitation rules
- Vacation home rules

ESTATE TAX INTEGRATION

Lifetime Gift Planning:
- Annual exclusion gifts ($17,000 for 2024)
- Lifetime exemption usage
- Basis step-up considerations
- Generation-skipping planning
- Family limited partnerships

Charitable Planning Integration:
- Qualified Charitable Distributions
- Donor Advised Funds
- Charitable Remainder Trusts
- Private Foundation options
- Appreciated asset donations

EQUITY COMPENSATION TAX STRATEGIES

With an increasingly complicated compensation package, I needed to change my approach to tax management. Rather than seeing this as a problem, Lacey approached this issue as a strategic opportunity. With her project management background, she created what we now call our "tax timeline"; a year-long calendar that maps income events, estimated tax payments, and planning opportunities.

"If we know exactly when each RSU vesting will happen," she reasoned, "we can prepare for the tax impacts months in advance." Our approach evolved to include quarterly tax planning sessions where we:
1. Projected total income including base salary and vesting equity
2. Calculated estimated tax liability using current-year tax brackets
3. Compared automatic withholdings to projected taxes
4. Created a dedicated "tax reserve" account for any shortfall
5. Identified timing opportunities for deductions and credits

This proactive approach transformed tax management from a reactive scramble each April into a strategic component of our overall financial planning. Rather than seeing taxes as something that happens to us, we began viewing tax management as an ongoing process integrated with investment, career, and life decisions.

One particularly effective strategy emerged from these discussions: timing our charitable giving to maximize tax efficiency. By concentrating donations in years with substantial RSU vesting, we offset some of the income spike while supporting causes important to us.

"What if we create a donor-advised fund contribution during high-income years?" Lacey suggested during one planning session. "We could take the deduction when we need it most while spreading the actual charitable giving over time."

This approach, which we implemented successfully during a particularly large vesting event, demonstrated how tax planning had evolved from simple compliance into strategic wealth management.

Previously, I viewed taxes as an afterthought; something to address once a year with minimal planning. Now, tax management is fully integrated into our financial system, with regular reviews and strategic decisions that account for both immediate impacts and long-term optimization.

RSU MANAGEMENT FRAMEWORK

RSUs (Restricted Stock Units) create unique tax challenges requiring specific strategies:
Vesting Preparation:
- Set calendar reminders 30 days before each vesting date

- Establish automatic withholding elections at your company's highest rate (typically 37% federal + applicable state taxes)
- Create a dedicated "tax reserve" account holding 10-15% of your RSU value to cover potential withholding shortfalls

Practical Example:

For a $100,000 RSU vest with automatic withholding of 37% federal and 10% state taxes:

- $47,000 automatically withheld
- Actual tax liability may reach $52,000-$55,000 depending on your total income
- Your tax reserve should hold $5,000-$8,000 to cover this gap

Immediate Post-Vest Decisions:

1. Hold vs. Sell Analysis
   - If your company stock already exceeds 10% of your portfolio, consider selling immediately
   - If selling, earmark proceeds specifically (e.g., 40% for taxes, 40% for diversified investments, 20% for goals)
2. Tax Planning Timeline
   - First 2 weeks post-vest: Verify withholding amounts in your payroll system
   - Within 30 days: Make estimated tax payments if withholding appears insufficient
   - Quarterly: Review YTD vesting and tax projections with your accountant

The RSU Tax Journey

Understanding Equity Compensation Taxation

RSU Grant	Vesting Date	Share Sale
No Immediate Tax	Taxed as Ordinary Income	Capital Gains/Loss
Zero Tax Impact	Full Fair Market Value Taxed	Additional Tax Consideration

Tax Calculation Example

- RSU Grant: 1,000 shares
- Fair Market Value: $150/share
- Ordinary Income at Vesting: $150,000

- Holding Period
- Short-term: Ordinary Income Rates
- Long-term: Preferential Capital Gains Rates

STOCK OPTIONS STRATEGY

For Non-Qualified Stock Options (NSOs):
- Exercise timing impacts both ordinary income (spread between strike price and FMV) and potential capital gains
- Specific calculation example:
    - 1,000 options with $50 strike price when stock is $150
    - Exercise creates $100,000 in ordinary income ($100 spread × 1,000 shares)
    - At 37% federal + 10% state: Approximately $47,000 in taxes due

For Incentive Stock Options (ISOs):
- Exercise-and-hold strategies may trigger Alternative Minimum Tax (AMT)
- AMT calculation example:
    - 1,000 ISOs with $50 strike price when stock is $150
    - Exercise creates $100,000 AMT income adjustment
    - For someone with $200,000 regular income, this could generate ~$28,000 in additional AMT liability

Advanced Strategy: Exercise laddering
- Instead of exercising all options at once, create a systematic schedule
- Example ladder for 10,000 options expiring in 2030:
    - 2025: Exercise 2,000 options
    - 2026: Exercise 2,000 options
    - 2027: Exercise 2,000 options
    - 2028: Exercise 2,000 options
    - 2029: Exercise remaining 2,000 options
- This approach spreads tax impact while reducing single-year concentration risk

Remember: Advanced tax planning requires coordinating multiple strategies while considering long-term implications. Focus on understanding how different approaches interact and affect overall tax efficiency. The most successful advanced planning often combines multiple strategies tailored to specific situations.

MANAGING TAX DOCUMENTATION AND COMPLIANCE

KEY PRINCIPLE
Effective tax management requires systematic documentation and organization rather than last-minute gathering of information.

Many people struggle with tax season not because of complex calculations, but because of poor record-keeping throughout the year.

The importance of tax documentation became painfully evident during my consulting years. After my first full year of independent work, I spent weeks trying to reconstruct business expenses from scattered receipts and incomplete records. "Tax season used to mean days of stress and searching for documentation," I explained to a fellow consultant. "Creating a simple digital system for tracking income and expenses transformed tax preparation from a dreaded project into a straightforward process."

This systematic approach not only reduced my stress but identified additional legitimate deductions I would have otherwise missed, creating substantial tax savings during a period when every dollar mattered.

UNDERSTANDING WHAT MATTERS

Effective documentation starts with understanding what records matter most. Income documentation extends beyond just W-2s and 1099s; bank interest statements, investment account reports, and records of any money-making activities all affect tax obligations. Business owners need particularly detailed records of both income and expenses, while employees should track job-related expenses even if they don't currently qualify for deductions.

Digital tools have transformed tax documentation management. Cloud storage solutions provide secure, accessible locations for storing receipts and important documents. Smartphone apps can categorize expenses in real-time, while accounting software generates reports needed for tax preparation. However, technology works best when backed by consistent documentation habits.

Regular review processes help you maintain documentation accuracy. Conduct a monthly review of income and expenses to identify missing documentation while your memories for that month remain fresh. Supplement this with quarterly reviews to analyze tax implications of your financial decisions for that time period, and adjust strategies as needed. Round this out with annual reviews where you should ensure documentation completeness before tax preparation begins.

Your Tax Organization System

Building audit-proof documentation

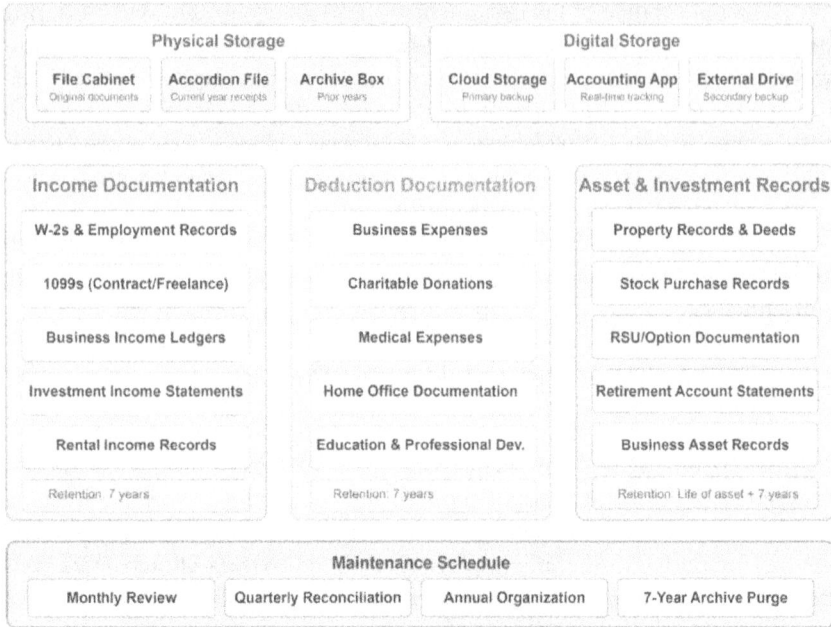

Physical Storage			Digital Storage		
File Cabinet Original documents	**Accordion File** Current year receipts	**Archive Box** Prior years	**Cloud Storage** Primary backup	**Accounting App** Real-time tracking	**External Drive** Secondary backup

Income Documentation	Deduction Documentation	Asset & Investment Records
W-2s & Employment Records	Business Expenses	Property Records & Deeds
1099s (Contract/Freelance)	Charitable Donations	Stock Purchase Records
Business Income Ledgers	Medical Expenses	RSU/Option Documentation
Investment Income Statements	Home Office Documentation	Retirement Account Statements
Rental Income Records	Education & Professional Dev.	Business Asset Records
Retention: 7 years	Retention: 7 years	Retention: Life of asset + 7 years

Maintenance Schedule			
Monthly Review	Quarterly Reconciliation	Annual Organization	7-Year Archive Purge

Professional document retention requirements vary by type:
- Tax returns and supporting documents: 7 years
- Property records: Throughout ownership plus 7 years
- Business asset records: Life of asset plus 7 years
- Employment records: 4 years minimum
- Investment purchase records: Until sale plus 7 years

Remember: Documentation success comes from consistent habits rather than intense effort at tax time. Focus on developing sustainable systems that work with your daily routine. The most effective tax documentation often combines simple, regular practices with appropriate support from technology and digital tools.

LONG-TERM TAX STRATEGY DEVELOPMENT

KEY PRINCIPLE
Sustainable tax management requires adapting strategies as your financial situation evolves rather than maintaining fixed approaches.

Creating long-term tax strategy resembles planning a cross-country journey; you need a clear destination, understanding of potential routes, and flexibility to adjust for changing conditions. Many people maintain the same tax approach year after year, missing opportunities to optimize their strategy as their financial situation changes.

My journey from corporate employee to consultant to Big Tech leader demonstrated how tax strategies must evolve with changing circumstances. As my income grew and became more complex; particularly with the addition of RSUs and rental property income; my tax strategy needed to evolve. "I realized that what worked when I had a simple W-2 wouldn't serve me well with multiple income streams," I explained during a financial workshop. Learning to think strategically about taxes helped me make better business, investment, and timing decisions throughout the year.

TAX BRACKET MANAGEMENT

Tax bracket management becomes increasingly important as income grows. Rather than simply trying to minimize current year taxes, successful long-term planning often involves strategic decisions about when to recognize income and claim deductions. Some higher-income years might benefit from maximum retirement contributions, while lower-income years present opportunities for Roth conversions or capital gains harvesting.

LIFE TRANSITIONS

Life transitions create both challenges and opportunities for tax planning. Marriage, divorce, career changes, and retirement all affect tax situations significantly. Understanding how these changes impact taxes helps make better financial decisions during transitions. For example, timing certain financial moves before or after marriage can create substantially different tax outcomes.

RETIREMENT PLANNING

Retirement planning requires particularly careful tax consideration. Traditional retirement accounts defer taxes but create future obligations, while Roth accounts offer tax-free growth but require after-tax contributions. Balancing these options while considering future tax rates, Required Minimum Distributions, and estate planning goals often determines long-term financial success.

Investment decisions increasingly affect your tax outcomes as wealth grows. Deciding which investments belong in tax-deferred, tax-free, or taxable accounts can significantly impact your after-tax returns. Understanding how different investment choices affect tax liability helps you create more efficient portfolios.

Estate planning adds another layer to tax strategy. Current estate tax exemptions may change, making flexibility crucial in long-term planning. Regular review of estate plans ensures they remain aligned with both tax law and personal goals. Sometimes, accelerating wealth transfer or charitable giving can create better long-term tax outcomes.

TAX LAW CHANGES

Legislative changes require strategy adaptation. Tax laws change regularly, creating both challenges and opportunities. Maintaining awareness of potential changes while building flexible strategies helps you manage legislative uncertainty. Working with tax professionals to understand the implications of new tax laws is a good way to ensure you're on top of all relevant changes.

Remember: Long-term tax strategy requires regular review and adjustment rather than set-and-forget approaches. Focus on building flexible strategies that can adapt to changing circumstances while maintaining core tax efficiency principles. Successful tax planning often combines clear long-term objectives with tactical flexibility to address changing conditions.

CHAPTER SUMMARY AND KEY TAKEAWAYS

Through my journey, I've learned that effective tax management combines technical knowledge with practical application. The lessons from both personal experience and helping others show that successful tax planning requires active management rather than annual reaction.

CORE TAX MANAGEMENT PRINCIPLES:

Planning Over Reaction: During my recovery years, I discovered that proactive tax planning matters more than last-minute tax preparation. One colleague's experience reinforced this; by planning throughout the year, she reduced her tax burden significantly compared to her previous reactive approach. Understanding how financial decisions affect taxes before making them creates better outcomes than trying to optimize at tax time.

Integration Over Isolation: Working with others showed how coordinating different tax strategies creates better results than focusing on single approaches. A small business owner's experience demonstrated this when combining retirement planning, business structure, and investment strategies reduced his total tax burden more effectively than any single strategy could achieve.

Documentation Over Memory: Through both success and failure, I've learned that systematic record-keeping matters more than trying to reconstruct information at tax time. Recent experiences helping others through audits showed how good documentation protects against unnecessary tax problems while creating peace of mind.

ACTION PLAN

First 30 Days: Tax Assessment
- Review your current tax situation
- Organize all existing documentation
- Identify planning opportunities
- Create your tax documentation system
- Schedule regular reviews

60-Day Implementation
- Begin strategic tax planning
- Implement documentation habits
- Establish professional relationships
- Create a tax calendar
- Build emergency reserves

90-Day Establishment
- Review and adjust strategies
- Strengthen your documentation systems
- Plan for future changes
- Create long-term tax vision
- Build flexibility for uncertainty

FINAL THOUGHTS

Remember: Tax management success isn't about finding perfect loopholes; it's about making informed decisions that legally optimize your tax situation. Through bankruptcy and recovery, I learned that effective tax planning combines understanding fundamentals with strategic decision-making.

YOUR NEXT STEP

Find last year's tax return. Look at your effective tax rate; the percentage you actually paid after all deductions and credits. Is it higher or lower than you expected? Understanding your real tax burden is the first step toward optimizing it.

Tax planning isn't about tricks or loopholes. It's about making informed decisions throughout the year so April doesn't bring surprises.

MOVING FORWARD

You've built your foundation, protected it, grown it, and optimized your income. For many readers, this is enough; and that's perfectly valid. Financial security and independence are worthy goals in themselves.

But money doesn't exist in isolation. It flows through relationships, shapes family dynamics, and ultimately outlives us. The final section of this manual addresses what happens when personal finance becomes interpersonal finance.

Section V isn't just for parents or those planning estates. Whether you're navigating money conversations with a partner, wondering how to help the next generation avoid your mistakes, or thinking about what you'll leave behind, these chapters offer frameworks for the human side of financial life. After all, the ultimate purpose of financial success isn't the money itself; it's what that security enables for the people we love.

SECTION V
FAMILY FINANCES

Money touches every relationship in your life. It shapes how you connect with partners, what you teach children, and what you leave behind. This section addresses the human side of finance; the part that matters most but gets discussed least.

These chapters apply whether you're single or partnered, childless or raising a family, just starting out or planning what comes next. Money and relationships intersect for everyone.

Chapter 13: Money in Relationships explores building financial partnerships. Every couple navigates money differently. This chapter offers frameworks for finding your approach; one that respects both individual autonomy and shared goals.

Chapter 14: Financial Literacy for Families addresses how financial wisdom passes between generations. Children learn about money whether we teach them intentionally or not. This chapter helps you teach intentionally.

Chapter 15: Estate Planning covers protecting and transferring your legacy. The over ten-year age difference between Lacey and me adds complexity to our estate planning, requiring both immediate protection and long-term strategy. From basic protection during recovery to managing substantial assets now, understanding estate planning helps secure your family's future.

CHAPTER 13
MONEY IN RELATIONSHIPS

LEARNING OBJECTIVES

- Master effective money conversations in relationships
- Build sustainable financial partnerships that respect both parties
- Navigate financial power dynamics with grace and understanding
- Create systems that support both shared goals and individual growth
- Develop lasting financial harmony through life's changes

OPENING STORY

The hardest money conversation of my life wasn't with a bankruptcy trustee or with Big Tech leadership during negotiations; it happened over coffee on my third date with Lacey. At forty, I had rebuilt my finances from bankruptcy through consulting to a growing career. I knew this early conversation would shape not just a potential relationship, but how we'd approach money together. Her response to my financial history; "I see someone who's learned from mistakes, not someone defined by them"; taught me that financial partnership isn't about perfect records but about honesty and growth together.

INTRODUCTION

Money conversations shape relationships in profound and lasting ways. Whether discussing who pays for dinner on a first date or planning retirement together after decades of marriage, how couples approach financial discussions often determines relationship satisfaction and longevity.

Financial partnership resembles dancing; requiring coordination, communication, and adaptability from both partners. Many couples struggle with money discussions, creating patterns of misunderstanding or conflict that affect all aspects of their relationship.

The most successful approach to money in relationships combines practical systems with emotional intelligence. Like any important relationship skill, financial partnership requires both technical knowledge and interpersonal awareness.

UNDERSTANDING FINANCIAL PARTNERSHIPS

KEY PRINCIPLE
Successful financial partnerships require open communication about both past and present money situations rather than avoiding difficult conversations.

Financial partnership begins with honest communication about money histories, values, and habits. Many couples avoid these conversations, fearing judgment or conflict, only to discover that unaddressed financial differences eventually create deeper relationship problems.

Our own financial partnership began with unusual transparency. After my third-date confession about bankruptcy, Lacey and I quickly moved to deeper financial discussions. One evening over takeout Indian food in my modest apartment, we compared our complete financial pictures; not just numbers, but our attitudes toward money.

"I've always been careful with money," Lacey explained, sorting through her meticulously categorized expense spreadsheet. "My parents taught me to save first, then spend what's left." Her natural financial prudence contrasted with my more complex money history. Yet instead of judging my past financial collapse, she was curious about the systems I'd built during recovery. "These tracking methods you developed after bankruptcy are actually more detailed than mine," she observed, examining my rebuilding strategy. "I think we can learn from each other."

This early conversation revealed our different financial personalities; Lacey's innate conservatism balanced against my hard-won discipline after experiencing both extremes. Understanding these differences helped us build a partnership that leveraged both perspectives rather than forcing either of us to abandon our natural approach.

RECOGNIZING DIFFERENT MONEY STYLES

Partners typically bring different financial perspectives shaped by family background, personal experiences, and natural tendencies. Understanding these differences helps create mutual respect rather than judgment about approaches to money. Financial personalities often reflect different values and priorities:
- Savers prioritize security and future planning
- Spenders value experiences and current enjoyment

- Planners need structure and predictability
- Improvisers prefer flexibility and spontaneity
- Investors focus on growth and opportunity
- Protectors emphasize safety and risk management

CREATING SHARED MONEY VALUES

Building financial partnership requires identifying shared values while respecting individual differences. This foundation helps create systems that support both partners' needs while working toward common goals.

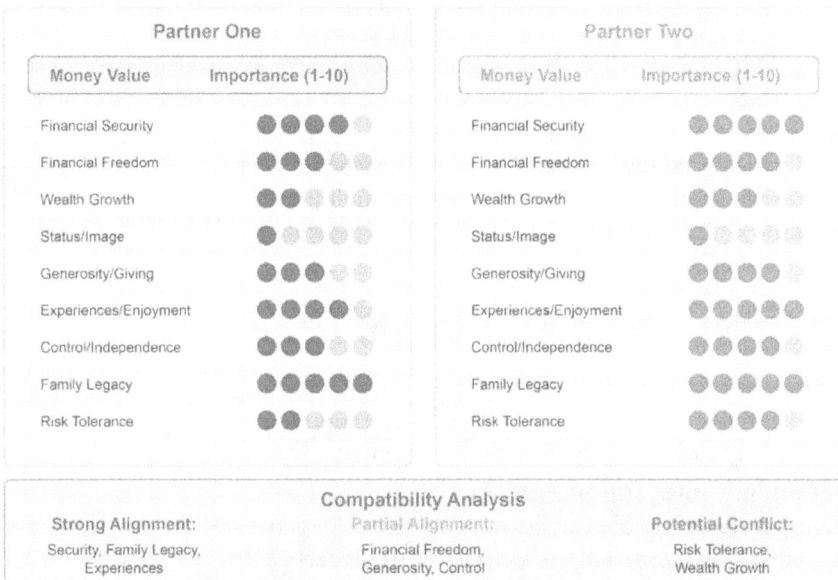

Partner One		Partner Two	
Money Value	Importance (1-10)	Money Value	Importance (1-10)
Financial Security	●●●●	Financial Security	●●●●●
Financial Freedom	●●●	Financial Freedom	●●●●
Wealth Growth	●●●	Wealth Growth	●●●
Status/Image	●	Status/Image	●
Generosity/Giving	●●●	Generosity/Giving	●●●
Experiences/Enjoyment	●●●●	Experiences/Enjoyment	●●●●●
Control/Independence	●●●●	Control/Independence	●●●●
Family Legacy	●●●●●	Family Legacy	●●●●●
Risk Tolerance	●●	Risk Tolerance	●●●●

Compatibility Analysis		
Strong Alignment:	Partial Alignment:	Potential Conflict:
Security, Family Legacy, Experiences	Financial Freedom, Generosity, Control	Risk Tolerance, Wealth Growth

NAVIGATING FINANCIAL DIFFERENCES

Even the strongest financial partnerships encounter occasional disagreements. Lacey and I discovered this when considering whether to purchase a second investment property in 2022.

I felt eager to expand our real estate portfolio, seeing clear potential in the Nashville market. "The numbers make sense, and we have the capital available," I argued, presenting detailed projections during our monthly financial review.

Lacey, however, felt more cautious. "I agree the opportunity looks good," she acknowledged, "but I'm concerned about concentrating too much of our net worth in real estate, especially while the market seems volatile." Rather than allowing this difference to create conflict, we developed a structured approach to financial disagreements:

1. We committed to a 48-hour reflection period before any major decision
2. Each of us wrote out our perspective with supporting data
3. We identified precisely where our views diverged
4. We researched external perspectives on the specific point of disagreement
5. We set a specific time to revisit the decision with fresh insights

This process helped us recognize that our disagreement wasn't about the property itself but about portfolio diversification principles. By focusing on this specific concern rather than the broader decision, we found a compromise; proceeding with the investment but simultaneously increasing our index fund investments to maintain overall diversification.

"What I appreciate about our approach," Lacey noted afterward, "is that we transformed a potential argument into a better investment strategy than either of us would have created alone."

Financial disagreements, when approached constructively, often lead to more robust decisions that incorporate multiple perspectives. The key is creating a structured process that respects both viewpoints while focusing on shared long-term goals.

UNDERSTANDING PARTNERSHIP MODELS

Different relationship structures require different financial approaches. The models range from complete financial integration to mostly separate finances, with many variations between these extremes.

Complete Integration Approach

Some couples combine all finances into joint accounts and make all decisions together. This approach works well when partners share similar money values and spending habits, offering simplicity and unity but potentially reducing individual financial identity.

Independent Partnership Model

Other couples maintain largely separate finances while sharing key expenses. This approach preserves individual financial autonomy but requires more complex coordination for shared goals and responsibilities.

Hybrid Systems

Most successful couples develop personalized systems combining elements of both approaches:

- Joint accounts for shared expenses
- Individual accounts for personal spending
- Shared decision-making for major financial choices
- Clear agreements about financial responsibilities
- Regular communication about money matters

Remember: Financial partnership success requires open communication and mutual respect rather than finding the "perfect" system. Focus on understanding both partners' needs while developing approaches that support your specific relationship dynamics.

EXPENSE SHARING APPROACHES

> **KEY PRINCIPLE**
> Effective expense sharing requires finding methods that feel fair to both partners rather than following standard formulas or one-size-fits-all advice.

Expense sharing creates a foundation for financial partnership, yet "fair" distribution looks different for each relationship. Many couples adopt standard approaches without considering their specific circumstances, creating imbalance or resentment.

When Lacey and I decided to move in together in 2016, we faced the expense-sharing question directly. With my consulting income at approximately $150,000 and Lacey's project management salary around $75,000, we had a significant income disparity to navigate.

"I want to contribute my fair share," Lacey insisted during our planning discussion. "But if we split everything 50/50, I'd have almost nothing left for savings while you'd have substantial discretionary income."

Together, we calculated what proportional sharing would look like:
- My income represented 67% of our combined earnings
- Lacey's income represented 33%

"What if we split our major expenses in that same ratio?" I suggested. "You'd contribute 33% toward housing and shared expenses, I'd cover 67%." This approach immediately felt more equitable to both of us. For our $1,800 apartment, I would pay $1,200 while Lacey contributed $600. The arrangement allowed each of us to maintain similar savings rates relative to our incomes while preventing either person from feeling financially strained.

"This feels balanced," Lacey agreed. "I'm not being subsidized, just contributing proportionally to what I earn." This decision proved crucial to building financial harmony. Rather than creating resentment or dependency, our proportional approach respected both our income differences and our shared commitment to building wealth together.

Financial Partnership Styles

Finding the right approach for your relationship

Complete Integration

$ — Joint — $

Pros:	Cons:
• Maximum transparency	• Limited financial autonomy
• Simplified management	• Requires complete trust
• Complete financial unity	• Potential for control issues

Best for: Couples with similar money values, strong trust, and similar earnings or traditional arrangements

Independent Partnership

$ ---- Bills ---- $

Mine   Yours

Pros:	Cons:
• Maximum individual autonomy	• Less unified financial vision
• Clear spending boundaries	• More complex management
• Good for different money styles	• Potential fairness issues

Best for: Couples who value financial independence

Hybrid System (Three-Account)

$ — Joint Account — $

Mine   Household   Savings   Yours

Pros:	Cons:	Best for:
• Balances autonomy and unity	• Requires more setup	Most modern couples, especially those with
• Proportional contributions	• Regular rebalancing needed	different incomes, money styles, or who want
• Personal spending freedom	• May evolve as income changes	balanced financial partnership

UNDERSTANDING DIFFERENT SHARING METHODS

Equal Splitting (50/50)

The simplest approach divides all expenses equally between partners. This works well when incomes and financial obligations are similar but can create hardship when significant income disparities exist.

Proportional Sharing (Income-Based)

This method calculates expense contributions based on income percentages. If one partner earns 60% of combined income, they contribute 60% toward shared expenses. This approach often creates more equitable financial partnership when incomes differ substantially.

TAILORED HYBRID APPROACHES

Many couples develop customized systems that combine different sharing methods:

Expense Category Allocation

Some couples divide financial responsibilities by category rather than percentage:

- Higher earner covers housing costs
- Lower earner handles utilities and groceries
- Joint contribution to savings goals
- Individual responsibility for personal expenses

- Shared approach to entertainment and vacations

Threshold Method

This approach combines equal and proportional sharing:

- Basic expenses split 50/50
- Premium choices paid by partner preferring upgrade
- Additional expenses shared proportionally

IMPLEMENTATION STRATEGIES

Effective expense sharing depends on mutual understanding of actual costs and contributions. Regular financial reviews help maintain clarity while preventing misunderstandings about who contributes what. Successful expense sharing requires clear systems:

Tracking Technologies

Modern financial apps can simplify expense sharing:

- Split expense tracking applications
- Joint account monitoring tools
- Shared budgeting platforms
- Expense notification systems
- Payment request features

Adjusting Through Life Changes

Effective expense sharing evolves with changing circumstances:

- Income changes
- Career transitions
- Family additions
- Housing changes
- Financial goal shifts

Remember: Expense sharing success requires finding approaches that respect both partners' financial realities. Focus on creating systems that feel fair to both people rather than following generic formulas. The most effective expense sharing often combines multiple approaches tailored to your specific relationship.

ACCOUNT MANAGEMENT STRATEGIES

KEY PRINCIPLE

The best account systems are ones that both partners feel comfortable with rather than following prescribed financial advice that doesn't match your relationship.

Account structure provides the practical framework for financial partnership. Many couples adopt traditional approaches without considering whether these systems actually support their relationship's unique dynamics and needs.

The question of how to structure our accounts emerged as Lacey and I prepared for marriage. After trying several approaches during our first year living together, we discovered the "three-account system" that worked perfectly for our relationship.

"I value having some financial independence," Lacey explained during a Sunday morning financial check-in at our favorite coffee shop. "But I also want us to build together toward shared goals."

I understood her perspective completely. After rebuilding my finances from scratch following bankruptcy, maintaining some personal financial autonomy felt important to me as well. We established three primary accounts:

1. A joint household account for rent, utilities, groceries, and shared expenses
2. A joint savings account for emergency funds and vacation savings.
3. Individual accounts for personal spending, gifts, and professional expenses

Our contributions followed our proportional income ratio; I deposited 67% of the joint account requirements while Lacey contributed 33%. We each kept the remainder of our incomes in our personal accounts.

"What I love about this system," Lacey noted a few months after implementation, "is that I never have to ask permission to buy something for myself, but I also feel completely invested in our shared future."

THE THREE-ACCOUNT FOUNDATION

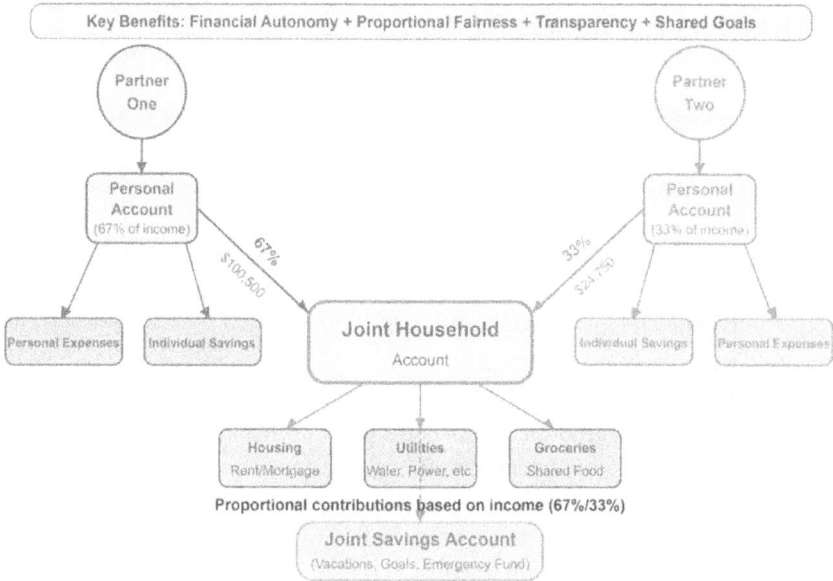

Key Benefits: Financial Autonomy + Proportional Fairness + Transparency + Shared Goals

Partner One — Personal Account (67% of income)

Partner Two — Personal Account (33% of income)

Personal Expenses | Individual Savings

Joint Household Account

67% $100,500 — 33% $24,750

Individual Savings | Personal Expenses

Housing Rent/Mortgage | Utilities Water, Power, etc | Groceries Shared Food

Proportional contributions based on income (67%/33%)

Joint Savings Account (Vacations, Goals, Emergency Fund)

A balanced account structure often includes:

Joint Operating Account

This account typically handles regular shared expenses:

- Rent or mortgage payments
- Utility bills
- Grocery expenses
- Shared subscriptions
- Joint insurance costs

Joint Savings Account

Dedicated to shared goals and future planning:

- Emergency fund
- Vacation savings
- Home down payment
- Major purchase funds
- Shared investment goals

Individual Accounts

Providing personal financial space:

- Personal discretionary spending
- Individual hobbies and interests
- Gifts for partner
- Professional expenses

- Separate savings goals

CREATING CLEAR PROTOCOLS

Successful account management requires clear agreements:

Contribution Systems

Partners need clear understanding about how money moves between accounts:

- Direct deposit allocations
- Transfer timing
- Contribution amounts
- Balance maintenance
- Responsibility divisions

Access Guidelines

Understanding account access helps prevent misunderstandings:

- Who manages which accounts
- Spending consultation thresholds
- Financial notification expectations
- Emergency access provisions
- Privacy boundaries

SPECIAL SITUATION PLANNING

Variable Income Management

When one or both partners have irregular income, additional planning helps maintain financial stability:

- Base expense coverage plans
- Percentage-based contributions
- Buffer account maintenance
- Lean period preparations
- Surplus allocation agreements

Business Owner Considerations

Entrepreneurs and business owners face unique partnership challenges:

- Business/personal separation
- Irregular income management
- Reinvestment decisions
- Risk management
- Long-term planning

LONG-TERM FINANCIAL HARMONY

> **KEY PRINCIPLE**
> Lasting financial harmony requires adapting to changing circumstances while maintaining core partnership principles rather than expecting initial arrangements to work forever.

Financial partnerships evolve throughout relationships. Many couples establish money systems early but fail to adapt them as circumstances change, creating disconnects between their financial arrangements and current needs.

Our over ten-year age difference created unique long-term planning considerations that Lacey and I needed to address openly. During a weekend trip to Nashville in 2021 (which would eventually become our home), we had a pivotal conversation about our different financial time horizons.

"I'll likely retire while you're still in your peak earning years," I noted as we discussed our future plans over dinner. "How do we build a financial partnership that accounts for our different life stages?"

Lacey approached this challenge with remarkable clarity. "I see it as an opportunity, not a problem," she replied. "Your earlier retirement lets us test our financial independence strategies while I still have active income as backup." Together, we developed a "staged independence" approach:

- Build a financial base sufficient for my retirement by 2030
- Use my retirement as a real-world test of our withdrawal strategies
- Leverage Lacey's continuing income to adjust and refine our approach
- Create a fully independent portfolio by 2045 for Lacey's retirement

This framework transformed our age gap from a planning challenge into a strategic advantage. It also prompted important discussions about estate planning, healthcare considerations, and legacy goals much earlier than most couples face them.

"Most people have to jump into retirement together, hoping they've calculated everything correctly," Lacey observed. "We get to implement our strategy in phases, with time to correct course if needed."

This approach exemplifies how financial partnership evolves through changing circumstances. Rather than avoiding difficult conversations about our different life stages, we integrated these realities into our planning, creating stronger trust and more robust financial strategies.

COMMUNICATION SYSTEMS THAT LAST

Sustainable financial partnership requires ongoing dialogue:

	Short daily check-ins Regular monthly reviews Deep annual discussions
Daily	**Quick Money Check-ins (2-3 minutes)** • Upcoming bills or expenses for the day • Quick alerts about account balances or unexpected charges
Weekly	**Money Date (15-30 minutes)** • Review spending for the past week • Plan for upcoming expenses and bills • Address any immediate financial concerns
Monthly	**Budget Review (30-60 minutes)** • Complete review of last month's income and expenses • Track progress toward savings goals • Adjust budget categories as needed • Discuss any upcoming large expenses
Quarterly	**Financial Goal Review (60-90 minutes)** • Review investment performance and strategies • Reassess short and long-term financial goals • Discuss major life changes that might affect finances
Annual	**Financial Review Summit (2-3 hours)** • Complete annual financial health check • Tax planning, estate planning, insurance review, and long-term goals

NAVIGATING FINANCIAL TRANSITIONS

Major life changes require financial partnership adjustments:

Career Transitions

Professional changes often necessitate financial system updates:

- Income changes
- Benefit adjustments
- Location considerations
- Schedule adaptations
- Professional expense shifts

Family Growth

Adding children transforms financial partnerships:

- Expense increases
- Income adjustments
- New financial goals
- Changed priorities

256

- Additional planning needs

BUILDING FINANCIAL PATTERNS

Deepening financial partnership requires ongoing effort:

Beyond Numbers

True financial intimacy extends beyond practical systems:
- Sharing financial hopes and fears
- Understanding money triggers
- Supporting financial growth
- Celebrating financial achievements
- Creating shared financial legacy

Learning Together

Financial education becomes more powerful when shared:
- Reading financial books together
- Attending financial workshops
- Discussing economic news
- Sharing financial insights
- Teaching others together

Remember: Financial harmony requires continuous adaptation while maintaining core partnership principles. Focus on building systems that can evolve with your relationship while preserving fundamental values. The most successful financial partnerships often combine flexible practices with consistent communication.

CHAPTER SUMMARY AND KEY TAKEAWAYS

Through my journey from bankruptcy through rebuilding to financial success with Lacey, I've learned that money in relationships requires both practical systems and emotional intelligence. The lessons from both personal experience and helping other couples show that financial partnership success comes from open communication and mutual respect rather than finding perfect systems.

CORE PARTNERSHIP PRINCIPLES:

Communication Over Avoidance: During relationship development with Lacey, I discovered that honest financial discussions create stronger bonds than avoiding difficult money topics. One couple's experience reinforced this; by discussing financial differences openly, they built deeper trust while preventing future conflicts. Success comes from creating safe spaces for regular money conversations.

Systems Over Rules: Working with couples showed how personalized financial approaches create better outcomes than following generic advice. A young couple's experience demonstrated this when their custom hybrid system worked better than either traditional joint accounts or completely separate finances. The most successful financial partnerships often combine elements from different approaches.

Evolution Over Rigidity: Through both success and failure, I've learned that financial partnerships must adapt to changing circumstances. Recent experiences helping long-term couples navigate transitions showed how flexible systems support relationship strength through life changes.

ACTION PLAN

First 30 Days: Foundation Building
- Share complete financial information
- Discuss money histories and values
- Identify financial goals and priorities
- Explore partnership models
- Create initial sharing approach

60-Day Implementation
- Establish account structure
- Develop contribution systems
- Create communication methods
- Build joint decision processes
- Establish individual autonomy areas

90-Day Establishment
- Review initial system effectiveness
- Adjust approaches as needed
- Strengthen communication practices
- Plan for upcoming changes
- Celebrate financial partnership progress

FINAL THOUGHTS

Remember: Financial partnership success isn't about finding perfect systems; it's about creating approaches that respect both partners while supporting shared goals. Through bankruptcy, recovery, and building a life with Lacey, I've learned that money in relationships requires ongoing communication and mutual adaptation.

Your financial partnership will be unique. Whether you're:
- Starting a new relationship

- Strengthening existing partnership
- Navigating major transitions
- Planning long-term future

The principles remain consistent: communicate openly, respect differences, and create systems that work for your specific relationship. With thoughtful development, money becomes a source of connection rather than conflict in your relationship.

Remember that financial partnerships evolve with life circumstances. Stay connected through regular money conversations, adapt systems as needed, and maintain focus on both individual well-being and shared goals. Your financial relationship success depends more on how you communicate and adapt than on which specific systems you choose.

CHAPTER 14
FINANCIAL LITERACY FOR FAMILIES

LEARNING OBJECTIVES

- Understand how to teach financial concepts across generations
- Learn age-appropriate methods for money education
- Master techniques for building lasting financial habits
- Develop strategies for teaching complex financial concepts
- Create sustainable approaches to family financial education

OPENING STORY

Watching my son navigate his first equity compensation package at Meta showed me how crucial early financial education becomes. Despite his six-figure starting salary, he called seeking guidance about RSU vesting and tax implications. This moment crystallized the difference between simply having money and truly understanding it. The contrast between his starting point and my bankruptcy journey reinforced that financial wisdom needs active teaching rather than hoping children learn through observation.

INTRODUCTION

Financial literacy in families resembles passing down a family recipe; each generation adds their own understanding while maintaining core principles. Many parents feel uncomfortable discussing money with their children, missing crucial opportunities to build financial wisdom early.

Teaching financial literacy differs fundamentally from other types of education because it combines practical skills with values and behavior patterns. Like teaching a child to ride a bike, it requires both instruction and supported practice, with plenty of opportunity for safe learning from mistakes.

The most successful financial education adapts to each child's developmental stage while maintaining consistent core principles. Similar to teaching language, early exposure creates natural understanding that grows more sophisticated over time.

Most importantly, you'll discover that family financial education isn't about creating perfect money managers; it's about building confident, capable decision-makers who understand both the practical and ethical aspects of money management.

STARTING MONEY CONVERSATIONS

KEY PRINCIPLE
Financial education begins with open family discussions rather than formal lessons or lectures.

Financial conversations flourish in everyday settings rather than formal lessons. Many parents avoid money discussions entirely or attempt structured "financial lectures" that feel forced and ineffective. Understanding how to incorporate financial concepts into daily activities creates more impactful learning opportunities.

My approach to teaching financial concepts with my children transformed after our restaurant failure. With no income coming in and rapidly depleting savings, I turned grocery shopping into desperate financial education by involving them in comparing prices, calculating unit costs, and making difficult budget-conscious decisions. "I realized crisis creates powerful teaching moments," I shared during a parenting workshop. "Our trips to discount stores became necessary lessons in distinguishing needs from wants." These real-world lessons during our financial crisis taught them more about money management than all the years of comfortable living had ever done.

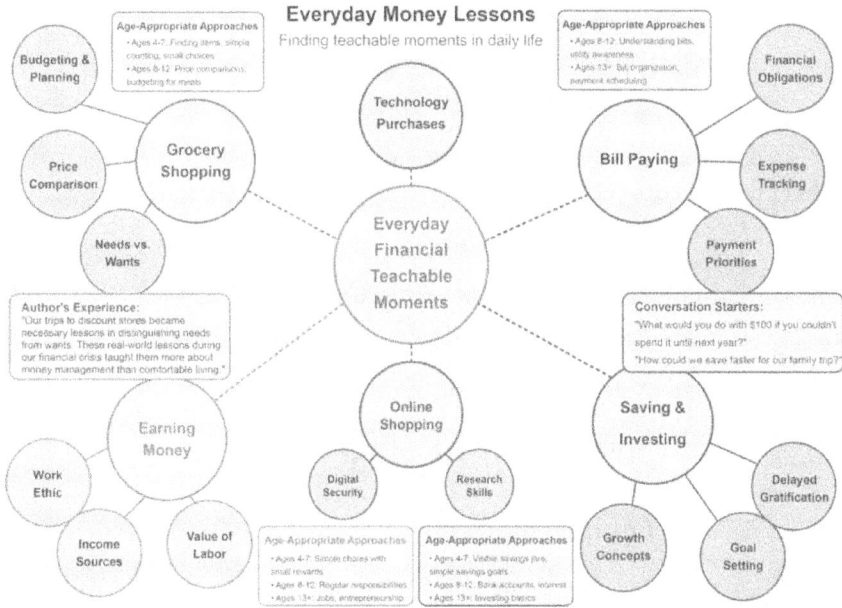

Everyday Money Lessons
Finding teachable moments in daily life

(Diagram: "Everyday Financial Teachable Moments" mind map)

Age-Appropriate Approaches
• Ages 4-7: Finding items, simple counting, small choices
• Ages 8-12: Price comparisons, budgeting for meals

Budgeting & Planning

Price Comparison

Grocery Shopping

Needs vs. Wants

Technology Purchases

Author's Experience:
"Our trips to discount stores became necessary lessons in distinguishing needs from wants. These real-world lessons during our financial crisis taught them more about money management than comfortable living."

Earning Money

Work Ethic

Income Sources

Value of Labor

Online Shopping

Digital Security

Research Skills

Everyday Financial Teachable Moments

Age-Appropriate Approaches
• Ages 8-12: Understanding bills, utility awareness
• Ages 13+: Bill organization, payment scheduling

Financial Obligations

Bill Paying

Expense Tracking

Payment Priorities

Conversation Starters:
"What would you do with $100 if you couldn't spend it until next year?"
"How could we save faster for our family trip?"

Saving & Investing

Growth Concepts

Goal Setting

Delayed Gratification

Age-Appropriate Approaches
• Ages 4-7: Simple chores with small rewards
• Ages 8-12: Regular responsibilities
• Ages 13+: Jobs, entrepreneurship

Age-Appropriate Approaches
• Ages 4-7: Visible savings jar, simple savings goals
• Ages 8-12: Bank accounts, interest
• Ages 13+: Investing basics

BUILDING FINANCIAL VOCABULARY

Children develop financial understanding gradually through exposure to key concepts. Introducing terms like "saving," "spending," "sharing," and "investing" in everyday contexts helps build fundamental financial vocabulary. This language development creates the foundation for more complex financial discussions later.

Money conversations provide opportunities to discuss family values. Explaining why you choose to spend on certain things while saving on others helps children understand the connection between values and financial decisions. These conversations go beyond basic money management to address deeper questions about priorities and purpose.

CREATING SAFE DISCUSSION SPACES

Effective financial education requires creating environments where questions are welcome and mistakes become learning opportunities. Many families inadvertently discourage financial curiosity by reacting negatively to money questions or concerns. Establishing open communication channels helps develop financial confidence.

AGE-APPROPRIATE STARTING POINTS

Different ages require different conversation approaches:
Preschool years (3-5):

- Simple concepts of waiting and saving
- Identifying coins and basic money recognition
- Concepts of wants versus needs
- Understanding that things cost money
- Simple earning opportunities for treats

Elementary years (6-10):
- Basic budgeting with allowance
- Saving for short-term goals
- Earning through age-appropriate chores
- Comparison shopping basics
- Introduction to banking concepts

AGE-APPROPRIATE TEACHING

KEY PRINCIPLE
Effective financial education matches concepts with developmental stages rather than forcing advanced ideas too early.

Financial concepts must align with cognitive and emotional development. Many parents either underestimate children's capacity to understand money or attempt to teach concepts beyond their developmental readiness. Understanding how financial comprehension develops helps create more effective teaching approaches.

My experience teaching my children about money during our post-restaurant crisis demonstrates the importance of age-appropriate approaches. When we suddenly had to cut all discretionary spending, my son and daughter responded differently to our new financial reality.

My daughter understood the abstract concept of "temporary sacrifice," while my son needed concrete explanations for each "no." "I learned that even children in the same family need different approaches during financial hardship," I explained to Lacey. "When I adjusted my explanations to match each child's emotional and cognitive understanding, both adapted to our difficult circumstances with remarkable resilience."

EARLY YEARS FOUNDATION (AGES 3-7)

Young children develop financial understanding through concrete experiences. At this stage, physical money interactions, simple sorting activities, and immediate cause-effect relationships create fundamental awareness. Abstract concepts like interest or future planning typically exceed developmental readiness.

ELEMENTARY BUILDING BLOCKS (AGES 8-12)

Middle childhood brings capacity for more structured financial learning:
Money Management Fundamentals
- Three-jar system (save/spend/share)
- Weekly allowance management
- Basic goal setting
- Simple earning opportunities
- Delayed gratification practice

Banking Introduction
    Children at this age benefit from hands-on banking experiences. Opening a savings account, making deposits, and watching balances grow helps transform abstract saving concepts into concrete understanding. Many banks offer youth accounts specifically designed for this age group.

TEEN MONEY MANAGEMENT (AGES 13-17)

    Adolescence brings capacity for more sophisticated financial concepts:
Expanded Responsibility
    Teenagers can handle increasing financial responsibility through structured independence. Managing a clothing budget, planning for larger purchases, and handling personal expenses helps develop practical money management skills within a supportive environment.

Employment and Taxes
    First jobs provide powerful learning opportunities. Understanding pay stubs, tax withholding, and the relationship between work and compensation creates fundamental employment literacy. These experiences build essential knowledge for adult financial independence.

YOUNG ADULT TRANSITION (AGES 18-23)

The transition to adulthood requires specific financial preparation:
Independence Preparation
    Young adults need guided practice with:
- Budget creation and management
- Credit building and protection
- Insurance basics
- Educational and career planning
- Basic investment concepts

Age-Appropriate Money Lessons Matrix

Teaching Money by Age: Developmentally-appropriate financial education

Age Group	Core Concepts	Activities	Tools	Learning Goals
Ages 3-7	• Money has value • Saving for later • Needs vs. wants	• Coin recognition games • Grocery store math • Simple saving practice	• Clear piggy banks • Picture books about money • Pretend store/restaurant	• Basic money recognition • Patience development • Simple choices
Ages 8-12	• Basic budgeting • Simple interest • Earning and goal setting	• Opening savings account • Allowance management • Simple entrepreneurship	• Three-jar system • Goal charts • Bank visit field trips	• Planning skills • Delayed gratification • Work-reward connection
Ages 13-17	• Compound interest • Credit basics • Taxes & employment	• First job experience • Clothing/personal budget • Long-term saving projects	• Debit card (supervised) • Budget apps • Stock market games	• Financial autonomy • Work-income connection • Long-term perspective
Ages 18-23	• Investing fundamentals • Insurance & risk management • Retirement & student loans	• Investment simulation • Career planning • Independent budgeting	• Investment apps • Credit monitoring • Financial mgmt tools	• Long-term planning • Financial independence • Wealth building mindset

FAMILY FINANCIAL HABITS

KEY PRINCIPLE
Strong financial habits develop through consistent family practices rather than occasional lessons or discussions.

Financial habits develop through regular practice rather than occasional instruction. Many families discuss money sporadically or during crises, missing opportunities to build consistent financial behaviors. Understanding how habits form helps create effective family financial practices.

Our family approach to grocery shopping during recovery illustrates how routine practices build financial awareness. Each week after bankruptcy, my children participated in meal planning, creating shopping lists, comparing prices online, and finding coupons before our actual shopping trip. "We didn't set out to teach budgeting formally," I explained to another recovering family. "But through our weekly routine of stretching limited resources, the children developed price awareness, planning skills, and value assessment naturally." These lessons stuck with them even after our financial situation improved.

PRACTICAL APPLICATION SYSTEMS

Theoretical knowledge transforms into practical understanding through regular application. Creating systems that allow children to practice financial decision-making helps develop both knowledge and confidence. These systems should grow in complexity as children develop greater capacity.

Allowance Management

Strategic allowance systems provide powerful teaching opportunities:

- Regular payment schedules
- Clear earning parameters
- Spending freedom within boundaries
- Saving expectations
- Natural consequences

GOAL SETTING PRACTICES

Regular goal-setting helps develop planning skills and delayed gratification. Family financial goals, individual saving targets, and shared projects all provide opportunities to practice purposeful money management. These experiences help children connect current decisions with future outcomes.

FINANCIAL DECISION PARTICIPATION

Including children in appropriate family financial decisions helps develop judgment and understanding. While children shouldn't bear adult financial concerns, age-appropriate involvement in certain decisions provides valuable learning opportunities. These experiences help develop critical thinking about money matters.

CREATING LEARNING ENVIRONMENTS

Physical elements in the home environment can support financial education:

- Visible saving containers for young children
- Family goal charts or thermometers
- Budget planning areas
- Financial responsibility charts
- Resource centers for money questions

Remember: Financial habits develop through consistent practice rather than theoretical knowledge. Focus on creating regular financial activities while providing appropriate responsibility levels. The most successful financial education often comes through systematic family practices rather than isolated teaching moments.

LONG-TERM FINANCIAL EDUCATION

KEY PRINCIPLE
Lasting financial literacy requires ongoing education that evolves with family circumstances rather than treating learning as a completed task.

Financial education functions as a lifelong process rather than a completed achievement. Many families treat financial education as a checklist to complete rather than an ongoing journey. Understanding that financial knowledge needs continuous development helps create sustainable learning approaches.

Our family approach to technology purchases demonstrates evolving financial education. As my children grew from elementary school through high school after our financial recovery, the decision-making process for electronics evolved from simple parent-guided choices to increasingly sophisticated discussions. "We kept increasing the complexity of the analysis as they matured," I explained to a parenting group. "By high school, they were handling multi-factor decisions that considered features, longevity, total cost of ownership, and opportunity costs."

This progression helped them develop critical thinking skills that extended far beyond technology purchases into broader financial decision-making.

ADAPTING TO LIFE STAGES

Financial education needs change with life progression. Different stages; childhood, adolescence, young adulthood, family formation, career advancement, and retirement preparation; each require specific financial knowledge. Recognizing these changing needs helps maintain relevant financial education.

ADDRESSING LIFE TRANSITIONS

Major life events create crucial financial teaching moments:
- First jobs and income management
- College planning and education costs
- First independent housing
- Career transitions and changes
- Family formation and planning
- Retirement preparation

CREATING LEARNING RESOURCES

Family financial libraries provide ongoing educational support. Curating age-appropriate books, articles, podcasts, and videos helps family members continue their financial education independently. These resources support continuous learning between more formal discussions.

MAINTAINING FINANCIAL COMMUNICATION

Regular financial discussions help maintain continuous education:

- Monthly family budget reviews
- Quarterly financial goal check-ins
- Annual financial planning sessions
- Regular money management conversations
- Ongoing financial question opportunities

Remember: Financial education requires continuous development rather than one-time instruction. Focus on creating ongoing learning opportunities while adapting teaching to changing life stages. The most successful family financial education often evolves naturally with life circumstances rather than remaining static.

CHAPTER SUMMARY AND KEY TAKEAWAYS

Through my journey from bankruptcy to building wealth, and especially watching my children develop their own financial understanding, I've learned that family financial education combines consistent teaching with practical application. The lessons from both personal experience and helping others show that financial literacy requires ongoing effort rather than one-time instruction.

CORE FINANCIAL EDUCATION PRINCIPLES:

Practice Over Theory: During my recovery years, I discovered that hands-on money management teaches more effectively than abstract concepts. One family's experience reinforced this; by involving children in real financial decisions, they developed better money skills than those taught through lectures alone. Success comes from creating practical application opportunities rather than theoretical instruction.

Process Over Perfection: Working with families showed how consistent financial education creates better outcomes than seeking perfect financial understanding. A colleague's experience demonstrated this when his patient approach to financial teaching helped his children develop natural money management skills. The most successful financial education often emphasizes regular progress rather than flawless money management.

Values Over Techniques: Through both success and failure, I've learned that connecting money management with deeper values creates more lasting impact than focusing solely on financial techniques. Recent experiences helping families develop financial literacy showed how purpose-driven money management creates better long-term outcomes than just teaching technical skills.

ACTION PLAN

First 30 Days: Foundation Building
- Start regular money conversations
- Identify age-appropriate concepts
- Create simple learning activities
- Establish allowance systems
- Begin family financial discussions

60-Day Implementation
- Develop regular financial routines
- Create learning opportunities
- Establish goal-setting practices
- Build financial responsibility areas
- Implement consistent practices

90-Day Establishment
- Review initial progress
- Adjust teaching approaches
- Strengthen weak areas
- Plan future learning
- Maintain consistent habits

FINAL THOUGHTS

Remember: Family financial literacy isn't about creating perfect money managers; it's about building lasting financial wisdom that grows over time. Through bankruptcy recovery and building wealth through my renewed career, I've learned that effective financial education requires both knowledge and consistent application.

CHAPTER 15
ESTATE PLANNING

LEARNING OBJECTIVES

- Understand essential estate planning components
- Learn effective wealth transfer methods
- Master protection strategies for different assets
- Develop comprehensive family legacy plans
- Create lasting generational impact

OPENING STORY

Estate planning took on new meaning when Lacey and I began discussing our over ten-year age difference. While managing substantial assets at Big Tech, including RSUs and rental properties, I realized that protecting our legacy meant more than just drafting a will. This journey taught me that effective estate planning combines both immediate protection and long-term strategy, especially when considering complex family dynamics and varying life expectancies.

INTRODUCTION

Estate planning extends far beyond writing a will; it encompasses protecting your loved ones, preserving your values, and creating lasting impact. Many people avoid estate planning due to discomfort with mortality or confusion about the process, missing crucial opportunities to protect their legacy.

Creating an estate plan resembles designing a comprehensive protection system; each component serves specific purposes while working together to create complete coverage. Like building a security system, different assets and family situations require different protective measures.

The most successful estate planning combines technical expertise with personal values. Similar to creating a family constitution, it requires understanding both legal requirements and family dynamics to create effective protection and transfer strategies.

Most importantly, you'll discover that estate planning isn't about controlling from the grave; it's about providing guidance and support that helps future generations thrive. The methods we'll discuss work whether you're protecting modest assets or substantial wealth, because they focus on fundamental principles that apply to any situation.

UNDERSTANDING ESTATE PLANNING FUNDAMENTALS

KEY PRINCIPLE
Effective estate planning requires understanding both protection and transfer rather than focusing solely on asset distribution.

THE CATALYST FOR PLANNING

Estate planning took on particular urgency for Lacey and me given our over ten-year age gap. What might have seemed like a distant concern became an immediate priority that required thoughtful consideration of our different life stages. "Standard estate plans assume spouses are roughly the same age," our attorney explained during our initial consultation. "Your situation requires more customized planning."

This reality became the catalyst for deeper conversations about our wishes and values. One Sunday afternoon, sitting on our back deck, we faced questions most couples defer until much later in life: "If something happens to me in the next ten years," I asked Lacey, "what financial structure would give you the most security while honoring my responsibilities to my adult children?"

CREATING YOUR ESTATE FRAMEWORK

These discussions went far beyond basic will creation. We needed to consider multiple time horizons and potential scenarios that spanned decades. The process revealed important insights about our priorities and values.

For Lacey, maintaining independence while having secure resources was paramount. "I don't want to be financially dependent on decisions made by trustees," she explained. "I need both security and autonomy." For me, balancing responsibilities to both my spouse and adult children required careful consideration. "I want to ensure Lacey's long-term security," I shared, "while also preserving assets for my children from my first marriage."

ESSENTIAL ESTATE COMPONENTS

Every effective estate plan needs four fundamental elements:

A Will serves as your basic instruction manual, directing asset distribution and naming guardians for minor children. However, like a book's table of contents, it provides structure but doesn't tell the complete story.

Powers of Attorney protect you during life, not just after death. Medical and financial powers of attorney ensure trusted individuals can make decisions if you become incapacitated. Without these documents, even spouses may face legal barriers to helping during emergencies.

Healthcare Directives communicate your medical wishes when you can't speak for yourself. These documents prove especially crucial for unmarried partners or blended families where multiple parties might claim decision-making authority.

Beneficiary Designations often matter more than your will for certain assets. Many people carefully craft wills but forget to update beneficiaries on life insurance, retirement accounts, or transfer-on-death accounts, potentially undermining their entire estate plan.

Implementation Priority:
1. Healthcare directives
2. Powers of attorney
3. Will/basic disposition
4. Beneficiary updates

Key Considerations:
- Age differences between spouses
- Blended family situations
- State-specific requirements

ADVANCED
Situation-Specific Planning

IMPORTANT
Asset-Specific Documents

ESSENTIAL
Foundation Documents for Everyone

Essential Documents:
- Will (or Pour-Over Will)
- Durable Power of Attorney
- Healthcare Directive/Proxy
- HIPAA Authorization

Important Documents:
- Beneficiary Designations
- Transfer/Payable on Death
- Real Estate Titles
- Digital Asset Inventory

Advanced Documents:
- Revocable Living Trust
- Business Succession Plans
- Irrevocable Trusts
- Complex Tax Planning

CREATING EFFECTIVE PROTECTION STRATEGIES

KEY PRINCIPLE
Asset protection requires matching specific strategies to different types of assets and family situations rather than using a one-size-fits-all approach.

THE BIG TECH COMPLEXITY

When I joined Big Tech, my compensation structure added significant complexity to our estate planning. With substantial equity compensation through RSUs, our assets suddenly required sophisticated protection strategies beyond basic wills or trusts. "I realized how vulnerable these digital assets could be without proper planning," I shared with Lacey during our estate review. "They required completely different protection approaches than our physical assets."

This insight led us to develop specific protection mechanisms for different asset types. My tech industry RSUs needed clear documentation and access protocols, while our rental properties required different ownership structures for liability protection and tax efficiency.

RETIREMENT ACCOUNT PROTECTION

My retirement accounts presented another unique planning challenge given our age difference. With Lacey likely to outlive me by decades, maximizing the growth potential of inherited retirement assets became crucial. We structured our beneficiary designations to allow for the longest possible tax-deferred growth while ensuring immediate access if needed.

"The stretch provisions for inherited IRAs could provide substantial additional growth over Lacey's lifetime," I explained to our advisor. "But we needed to balance that with ensuring immediate liquidity for unexpected needs." This led to strategic beneficiary planning that maximized flexibility.

IMPLEMENTING TRANSFER STRATEGIES

> **KEY PRINCIPLE**
> Effective wealth transfer requires careful timing and method selection rather than simple one-time decisions.

STRATEGIC TIMING DECISIONS

After rebuilding my finances from bankruptcy to substantial assets, I became keenly aware of the importance of strategic transfer timing. Working with Lacey, we developed a multi-phase transfer strategy that balanced current tax efficiency with future needs.

"Our significant age difference means we need to think about transfers across different time horizons," I explained during our planning session. "Some transfers make sense now, while others should happen later based on tax law and our changing needs." This led to a staged approach rather than a single transfer plan.

Last Will and Testament	Revocable Living Trust	Transfer on Death (TOD)	Beneficiary Designations
Process	**Process**	**Process**	**Process**
• Goes through probate	• Avoids probate	• Automatic transfer	• Immediate transfer
• Court-supervised	• Managed by trustee	• Assets pass directly	• No probate required
• Executor manages	• Private transfer	• No court involvement	• Contract-based
• Public process	• Functionals during life	• Simple to establish	• Form-based setup
Advantages	**Advantages**	**Advantages**	**Advantages**
• Lower initial cost	• Privacy maintained	• Very low cost	• No cost typically
• Court oversight	• Faster asset transfer	• Quick asset transfer	• Immediate distribution
• Can appoint guardians	• Incapacity planning	• Easy to establish	• Bypasses probate
• Simple to create	• Works across states	• Can change anytime	• Easy to update
• Familiar to most people	• Can control distribution	• Works for many assets	• Tax advantages possible
Disadvantages	**Disadvantages**	**Disadvantages**	**Disadvantages**
• Probate costs/delays	• Higher setup costs	• Limited to specific assets	• Only for specific assets
• Public record	• Requires maintenance	• No control after death	• No distribution control
• No incapacity planning	• Must re-title assets	• No incapacity planning	• May conflict with will
• Only covers probate assets	• More complex	• No contingent planning	• Easy to forget updating
• Can be contested	• Still need a will	• Can create confusion	• Potential tax issues
• State-specific rules	• Ongoing management	• Still need a will	• No creditor protection
Best For	**Best For**	**Best For**	**Best For**
• Simple estates	• Larger estates	• Simple asset transfers	• Retirement accounts
• Naming guardians	• Privacy concerns	• Single beneficiaries	• Life insurance
• Lower cost solutions	• Multi-state property	• Supplemental transfers	• Financial accounts

LIFETIME GIVING APPROACH

Our Nashville move created an opportunity to implement a strategic giving program. By timing certain gifts with our relocation, we optimized tax results while beginning the gradual process of asset transition.

Our lifetime giving strategy includes:

- Annual exclusion gifts to family members
- Direct payment of educational expenses
- Strategic charitable contributions
- Real estate fractional interest transfers

TAX-EFFICIENT MECHANISMS

My experience with both financial collapse and subsequent rebuilding made me particularly sensitive to tax efficiency in transfers. We implemented a strategy that balanced immediate tax benefits with long-term wealth preservation. "Having lost everything once, I'm determined to ensure efficient transfers that don't lose value unnecessarily to taxes," I explained to our planning team. This perspective led us to carefully coordinate income tax, gift tax, and estate tax considerations in a comprehensive approach.

BUILDING LASTING LEGACY

KEY PRINCIPLE

True legacy involves transmitting values and wisdom alongside assets.

The Evolving Estate Plan: Key Planning Milestones by Age

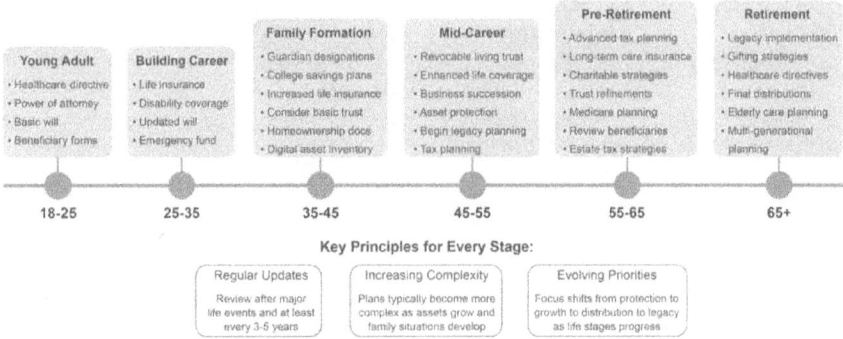

		Family Formation	Mid-Career	Pre-Retirement	Retirement
Young Adult	**Building Career**	• Guardian designations	• Revocable living trust	• Advanced tax planning	• Legacy implementation
• Healthcare directive	• Life insurance	• College savings plans	• Enhanced life coverage	• Long-term care insurance	• Gifting strategies
• Power of attorney	• Disability coverage	• Increased life insurance	• Business succession	• Charitable strategies	• Healthcare directives
• Basic will	• Updated will	• Consider basic trust	• Asset protection	• Trust refinements	• Final distributions
• Beneficiary forms	• Emergency fund	• Homeownership docs	• Begin legacy planning	• Medicare planning	• Elderly care planning
		• Digital asset inventory	• Tax planning	• Review beneficiaries	• Multi-generational
				• Estate tax strategies	planning
18-25	25-35	35-45	45-55	55-65	65+

Key Principles for Every Stage:

Regular Updates	Increasing Complexity	Evolving Priorities
Review after major life events and at least every 3-5 years	Plans typically become more complex as assets grow and family situations develop	Focus shifts from protection to growth to distribution to legacy as life stages progress

VALUES-BASED PLANNING

My journey from financial collapse to rebuilding taught me that assets without wisdom often don't last. This insight fundamentally shaped our legacy planning with Lacey. "Having lost everything once," I shared during our legacy planning session, "I understand that transferring financial assets without the knowledge to manage them responsibly is like giving someone a high-performance car without driving lessons."

This realization led us to create a comprehensive legacy plan that documents not just what assets will transfer but why certain decisions were made and what principles should guide their use. Our approach focuses on transferring the financial wisdom that came from both my success and failure.

PERSONAL HISTORY DOCUMENTATION

Our legacy plan includes personal financial narratives that explain critical moments in our journey. "My bankruptcy story contains crucial lessons that future generations shouldn't have to learn firsthand," I explained to Lacey. "Documenting both our successes and failures provides context for the assets we're transferring."

This documentation helps ensure that future generations understand both the how and why behind our financial decisions. Rather than just receiving assets, they inherit the wisdom gained through experience.

Beyond Assets: The Six Dimensions of Meaningful Legacy

A comprehensive approach to legacy planning

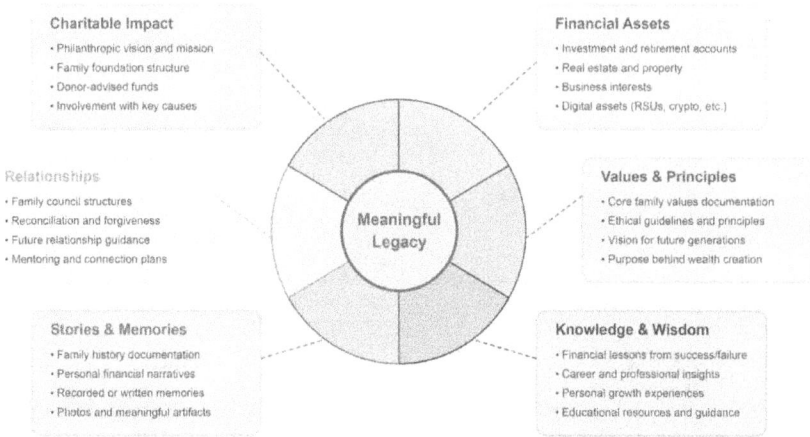

Charitable Impact
- Philanthropic vision and mission
- Family foundation structure
- Donor-advised funds
- Involvement with key causes

Financial Assets
- Investment and retirement accounts
- Real estate and property
- Business interests
- Digital assets (RSUs, crypto, etc.)

Relationships
- Family council structures
- Reconciliation and forgiveness
- Future relationship guidance
- Mentoring and connection plans

Meaningful Legacy

Values & Principles
- Core family values documentation
- Ethical guidelines and principles
- Vision for future generations
- Purpose behind wealth creation

Stories & Memories
- Family history documentation
- Personal financial narratives
- Recorded or written memories
- Photos and meaningful artifacts

Knowledge & Wisdom
- Financial lessons from success/failure
- Career and professional insights
- Personal growth experiences
- Educational resources and guidance

PHILANTHROPY AS LEGACY

Our move to Nashville created an opportunity to establish meaningful philanthropic involvement that reflects our values. Rather than just donating money, we developed relationships with organizations focused on financial education and second chances—causes that resonate deeply given my own experience.

"Having received a second chance after bankruptcy," I shared with our philanthropy advisor, "supporting others in similar situations gives meaning to our financial recovery." This approach ensures our values continue to create impact beyond our lifetimes.

FAMILY COUNCIL CREATION

Following our relocation, we established a family council structure that brings together multiple generations for regular discussions about both finances and values. This forum creates opportunities for explicit transmission of financial wisdom rather than hoping it happens naturally.

Our family council meetings include:
- Financial education components
- Legacy story sharing
- Philanthropic decision-making
- Investment review and learning
- Next generation mentoring

Finding Your Trust Fit

Comparing different trust structures

Trust Type	Key Features	Appropriate Situations	Complexity & Cost
Revocable Living Trust (Also called a Family Trust)	• Amendable during your lifetime • Avoids probate • Provides privacy • Can include incapacity provisions • No tax advantages	• Most common trust type • Ideal for basic estate plans • Good for blended families • Helps manage incapacity • Provides clear distribution instructions	• Moderate initial setup • Low ongoing maintenance • $1,500-$3,500 to establish • Requires proper funding • May need periodic updates Medium ••
Irrevocable Trust (Various Types)	• Cannot be changed once established • Assets no longer owned by you • Potential tax advantages • Asset protection benefits • Specific rules for distributions	• Estate tax concerns • Asset protection needs • Special needs planning • Multi-generational planning • Professional liability concerns • Spendthrift beneficiaries	• High initial setup • Ongoing administration costs • $3,000-$10,000+ to establish • Requires professional management High •••
Survivorship Trust (Author's Choice for Age Gap Situation)	• Provides for surviving spouse • Balances current spouse and children's needs • Can become irrevocable after first spouse's death • Flexible access provisions • Clear benefit beneficiaries	• Age differences between spouses • Blended family situations • Complex family dynamics • Balancing spouse care with children's inheritance • Long-term care planning	• Medium-high initial setup • Moderate ongoing management • $2,500-$5,000 to establish • Possible trustee fees after first death • May require regular accounting Medium-High •••
Specialized Trusts (Special Needs, ILIT, QPRT, CRUT, etc.)	• Purpose-built for specific needs • Typically irrevocable • Targeted tax advantages • Highly structured provisions • Complex administration • Specific regulatory compliance	• Special needs beneficiaries • High-value life insurance • Charitable giving goals • Estate tax minimization • Business succession planning • High-value real estate	• Very high initial setup • High ongoing costs • $5,000-$15,000+ to establish • Requires specialized attorneys • Complex tax reporting Very High ••••

Remember: Legacy building combines financial assets with family values and wisdom. Focus on creating opportunities for meaningful transmission of both practical knowledge and core principles. The most valuable legacies often grow from thoughtful combination of financial and personal inheritance.

CHAPTER SUMMARY AND KEY TAKEAWAYS

Through my journey from bankruptcy to building a legacy with Lacey, considering our over ten-year age difference, I've learned that effective estate planning combines technical expertise with deep personal meaning. The lessons from both personal experience and helping others show that lasting legacies require active cultivation rather than just legal documentation.

CORE LEGACY PLANNING PRINCIPLES:

Purpose Over Paperwork: During our estate planning process, I discovered that understanding why we make certain choices matters more than just making them. One family's experience reinforced this; when they shared their estate planning reasoning with their children, it transformed legal documents into meaningful family guidance. The most successful estate plans often reflect clear purpose behind every decision.

Values Over Valuables: Working with families showed how transferring values creates more lasting impact than transferring assets alone. A business owner's experience demonstrated this when his children's understanding of his work ethic and business principles proved more valuable than the business assets they inherited. True legacy combines financial wealth with family wisdom.

Flexibility Over Rigidity: Through both success and failure, I've learned that estate plans need adaptability to serve changing family circumstances. Recent experiences helping families navigate unexpected situations showed how flexible planning creates better outcomes than rigid structures.

ACTION PLAN

First 30 Days: Foundation Building
- Review current estate documents
- List all assets and obligations
- Identify key family considerations
- Document important relationships
- Begin value discussion with family

60-Day Implementation
- Create basic protection structures
- Develop communication plans
- Start legacy documentation
- Build family understanding
- Establish regular reviews

90-Day Establishment
- Refine protection strategies
- Deepen family involvement
- Create teaching opportunities
- Build lasting structures
- Maintain flexible adaptation

FINAL THOUGHTS

Remember: Estate planning isn't about controlling from the grave; it's about providing guidance and support that helps future generations thrive. Through financial rebuilding and creating new family bonds, I learned that effective estate planning requires both technical skill and emotional intelligence.

Your legacy journey will be unique. Whether you're:

- Starting basic protection
- Managing complex assets
- Building family business legacy
- Creating charitable impact

The principles remain consistent: understand your purpose, communicate your values, and create flexible structures that support family success. With proper development, estate planning becomes an expression of family care rather than just asset distribution.

Remember that family circumstances constantly evolve. Stay flexible, maintain open dialogue, and don't hesitate to adjust plans as situations change. Your goal isn't perfect control but creating supportive structures that help future generations build on your foundation while adding their own wisdom to the family legacy.

CONCLUSION
YOUR FINANCIAL
JOURNEY - BEYOND
NUMBERS TO MEANING

My path from Marine Corps service through bankruptcy to Big Tech leadership taught me that money is never just about numbers. Each financial decision we make reflects our values and shapes our future possibilities. The contrast between my bankruptcy recovery, starting with $25 weekly investments, and helping my son navigate six-figure compensation decisions demonstrates how financial wisdom transcends income levels.

THE HUMAN ELEMENT OF FINANCE

Working with Lacey to align our financial goals despite our over ten-year age difference reinforced that money management is fundamentally about human connection and understanding. When she responded to my third-date financial confession with wisdom beyond her years; seeing someone who had learned from mistakes rather than someone defined by them; I understood that financial partnership requires emotional intelligence as much as technical knowledge.

Through both teaching and learning, I've discovered that financial success involves three core elements:

First, an understanding that money serves as a tool for creating possibility rather than a measure of worth. During my darkest financial days, this perspective helped me focus on rebuilding rather than self-judgment.

Second, recognizing that financial wisdom grows through both success and failure. My bankruptcy taught me lessons that no MBA program could, while helping my children navigate their own financial journeys showed me how sharing both triumphs and mistakes creates deeper understanding.

Third, acknowledging that lasting financial success requires aligning money management with personal values. Whether managing substantial assets or starting fresh, choices that reflect our core values create more sustainable outcomes than those based purely on numbers.

A NEW FINANCIAL PARADIGM

The traditional narrative of financial success; graduate college, climb the corporate ladder, retire comfortably; no longer fits our modern reality. Today's professionals navigate multiple career iterations, complex compensation structures, remote work opportunities, and changing definitions of success.

Success in this new landscape requires emotional intelligence alongside financial acumen. I witnessed this when helping my son navigate his tech compensation. Despite his technical brilliance, his most crucial questions weren't about stock vesting schedules or tax implications; they centered on using his sudden wealth responsibly and maintaining perspective despite his peers' lavish spending.

BEYOND PERSONAL FINANCE

The most valuable financial lessons often emerge from sharing our experiences with others. During family dinner discussions, I've noticed how my grandchildren absorb more from our casual conversations about money decisions than from any formal teaching. When my granddaughter asked about my bankruptcy story, her thoughtful questions revealed how financial wisdom passes between generations through honest dialogue about both successes and failures.

Working with Lacey to plan our financial future while navigating our age difference has taught me that money conversations create bridges between different perspectives and life experiences. Our discussions about early retirement and legacy planning have evolved into deeper explorations of what we value most and how we want to impact future generations.

FINAL THOUGHTS

Money is never just about numbers. It's about the stories we create, the values we embody, and the impact we leave. Through bankruptcy and recovery, through career rebuilding and family building, I've learned that financial success comes not from perfect decisions but from continuous learning and growth.

Your most important investment will always be in yourself; your knowledge, your relationships, your capacity for growth. As you navigate your own financial journey, remember that every setback carries lessons, every success creates opportunity for positive impact, and every financial decision shapes not just your future but potentially generations to come.

The journey continues. Make yours count.

ACKNOWLEDGMENTS

Writing this book has been a journey of reflection and discovery, one that would not have been possible without the support, guidance, and wisdom of many individuals. Their contributions deserve more than just a brief mention; they are an integral part of both this book and my journey.

First and foremost, my deepest gratitude goes to my wife, Lacey. Your patience during the countless hours I spent writing, your insights that helped shape many of the concepts in this book, and your unwavering belief in the importance of sharing our story have made this book possible. Your perspective as someone building wealth alongside me while maintaining work-life harmony has added invaluable depth to these pages.

To my children, you've been both my inspiration and my teachers. Watching you navigate your own financial journeys, especially my son's entry into the tech world at Meta, has provided crucial insights that shaped many chapters in this book. Your resilience during our family's personal and financial challenges continues to inspire me.

I owe a tremendous debt of gratitude to my dear friend and mentor, Casey Robinson, who guided me through my darkest personal and financial days and showed me that bankruptcy and divorce could be a beginning, not an end.

My writing team has been extraordinary. To my development editor, David Gallegos, whose challenging questions and insightful feedback transformed my raw manuscript into a coherent narrative; your impact on this book cannot be overstated.

Finally, to my mother, whose immigrant journey taught me the value of hard work and financial responsibility. Though you didn't have the opportunity to teach me about investing or compound interest, you taught me something more valuable; resilience in the face of personal and financial adversity. This book is a testament to the principles you instilled in me.

And to my readers; thank you for allowing me to share this journey with you. My hope is that these pages will help you avoid some of the pitfalls I encountered while accelerating your path to financial security and peace of mind.

REFERENCES

BOOKS

- **Kiyosaki, Robert T.** (1997, updated 2017). *Rich Dad Poor Dad:* Plata Publishing. ISBN: 978-1612680194
- **Ramsey, Dave.** (2013). *The Total Money Makeover: A Proven Plan for Financial Fitness.* Thomas Nelson. ISBN: 978-1595555274
- **Sethi, Ramit.** (2019). *I Will Teach You to Be Rich* (2nd Edition). Workman Publishing. ISBN: 978-1523505746

ACADEMIC & RESEARCH

- **Lusardi, Annamaria & Mitchell, Olivia S.** (2014). "The Economic Importance of Financial Literacy: Theory and Evidence." *Journal of Economic Literature*, 52(1), 5-44. DOI: 10.1257/jel.52.1.5
- **Merton, Robert C.** (2014). "The Crisis in Retirement Planning." *Harvard Business Review*, July-August 2014.
- **Employee Benefit Research Institute.** (2024). *Retirement Confidence Survey.* Available at: ebri.org

GOVERNMENT RESOURCES

- **Internal Revenue Service.** Publication 970: Tax Benefits for Education. Available at: irs.gov/publications/p970
- **Social Security Administration.** *Understanding the Benefits.* Available at: ssa.gov/pubs/EN-05-10024.pdf
- **Federal Student Aid.** *Federal Student Loan Repayment Plans.* Available at: studentaid.gov/manage-loans/repayment/plans

ONLINE CALCULATORS & TOOLS (FOR READER REFERENCE)

- **Bankrate.com** - Mortgage, savings, and retirement calculators
- **NerdWallet.com** - Credit card and loan comparison tools
- **Investor.gov** - SEC's compound interest calculator
- **SSA.gov** - Social Security benefit calculators
- **TheRealMoneyGuide.com** - Companion tools for this book

ABOUT THE AUTHOR

David Kim brings over three decades of experience spanning military service, technology leadership, and financial planning to his work. As a former Marine who transitioned through corporate roles at Raytheon, Honeywell, Genpact, before reaching senior leadership at Big Tech, he offers unique insights into both career development and financial management. His professional credentials include:

- Master of Business Administration (MBA)
- Certified Financial Planner (CFP) coursework
- 10x Cloud Certifications (AWS, Azure, GCP)
- Project Management Professional (PMP)
- Licensed Real Estate Broker in multiple states

Beyond his corporate success, David has built and managed multiple businesses, including restaurants, a real estate investment portfolio, consulting practices, and AI startups. His experience with both financial collapse and subsequent recovery provides him with distinctive insights into building sustainable wealth and financial resilience.

As a speaker and mentor, David regularly shares his expertise at technology conferences and financial literacy workshops. His approach combines technical precision with practical wisdom, making complex financial concepts accessible to audiences at all levels.

David currently serves as a Senior Technical Leader at a Big Tech company while managing rental properties and pursuing FIRE goals with his wife, Lacey. He balances his professional commitments with personal interests in music, international travel, and mentoring the next generation of technology leaders. His story of resilience and recovery continues to inspire others on their journey to financial independence.

FINANCIAL TOOLKIT RESOURCES

The worksheets and calculators referenced throughout this book are available free at **tools.therealmoneyguide.com**

What You'll Find:

Financial Foundation Assessment ; Evaluate your current financial health and identify priority areas for improvement.

Debt Avalanche & Snowball Calculator ; Compare payoff strategies and create your personalized debt elimination plan.

Budget Builder ; Build a sustainable spending plan that adapts to your income type and life stage.

Emergency Fund Calculator ; Determine your target amount based on expenses, income stability, and family situation.

Insurance Coverage Analyzer ; Assess gaps in your protection and determine appropriate coverage levels.

Career Compensation Evaluator ; Analyze total compensation packages including equity, bonuses, and benefits.

RSU & Equity Tracker ; Manage vesting schedules, tax implications, and diversification strategies for stock compensation.

Real Estate ROI Calculator ; Analyze potential investment properties including cash flow, cap rate, and long-term returns.

Net Worth Tracker ; Monitor your complete financial picture with assets, liabilities, and progress over time.

FIRE Planning Calculator ; Project your path to financial independence with customizable assumptions.

Each tool includes instructions, examples, and the ability to save your work.

Scan to access your free toolkit
tools.therealmoneyguide.com